Broccoli
&
other
love
stories

To my beloved family.
The one I was born into,
the one that grew around me,
and the one I chose.

Notes and recipes from
an always curious, often
hungry kitchen gardener

Broccoli

&

other

love

stories

Paulette Whitney

Provenance Growers

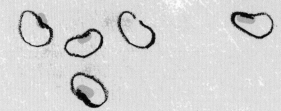

Contents

Acknowledgement of Country

Lutruwita (Tasmania) belongs to the Palawa who have nurtured this land for over 45,000 years and continue to do so today.

I feel immense gratitude to live in a place with an ancient, strong, living culture. My family lives and works on Muwinina land in the foothills of Kunanyi in south-eastern Lutruwita. I am of mixed European heritage — my father's family emigrated here from the Netherlands and the story of my mother's family is largely lost to the mists of time. We work with plants that are rooted in many living cultures from around the world.

We tend and are fed by land that should be in the ongoing care of the Palawa, who tend and are fed by it as they have been for countless generations in an ancient and continuing cycle of reciprocity. Many of the plants that pass our lips are vital cultural plants, and I am grateful to those who have shared the learning of generations with us so that we can grow a deeper relationship with this land and its legacy. I acknowledge that much of my knowledge of this land was stolen from the Palawa, and much of what I have read is written from the perspective of colonists rather than the perspective of the Palawa. I am committed to seeking out, supporting and paying for Palawa and First Nations knowledge where it is shared in culturally safe ways.

My heart aches at Lutruwita's history of violent dispossession, and at the ongoing prejudice cemented by the revisionist history lessons in the schools of my youth. The history I was taught perpetuated the myths of terra nullius and of the extinction of living Palawa culture and people. I am grateful that my children are being taught by Palawa educators, and that there are increasing opportunities for us to engage with, and learn from, the Palawa. To participate in cultural experiences in arts, food, history and land management and, most importantly, to listen, and through that listening learn to become better allies. Hand in hand with sharing knowledge and culture comes an obligation to respect boundaries, to accept that some knowledge belongs to the Palawa alone.

I am working to decolonise my writing and thinking, which is an ongoing process. Every book I open for research refers to plants being 'discovered', but those same plants have been cultivated, improved and used for food, ceremony, art, housing and tools for millennia. Much of what is deemed 'discovered' is stolen. Other plants are described as 'lost' when they have had ongoing cultural use and were never completely lost to their keepers. When we read, garden or cook, we have the opportunity to consider the true cultural roots of the plant we have in our hands. Try to seek out works by First Nations writers and migrants who have stewarded the plant or cooking technique you want to explore. I hope that the stories in these pages draw your thoughts to the people whose land you live upon and those whose cultural food plants you are cooking, eating and tending.

I write in hopes of a kinder and more curious future, one that embraces and lifts up the Palawa custodians of Lutruwita, and acknowledges the ongoing and systemic racism that blocks the path to sovereignty today. I will work as an ally for, treaty, reparations, adherence to Palawa protocols for caring for land, and a solid pathway to Palawa sovereignty here in Lutruwita.

Introduction

If I could have these pages do one thing, it would be this.

That you might pause. Hold an apple, then pierce the thick skin with your teeth. As its juice flows onto your tongue, think of the farm where it grew, the sun that fell on the leaves of the tree, and how those leaves made sugar from that sunlight, water and minerals from the soil that were shared with the tree by the creatures dwelling in the universe below its roots.

That, as you pause, you might remember the taste of a bruised apple from your school lunchbox that, even in its imperfection, helped you pass a dreary walk home. Maybe you'll think of Granny Smith and her fabled tree, sprouted from her compost, that was the mother of a million apple pies.

Perhaps as you pause, that apple in your hand and on your tongue, you'll see the brown calyx on the bottom of the apple, notice its resemblance to the end of a rose hip, and realise that you're eating the cousin of a rose every time you taste an apple.

How perfectly sublime is that?

Twenty years ago, a dye-induced headache pinching my temples, and a painful sales target–induced heartache clutching at my chest, I stumbled, blue-haired and black-clad, from the fug of a hair salon onto a sunny, sparkling Nipaluna (Hobart) street. Squinting, I looked up at towering Kunanyi (Mount Wellington), the mountain that holds the city in its arms. A half-hour walk west from that city salon and I could have been there, wandering to streams, grasslands, damp forests and mountain peaks that would cure any head or heart ache.

My lunchbreak wouldn't allow any healing walks, only longing glances to that precious mountain, before returning to the techno-beat gloom of the salon for my two o'clock client. There were whispers of hope there, though. Every day a dozen people — nurses, builders, gardeners, skateboarders, scientists, artists — sat before me and told stories, showing me a vast spectrum of other worlds out there.

In the street that day, drinking in the clean air, I met a Greenpeace hawker. He was, as they all are, young, beautiful, earnest and full of hope. He saw a world where your tuna sandwich didn't come with a side of dolphins, where ancient forests weren't turned to toilet paper, and where your worth wasn't measured by how many plastic bottles of goo you foisted upon unsuspecting people who just wanted their hair cut. I signed up to give him a chunk of my meagre wages, walked over to our local TAFE and enrolled to study environmental horticulture.

I can still feel it, the freedom of swapping that loud, moodily lit, cloying room for utes filled with thousands of trees that had to be planted, protected with tree guards and watered in, and the satisfaction of looking back after a hard week's work to see the nascent forest we'd created, where before there was only erosion, gorse and desolation.

It became a compulsion, feeling witch-like, conjuring life from seeds that I cast like spells onto soil. Watching them fall, then emerge and grow, was life-affirming. I began to work in a nursery where rather than selling over-priced shampoo, I helped my customers load miniature ecosystems into their car boots.

As well as a community of plant-lovers, this nursery had a library and I began to read.

First it was all about plants native to Lutruwita (Tasmania), the specialty of the nursery where I worked and learned under my mentor, Will Fletcher, who taught me as much about kind, gentle leadership as he did about the botanical and horticultural wonders of this island.

Then, as my reading crossed between the horticultural library at work and my chef husband Matt's cookbook library at home, an obsession grew.

I wonder sometimes if my path to growing food was unusual. Many small-scale food growers have had successful careers and entered agriculture or horticulture wanting a tree-change and feeling a pull to grow and produce quality food, while having a positive impact on their community and the environment. Others are idealists wanting to feed their communities and champion food sovereignty — for what is more important than safeguarding the means of producing our own sustenance? I was moved to grow food primarily to satisfy my rampant, hungry curiosity, but also from a deep love of the diverse and complex landscape here, naively thinking that if we used a degraded paddock in a suburb that was otherwise dedicated to horses and lawnmowers to instead grow food, then that might reduce demand for produce grown in less ideal circumstances. And I wanted everyone to taste as I do. To eat a tiny, dense French potato fresh from the earth, a fragrant alpine strawberry ice-cold and dressed with morning dew, or a tayberry warm from the sun, tasting richly of red wine and savoury–sweet.

While our business was in its infancy, with just a half-table stall at the farmers' market where I spent as much money as I made each Sunday,

Nipaluna (Hobart) changed. MONA, the Museum of Old and New Art, had opened its doors, and chef Luke Burgess partnered with Katrina Birchmeier and Kirk Richardson to start Garagistes, a long-table, no-bookings restaurant that would challenge and grow our appetites. Our eyes were opening. We were more playful. It seemed the whole city was learning to eat with curiosity — and people from all over were jumping on planes to join us.

The timing was serendipitous. My garden was full of radish and rocket flowers, of salvias that tasted of fruit salad or blackcurrants, of delicious weeds and obscure tomatoes — all of which would be discussed and fondled by many market customers, and rejected in favour of common thyme, red cherry tomatoes or old-fashioned 'Blackjack' zucchini. I adored these classics, but meeting Luke gave me a reason to invest in growing the things I love, to look wider, and to learn from the talented chefs who took our food from crate to plate, giving our horticultural oddities context.

Since then, restaurants have opened and closed, and we've had the privilege of working with incredible chefs, home cooks and gardeners. Our backs have become a little more tender, and I'm now growing my culinary curiosities in a plant nursery at bench height more than in the soil. My ethics have remained, and evolved. Our nursery has a no-new-plastic policy, which is labour intensive but non-negotiable in a world drowning in oceans of waste. Matt has taken up the knives again to pickle what he grows, and ease his back by growing a little less.

There is always a new plant, though. And every new plant must find its way into the kitchen.

The library at the nursery where I learned my trade had an encyclopaedia of plants arranged by botanical family. I found the relationships fascinating — that a tender, ephemeral herb could be related to a prickly shrub because of a structure in its flowers or a descent from a shared parent. I hope to share that wonder with you here... that seeing the kinship between a parsnip and the parsley on your plate might make your mind tingle.

The relationships between plants and their people hold the same fascination. Be it a recipe my mother taught me, one I found in a Spanish-speaking corner of YouTube, or one taught to me by a chef who experimented with our wares, there's a story left behind — the story of the cook, of the convivial meal shared, the thrill of discovering a new fact, or of the selfish indulgence of the first ripe peas eaten alone in the garden.

Hunger is certainly an excellent seasoning, and salt is quite good — but a story is the best seasoning of all for me.

Relationships

Everything is related. Tangled together by genetics, interdependence, by love — and the fact that we are, all of us, sculpted from the very same stardust.

A stain left in my grandmother's recipe book leaves echoes for me to trace the path to her favourite fruit cake, although I never met her.

A plant growing in Lutruwita (Tasmania) with close kin in South America leaves those same echoes, telling how we were once joined in the days of Gondwana.

An apricot pip on my daughter's bedside table reminds me of my childhood, and of stolen midnight feasts that span generations.

A stone I keep finding in my garden, given to me by a friend, makes me think of the magma it was formed in, the upwelling of which raised Kunanyi and the once sea-floor-land I live on, the wear of water on the mountain's slopes, and the river that carried the stone to my friend's feet. It makes me think of how the soil we grow our garden on was formed, and reminds me that I am a merely fleeting steward in a tiny speck of time here.

If I sit with the world this way, noticing not just the things around me but the stories they hold — stories of the stolen land I live on and its traditional owners, the Palawa, stories of my own family, stories of the plants I grow, cook and eat, the earth I stand on and the people I share it with — my life is richer, brighter, sometimes more painful, but all the better for it.

Noticing means you see injustice. I write with trepidation about many of the plants in this book whose stories belong to others, and I think of the colonisation and theft that brought them to these shores.

Noticing means you see decay. As I move through my neighbourhood I see invasive species, development and climate change wreaking death by a thousand cuts on this precious island and across the globe. Even the once-innocent night sky is now lit up by billion-dollar hunks of technology that chill my heart.

Noticing means I see the futility of my worry about how to best cook a quail egg, when so many have no access to a stove, let alone such ostentatious ingredients.

Without that noticing, how can I value what we do have? How can I question change and feel moved to respect and preserve the bounty around me? Though the noticing brings discomfort, it also brings with it gratitude, connection and a fierce desire to protect.

My mother

My mother gave me a gift. I wanted trackpants with zips on the cuffs. A phone with a long cord, not one on the kitchen wall where everyone could listen in. I wanted the Adidas Romes and to read *Cosmopolitan* before I was old enough. And while I was busy wanting, with all the wistful, angst-laden need of youth, I was getting things that the popular girls with the Rome sneakers and sparkly scrunchies were probably missing. My mum gave me skills, adventures and time.

By the banks of Timtumili Minanya (the River Derwent), as my stepdad hunted slick, spotted brown trout, Mum handed us ice-cream tubs and asked us to fill them with blackberries. We picked and ate. One for the bucket, two for the mouth, sibling rivalry making us work harder than we otherwise might've. I preferred them barely ripe, firm with a bit of sourness, and ate until my stomach hurt. The properly ripe ones Mum would stir through stewed Granny Smith apples, top with a crumble and bake into a sweet, sour, pink delicacy with a crisp, browned top.

Her hands made ours capable. We learned by watching, then by helping, to quickly halve apricots and flick out stones, and how long to cook them before covering them in the same crumble or topping with a sponge batter. We tasted mussels cooked over smoky fires on beaches, little river trout with slices of lemon tucked inside and cooked the same way, and we learned the golden rule of camping: always start the fire and boil a billy for tea before anything else.

She grew a little garden where we stole still-forming peas, well before they swelled in their pods, savouring each tiny green pearl. I won Mum's favour by learning to relish broad beans at the opposite end of ripeness, single-podded when they were fat and starchy, their thick skins tasting deliciously metallic, oily with butter, salt and pepper. A lamb roast wasn't complete without freshly plucked mint, minced finely with a little sugar and salt, a touch of boiling water to draw the flavour out, and malt vinegar added to the little glass jug with a flippy stainless steel lid that made our family's mint sauce ritual complete.

We ate fish to their bones, made glorious soups with barley, vegetables and the remains of a roast, and sat on stools at the kitchen bench grabbing green spirals of apple skins as they fell from her knife, nibbling them all the way to their curly ends with relish. Food was nourishing and we understood it, her curiosity and continual learning and resourcefulness normalising that way of living. If life drops a whole fallow deer, a gigantic bluefin tuna or a basket of apricots at your door, you roll up your sleeves, feed your family and fill the freezer.

At the time, of course, I had no idea of what I'd been given. I would've chosen a TV with a remote control — imagine not having to get up to change the channel! — over a day by a lakeside with nothing to do but walk, read and gather blackberries... but forty years later, that gift still echoes.

I still love to walk with no destination. I look forward to a bite of silverbeet as much as I relish a lobster. I can't abide wasting food, and I know how to look for a dozen ways to use the food that finds its way into my kitchen.

Home

My family and I live in the foothills of Kunanyi, not far south of Nipaluna, on unceded Palawa land.

We work together growing seedlings, herbs, vegetables and seed crops. Matt, a former chef, makes pickles and preserves and sells our harvests on Saturday mornings at the Salamanca Market. I tend the nursery, sow the seeds and collect plants we can eat.

It's an intense life, lived in burning sun and bone-jarring frosts. Our living is at the mercy of wind, rain, hail and sometimes-fickle chefs. We also have freedom. We get to live outdoors, look up and see wedge-tailed eagles soar over our farm. If our daughters miss school, we are home to care for them. Through our work we have grown relationships with herbalists, gardeners, chefs, kitchen hands, botanists and cooks who teach us every time we talk. We eat well. Not a plant passes through our hands untasted, and although we live a small life, rarely able to travel, we can taste the world through our garden.

The garden

Lutruwita has a cool-temperate climate and sits at a latitude between 41 and 43 degrees south. In the southern foothills of Kunanyi, where my family and I live and work, we have chilly winters, but it rarely drops much below 0°C (32°F), and even in the coldest part of the year, daytime temperatures are usually above 10°C (50°F). Our last frost is usually in September and our first in May, although there are always surprises. Between those two frosts is our warm season when we can grow summer crops. Some years we have October days up to 30°C (85°F). In other years our Octobers are cold and wet, the thermometer staying below 20°C (68°F), giving our summer crops a challenging start. Summers can be hot and dry, with occasional days in the thirties, but rarely nights over 20°C (68°F).

The land we work on was once a sea floor. Rocks that find their way to the surface are marked with fossils of bryozoans, brachiopods and molluscs that are more than 200 million years old. The rock that dominates south-eastern Lutruwita is dolerite, which intruded as magma around 150 million years ago, pushing the land we now live on from below sea level to 300 metres (1000 feet) above it. Since then, the sandstone and mudstone that capped the dolerite has weathered away, exposing magnificent dolerite landforms such as Kunanyi's 'Organ Pipes', and giving much of south-eastern Lutruwita dolerite soils.

But our pocket must have been protected from that erosion. All our neighbours have rusty red tones in their soil from the iron in the dolerite, and soil that is a foot or two deep, and slightly more amenable to cultivation than ours. Our soil is shallow and pale, with ledges of mudstone, and fossils breaking the surface here and there. It is far from ideal, growing food on such ancient, thin soil — but, gently coaxed with compost and crop rotation, our garden feeds us, and our community, admirably.

We chose this patch of land because it was bare and had been neglected. We wanted to garden but couldn't, in good conscience, clear bushland to do it. I'm happy with our decision from that perspective, but I often regret that I didn't take a moment to dig a hole and see the thinness of the soil before we made it our home.

A note on botanical nomenclature: I am a layperson who places great value in science. I've tried my best to be botanically accurate, but may make the odd mistake or lag a little in the always-changing classification of plants. Latin names are vital when discussing edible plants, particularly those that are less familiar to us, as unpalatable or even toxic species could be consumed if a plant is incorrectly labelled or misidentified. There are different conventions in different regions; I have used those that are currently recognised in Lutruwita (Tasmania) using the literature at my disposal.

It is far from ideal, growing food on such ancient, thin soil – but, gently coaxed with compost and crop rotation, our garden feeds us, and our community, admirably.

The plants

Meeting plants is like meeting new friends.

At first you're all gentle: 'Would you like some water, how much and when? Or maybe some shade, some sun, some fertiliser?'

Then, when you know each other better, things ease off. You let your new friend get a little dry, perhaps a bit pot-bound, because you've learned what they'll tolerate. There are others — I'm looking at you, basil — who are needy friends. If you leave a droplet of water on their foliage at night they throw up their leaves and invite every pathogenic fungal spore over for a party, and then turn slimy by dawn — so you learn to water early, and to keep the hose low to avoid wetting those delicate leaves, and your finicky friend rewards you with verdant pesto all summer.

It takes time, and enriches the both of you. The plant adapts to your ministrations, or lack thereof, and you get to know its foibles and learn just when to water, to offer food or shade, and when to harvest.

Eventually, you'll end up in the kitchen together. I have a few friends who know where the knives are and join in, others who take a little coaxing, and perhaps a glass of wine, before they'll get their hands into the dough and help knead. Plants are the same. You'll throw your first oca in the roasting pan with potatoes and it will be savoury, familiar-tasting and comfortable at first bite. Others, like radicchio, might hit your delicate mouth with their feisty bitterness and take some time to learn to prepare, or for you to develop a taste for.

I've read countless books on plants that outline their cultivation needs, heights, days-to-harvest and preferred climatic ranges. I've scoured hundreds of cookbooks that have taught me how long to roast a pumpkin or how to soak and simmer white beans. I hope to take you with me, so you feel like you can comfortably hold an unfamiliar seed or fruit and not expect to know what to do with it, or even be able to find this out in a book or on a website. I hope you'll let your horticultural and culinary instincts guide you and safely enjoy the ride, successful or not. You might learn, as I did, that a tropical coffee tree survives cold if it's in the breeze of your heat pump, or that you can use the stem of sweet cicely as a drinking straw, to delight young and old. There will be plant deaths, and there will be toasted sandwiches for dinner after culinary failures, but sometimes that's okay!

The road to learning is never linear, and mine is never taken alone. A friend — human or botanical — always accompanies me, and together we work it all out and rejoice in the overwhelming beauty and romance of what nature provides. My work is driven by curiosity. If I read of a plant I haven't met yet, I research it.

Will it grow here? There's no point wanting to add something to my collection if it will die from the cold.

Is it invasive? This is a difficult path to tread. Perennial edible plants that need little care are very desirable, but those same plants could escape

There will be plant deaths,
and there will be toasted
sandwiches for dinner
after culinary failures,
but sometimes that's okay.

into wild areas and cause harm. I once germinated sea buckthorn seeds after a chef asked for them, but after thinking on the damage the superficially similar African boxthorn has caused to this landscape, I chose not to propagate a thorny, bird-dispersed plant that could thrive and spread here, delicious or not. Others, like miner's lettuce, *Claytonia perfoliata*, are invasive in a garden situation, but are eaten by herbivores once outside my fence, and produce wonderful salad greens in the depths of winter, so I still propagate those. This is an issue I will inevitably sometimes get wrong, but I will get it wrong after due consideration and much wringing of hands.

Is it delicious? One summer I grew a huge crop of kiwano, a spiky melon cucumber that was said to taste like cucumber, banana and passionfruit. Here it is too cool to ripen them properly, so they were bland and gave my tongue a strange sticky sensation. Our rule is usually to grow small batches of things until we know they taste good, but we still have experimental hiccups from time to time.

Is it interesting? I could probably be disciplined and grow big batches of staple crops such as Dutch Cream potatoes, red cherry tomatoes or smooth black zucchini. If I could work efficiently I might still make a living, but what a dull living it would be. Without curiosity, I would never have tasted silky Portuguese cabbage, a bittersweet tamarillo or the tiny, succulent greens of chickweed. I would never have felt the numbing sensation of sansho leaves on my tongue, smelled the chlorine-pool scent of epazote or gathered the sappy shoots of an unharvested salsify plant and found them delicious.

Is it ethical? I am wrangling with the ethics of growing food plants that are native to Lutruwita and have cultural significance to the Palawa people. I am choosing not to cultivate any other than the most common ones until I find a way to work with them that is culturally safe — which may mean not working with certain plants at all.

There are others that confuse me. Sweet grass, *Hierochloe odorata*, is culturally significant in North America and Canada and should not be traded for money there, but it is also native, and has a long history of human use, in northern Europe where our family has roots. I hope that acknowledging the stories and significance these plants hold is enough, and if I can freely share plants with people for whom they are significant, it is an honour to serve them.

You may notice my anthropomorphism when I talk about plants; they have that kind of presence in my life. When I hear of a new plant I first run it through my feasibility, flavour and ethics filters. By the time I've decided to grow it and tracked down, then planted, a seed or cutting, researched the plant some more as I watched it grow, finally tasting it and sharing it with other growers and eaters, that plant and I have developed a relationship. I care about it and want to share its stories with you.

Garden methods

My favourite tool is a tip-shop steak knife, Matt's is a tractor.

All farming couples will tell you that a middle ground is hard to find. I think our tools of choice reflect that disparity, and that the answer is often somewhere in the middle.

As we mature as farmers, I suspect I'll grow to value that tractor. Spreading compost, moving heavy produce and mowing aren't things for injured knees and tender spines, but I'll happily squat among the emerging carrots, after Matt has hoed the weeds from between the rows, using the point of my trusty steak knife to flick out the weeds hiding among the seedlings.

When we first bought our tractor, we had it fitted with a rotary hoe and bed former. It makes the garden appear neat and functional, but those tidy, fluffy rows of soil had been assaulted. Organisms that prefer to live deep down were thrust into the light, and fungal hyphae — the vast underground fungal network of which the mushrooms we see are merely the fruiting bodies — smashed. Holes made by worms that let water infiltrate the soil were broken, and tiny aggregate clumps of soil formed by tiny life forms or electrical charges were crumbled, making the soil appear looser, when in reality it was more like an overbeaten meringue. Deep down, where the tines of the rotary hoe hit the subsoil, a pan formed — a hard layer between that meringue and the subsoil. So we bought a ripper, a new tool to break that pan. We ripped, sowed green manures and cultivated less, and the soil improved a little, but even now that we barely cultivate at all, it will take time to repair our damage.

We're now working somewhere between the tractor and the little knife. Dutch hoes are magnificent, with sharp blades that make light work of young weeds, and long handles that make the work ergonomic. Our friend James Da Costa worked with us a while and fashioned a wire weeder, a simple tool made by bending an angular U-shape into a piece of wire and fastening it with a hose clamp to the end of a rake handle. It works as the Dutch hoe does, but can get into nooks and crannies near seedlings without slicing them off. We swap beer for wood chips when arborists pass by, then let the chips age before using them as mulch between our garden beds. When they break down after a season or two, we flip them, now brown and crumbly, on top of the beds and put fresh mulch on the paths.

Rather than burning the detritus that falls from the eucalypts growing near our home, we rake it into a pile, run over it with our mower, then mound it up again. After a few months it, too, breaks down and makes an excellent mulch for our paths, or keeps our chickens from getting muddy feet. It's a wonderful resource that many rake up and set fire to. It's a shame to see that carbon heading into the sky, rather than into the soil.

Instead of the big steel tractor ripper, we now have a broadfork — a wide, heavy, two-handled tool with thick steel tines welded to a bar that you stand on top of to push into the soil. Very occasionally, if we think a bed is compacted,

we work along it with the broadfork, inserting it every 10 inches or so, standing on it and giving it just a small wiggle. We don't want to disturb the soil — just to open up any compaction, allowing water, soil life and nutrients to pass between the layers. In a home garden, a normal fork will do the job, or the flat end of a crowbar if things are dire. It's tempting to buy new tools, but if you only need them once a year, see if you can adapt something you already have, or borrow from a friend.

We try to make our own compost, but beyond the home-garden scale, it is difficult to produce enough to contribute significantly to our garden without spending our days driving around gathering inputs. Nothing is wasted, though. Small weeds are thrown on paths where they quickly wilt and break down in the woodchips. Larger weeds, kitchen and garden waste go into the chook run, where they are eaten by the girls, or sit and cold-compost — pooped on and turned by scratching feet — until we shovel it all out for our pumpkins in spring. Spent potting mix from the nursery is formed into garden beds where stray seeds often germinate and give us surprise crops.

Mulch is a vital part of our work. Soil needs living plants to support the organisms that create it. But by weeding, harvesting and cultivating, we damage the soil and expose it to sun, fluctuating temperatures and erosion. Large crops that are in the ground for long periods — perennials, tomatoes, pumpkins, potatoes and corn — all have cultivation methods that leave empty space around plants. As well as protecting the soil from damage, mulch feeds the soil, slows evaporation and protects plants from soil pathogens that can splash up and infect susceptible plants. It's important to know the source of your mulch, though. My favourite, if I can find it, is spoiled silage from spray-free farms — a 'waste' product that is full of life, and contains few weed seeds, as these have mostly fermented away. Ask the supplier of your mulch if broad-leaf herbicides have been used, as their residues can affect any crops you use it on. And please look for local products. At my hardware store I see bales of sugarcane mulch on trolleys and wish there was a local alternative that was equally convenient for busy gardeners. Surely we don't need to ship straw from Queensland to Lutruwita?

We water with drip irrigation, as our garden can be cool and humid, and overhead watering can wet foliage, encouraging fungal and other diseases. And with limited water, we have to use it with care. To grow crops easily, a little irrigation set-up with timers is an excellent investment that allows you to take summer holidays with less worry and grow more food.

Seeds!

The life blood of our work, and my addiction, began with Michael Self's Phoenix Seeds catalogue, with irresistibly enticing listings of 'Thelma Sanders' sweet potato squash and 'Leicester Jones' tomatoes. From there I joined The Diggers Club... and then we got the internet.

Though my hopes were often dashed by blocky capital letters shouting 'NOT TO TAS' under tempting catalogue listings, due to our island state's strict biosecurity regulations, there were still plenty of seeds to get carried away with. As our business grew I became more selective, learning which suppliers were reliable, which had seeds that sometimes failed but were still worth supporting because they stewarded important collections, and a couple whose packets were too tiny to grow a decent trial.

I'd click 'add to cart' and have multiple tabs open so I could review each supplier's prices and, most painfully of all, cull the new varieties that my heart was screaming out for, but my head firmly dismissed, to shrink the seed bill to meet our budget. Now I'm a little more careful. Our garden is at capacity, so I try to explore only a couple of new things every season, and don't force my poor husband to get every single plant in the ground.

I'm also working harder at saving our own seeds, although seed-saving is more complicated with some plants than others. If you have only a single variety from a particular genus — only one kind of mustard, pumpkin or lettuce — in your garden, and your neighbours aren't gardeners, it's relatively easy.

Most important is to cull undesirable plants before they flower, so they don't share pollen with plants you *do* want. If they're a plant grown for roots or leaves — such as carrots, coriander or parsley — and they run to seed and flower too quickly, cull these individual plants in favour of leafier, rootier specimens in your garden. If any plants are sickly, cull those too. And if they're not 'true to type' — for instance, you find a red lettuce in your green lettuce patch, and you prefer to maintain the green variety — then eat that red lettuce before it flowers.

If you're not intending to sell the seeds, or trying to improve or maintain a named variety, then let it rip! There's fun to be had by crossing plants and seeing what new varieties emerge from your melting pot.

Some plants are 'free lovers', crossing with near relatives with wild abandon, and the seeds from such uncontrolled unions may result in poor-quality produce. Saving seeds of wanton pumpkins or zucchini can give you watery, stringy or bitter fruit — an outcome you don't want for the sake of saving a few dollars on seeds. To save seeds from your favourite cucurbit, get up at daybreak before the bees do and find mature but unopened flowers. Gently tease them open and share pollen from a desirable plant's male flower onto a female flower of your intended mother. Tie the female flower shut so no bees can thwart your plans, then tie a ribbon on the stem so nobody picks and cooks your intended seed source.

Kale will cross with cabbages, kohlrabi and others, so while your seeds will produce a brassica, it may not yield the heart you desire.

The kitchen

Thrift and decadence are comfortable companions in my kitchen. Along with everybody's less desirable but inevitable companions, drudgery and dishes.

It's too easy to see only the sticky drips on cupboard doors, plastic lunchboxes missing lids or the avocado somebody burrowed into and left its destroyed remnants on the bench. Sometimes, finding myself overwhelmed by this minutiae, I forget that I too am messy and wasteful and should try to let it go and make a cake.

My dear friend Beck, a mother to four boys and familiar with such chaos, gave me the best advice. Pick a bunch of flowers before you tackle the mess so at least you have somewhere beautiful to rest your eyes.

Such wisdom flies in the face of the perfectionism that has a stranglehold on so many of us, but frees us to bake in a messy kitchen, to sweep the washing from the couch and read a book, or to find a favourite vase and spend a moment recharging, gathering flowers, rather than feeling like we have to earn those pleasures by doing everything else first.

Waste is the thing I can't abide, so that ruined avocado is probably the hardest mess for me to ignore. I sometimes call my style of cooking 'food recycling', which I admit sounds rather unappetising, so I loved Tony Tan, a wonderful chef and cooking teacher, describing a dish as a 'leftover makeover'. Much better.

If I've sown, grown and harvested something, I want to use it to its best advantage, and if I've bought a kitchen implement into the house, I want it to last my lifetime and beyond. A few consumables are inevitable. I love baking paper and use it until it crumbles before composting it, but I refuse to have plastic wrap in the kitchen when beeswax wraps or upturned plates will always suffice. This feels a little futile in the face of pasta packets, chip wrappers, wine bottles and a never-ending parade of bubble tea cups that my daughters bring into our kitchen, but it gives me some sense of agency. Setting boundaries, even small ones, feels like positive action.

The same applies to energy. If I've warmed the oven, I might cook tonight's tagine on one shelf and tomorrow's baked beans on the other, or slip in some shortbread while a cake is baking for an hour. There's nothing more soothing on a cold day than a pot of something simmering on the wood stove while it warms the house. We use that same energy to dry heels of bread for crumbs, dehydrate chillies and dry our tea towels.

Learn to make my sponge topping (page 244) and pour it over apples, quinces, apricots and raspberries. Spy a bowl of plums softening on the bench and cover them with crumble — or put them in a jar, pour a bottle of vodka and a little sugar over them, hide the jar away for a year, and enjoy the surprise when you clean out the pantry and discover a wonderful purple libation.

Introduction

Gather all of those green leafy things — parsley, mint, coriander, kale, lovage — that won't get used before you shop again, toss them in a smoothie maker, blend it all together with garlic, lemon, olive oil and salt, and pour the resulting green sauce over hot steamed potatoes.

Make your grandmother's shortbread dough and spike it with anise hyssop flowers or chopped lemon thyme, or even try swapping some of the wheat flour for milled buckwheat or quinoa.

If you let go in the kitchen and 'fail upwards' sometimes, chances are you'll enjoy it more. Besides, what's a kitchen garden without an experimental cook? Make substitutions. Read a whole book on an unfamiliar culinary tradition, then improvise while your mind is still simmering with ideas.

There will still be sticky cupboard doors and mushy grey avocados, but time spent in the kitchen is a lesson in being in the moment. The food you prepare as an act of love for others, or for yourself, will be gone tonight, and more will be made tomorrow — and won't that be fun.

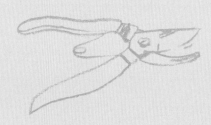

If you let go in the kitchen and 'fail upwards' sometimes, chances are you'll enjoy it more. Besides, what's a kitchen garden without an experimental cook?

33

Alliaceae

THE ONION FAMILY

I'm sure I'm not alone in harbouring a faint longing for an apocalypse.
I'm not a secret bunker-building, armoury fantasist, though. The apocalypse of
my imagining is zombie-free — a gentle, agrarian end of days that will happen
without bloodshed. Useful things like insulin and pacemakers will remain,
but all of the 'stuff' that absorbs us — phones, lip filler, bitcoin and TikTok —
will vanish, leaving us ample time for reading, walking, making cakes for our
dear ones... and for growing food.

My prepper instinct makes me stockpile books I may never find time to
read, mentally catalogue the edible plants growing in footpath cracks, fill my
larder with dried beans, and admire perennial plants that provide gardeners with
food, year after year, with little intervention. Plants that store beautifully, and
boast a variety of edible and medicinal parts — leaves, stems, corms and flowers.
The allium tribe stands proudly, front and centre, offering all of that and more.

There need not be zombies outside the barricades for these plants to be
useful. When we first moved into our home as a broke young family, there was
a patch of Egyptian walking onions here to welcome us. Sprawling, untended
for years by the people who last owned our house, whose only garden tool was
a backhoe, the onions claimed a dry corner under a peach tree, and whenever
the need for alliums arose I only had to step outside.

The succulent side shoots of perennial onions are perfect in place of spring
onions, and the corms of walking onions, potato onions and shallots are always
a little more luxurious than work-a-day brown onions. For some of us there can
be no life without garlic, the beginning of almost every savoury meal, and a plant
easily grown and stored. Edible allium flowers are beautiful and offer a gentle
oniony seasoning with little effort, turning a humble salad into a thing of majesty.

There are hosts of ornamental onions, and many invasive ones, that offer
every shade of allium flavour, from honey-sweet to sulphurous and pungent —
alliums for use raw or cooked, fresh or dried, as seasonings to use sparingly,
or as vegetables hearty enough to be the focus of a meal.

Garlic

ALLIUM SATIVUM

My kitchen is laid out so that as I face my workbench, I can reach out my right hand and take a knife, and, just as smoothly, reach out my left and lay my hand on garlic.

Cooking without garlic is unimaginable to me. Rare is the savoury dish begun without cracking a few cloves loose from a bulb, halving whole heads in cross-section before tossing them in a stockpot, or putting whole heads in a roasting pan. Cooked garlic's mouth-filling flavour sits somewhere between the sweetness of onions and the savouriness of browned meat, the slightly sulphurous funk giving a wholeness of flavour. Raw garlic offers a delicious, daring heat; I find myself making osso buco as an excuse to crush and chop half a dozen cloves of garlic to mix with a bunch of finely minced parsley, lots of finely grated lemon zest and a little pepper to serve in heaping tablespoonfuls on top of the rich, meaty, tomatoey stew. Devour such a generous bounty of pungency and you'll feel it doing you good with every bite.

It took me a few years to let go of the fear of garlic breath learned in childhood. I'm not sure what has changed. Did 1980s garlic come from jars, and was it smellier as a result? Or was our personal hygiene worse? I can't remember the last time I smelled garlic on anyone, so either we eat better garlic now, or I just eat so much now that I'm immune to the scent — if so, I apologise wholeheartedly to all of my garlic-free FODMAP friends.

Although it's a staple we'd like to have on hand year round, garlic is most certainly seasonal. Late winter and early spring are the worst time for the local organic garlic eater. Last year's bulbs are sprouting in the pantry, and new-season 'green' or 'wet' garlic and garlic scapes are yet to materialise. To mitigate this terrible dearth, I slowly roast the fiddly small cloves left over after our planting is done. I rub off their loose skins, pack them in a heavy-lidded pot and submerge them in olive oil. After cooking slowly for an hour or so, I reserve the garlicky oil for later cooking, squeeze out the delicious pulp from the papery skins, and throw the emptied nutty, fragrant skins into the stockpot to eke every last wisp of flavour from my harvest. I spread my sticky confit garlic pulp loosely on baking trays and freeze it for a few hours, then crumble the resulting sheets and freeze the crumbled garlic in small containers, allowing me to scoop out what I need for a dish. While it hurts my heart to freeze garlic, rather than preserve it in oil in pretty jars in the fridge, it would hurt my heart more to see someone contract botulism, a potentially fatal form of poisoning caused by a pathogen that thrives in the kind of low-acid, low-oxygen environment preserving garlic in oil would provide — which is why this age-old method is no longer recommended.

Fermented garlic scapes

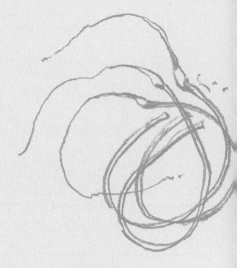

Pack the scapes into a clean glass jar with your flavourings of choice and fill the jar with water. Pour the water back out and weigh it. Work out what 3% of that water weight is, then weigh out that much salt — for instance, 3 grams (⅒ ounce) of salt for every 100 ml (3½ fl oz) of water.

Dissolve the salt in the water and pour it over your scapes, leaving an inch or more headspace at the top of the jar. Weigh the scapes down with a small saucer, or put a few bent bay sprigs on top, tucking them into the neck of the jar, to keep the scapes submerged.

Cover the top of the jar with muslin (cheesecloth), or a fermentation lid if you have one. Put the jar on a plate to save your kitchen bench from the overflow if things get too fizzy.

The liquid should start fizzing in a few days, depending on the ambient room temperature. Let it go on its merry, bubbly way for about a fortnight. You can stop the fermentation whenever you like; let your mouth be the guide. Just use clean utensils to pull out a scape — it should taste slightly fizzy, a little salty and deliciously tangy.

When fermented to your liking, pop the jar in the fridge, where the scapes will keep for a year or so. Be sure to keep the scapes under the brine as you use them and the level in the jar drops.

Enjoy the pickled scapes as snacks on their own, as an excellent addition to tartare sauce or fried rice, or as a tangy bite on a cheese plate.

garlic scapes

flavourings, such as fresh or dried chillies, peppercorns, thyme sprigs, savoury, bay leaves

water — filtered, or boiled and cooled

salt

When we plant our main crop of garlic — which in our southerly latitude is between March and May — I always add an extra patch of densely spaced plants to use as 'green garlic', an immature form of garlic that I can gather from early July when it has grown to the thickness of a pencil and looks a little like spring onions. It's an easy way to extend the garlic season; you can plant the cloves that sprout in your pantry in a pot on your balcony to use in the same way.

The next big garlic harvest comes in early November, when the 'hard neck' garlics produce their scapes — long, tender flower stems with hypnotic curls at their ends. Garlic has been tended by human hands for so long that it's rare for it to grow a true flower — that is, a flower that has sexual reproductive parts that produce true seed from two parent plants. If you don't pick the scapes, each head, instead of flowering, will grow a cluster of bulbils — clones of the parent plant produced without transfer of pollen and fertilisation of an ovary. The bulbils are miniature garlic cloves that are excellent pickled if you catch them before they form papery skins. I usually pick the scapes well before this, because they're delicious. So delicious that my daughter, when she was about eight, had a tantrum, telling me 'I'll die if I don't get scapes for dinner'. The simplest and best thing is to coat them in oil and salt and grill them, as they sit very happily on summer barbecues. I also love to pickle them, either in a hot vinegar pickle, or fermented in brine.

The main garlic harvest comes for us, inconveniently, just before Christmas. We grow a few varieties, and all mature at different times, from very late spring into early summer. When the bulbs are a good size, we turn off the irrigation and keep watch on the leafy tops. The outer sheathing leaves begin to yellow, and when there are five or six healthy, green leaves remaining it's time to get the garlic out of the ground. These healthy green leaves will dry as you hang your garlic, and are vital to hold the bulb together and keep the garlic fresh.

It is, I think, the most stressful harvest for us. It always seems to rain when it's time to pull garlic, and it needs dry, airy conditions to cure — for the skins to harden, the plants to dry out and go into dormancy and store well. We gather the freshly pulled garlic into loose bunches, tied together by the ends of their leaves, and hang them under our back veranda for a fortnight or so to dry. Then we rub off the loosest skins, trim away the dirty roots and store them by hanging them in a cool, dark, airy shed.

Before curing, I find the plumpest bulbs, with their skins still juicy, and peel some while they're at their most pungent, oily, sticky stage, and use these to make ridiculously wonderful aioli. Garlic at this fleeting and vibrant stage of maturity is called 'wet garlic', and you should snap it up when you can.

Even though garlic is commodified, always available and sometimes very cheap, it is well worth growing, to taste all through the season in its many addictive, wonderful phases — easing colds and warding off viruses, and frightening vampires as you go.

Alliaceae

Walking onion, Egyptian onion

ALLIUM × PROLIFERUM

Imagine a plant that thrives on neglect. One that literally walks around your garden, making food for you as it goes. If you don't water it in summer it dies back, but only into dormancy, until you water it again. If you dig it up while it's dormant, the bulbs will last in a paper bag in your pantry for up to two years — and when you finely slice and gently sauté them in oil, adding a little vinegar, salt and a pinch of brown sugar at the end, you'll have an onion jam that will delight your guests.

When walking onions are in active growth, from autumn to early summer, you can harvest the tops and side shoots as a flavoursome, low-maintenance substitute for spring onions. Later the plant will begin to 'walk', producing little onions on top of its stems that eventually bend, allowing those top onions to take root, then grow tall and bend again, *ad infinitum*.

You can circumvent the 'walking' by picking off the little top onions, which you can then pickle or roast, or use in stocks if you find them too fiddly to peel. On top of all that, they are striking-looking plants; tiny clumps of onions hovering in the air are very beautiful. And they're easily gathered and shared with friends if they become too rampant in your garden.

Potato onion

ALLIUM CEPA VAR. AGGREGATUM

It's usual, in temperate Australia, to sow onion seeds in late autumn or early winter, plant out the resulting seedlings in winter or early spring, watch them swell through spring, then ripen for harvest as the soil dries out in early summer.

Our garden is cold and soggy in winter, so I find it almost impossible to nurture minuscule, hair-like onion seedlings, pulling weeds from soil clumped by frost or sodden with rain. When I do, I'm rewarded with wonderful crops. Often I persevere so we can enjoy sweet red salad onions, delicious long 'Tropeas' and pungent home-grown brown onions — but for the most reliable yield, and to avoid chilblains and icy weeding knees from tending those tiny seedlings, I plant potato onions.

A relative of shallots, but with a golden skin, a slightly spikier flavour and better keeping qualities, potato onions are a cool-climate prepper's dream. Plant one in good soil in winter, feed occasionally through the growing season, with side dressings of compost and drinks of worm castings or seaweed solutions, and you'll harvest anywhere between four and sixteen onions in summer for every one you planted in winter. In a normal season, if indeed we have those anymore, the rhythm of winter damp and summer dry means they don't need any supplemental water, and allowing the soil to dry out in summer, as soon as you notice the first green tops flopping, helps the papery outer skin to dry, which makes for better storage.

I pull them out in whole clumps, slicing under the base of each clump with my trusty steak knife to sever the roots and lift the plants without disturbing the soil too much, then I bunch them loosely to hang until I'm ready to eat them. The little ones make superb pickled onions. The larger ones, when juicy and freshly harvested, are lovely raw, and simply sliced and dressed in salads — but most of all we love to confit them in olive oil. A slow-cooked onion is the most luxurious of simple foods.

Confit potato onions

Peel the onions, trimming the root end as little as possible, to keep your onions whole after cooking. Place them in a casserole dish, fitting them fairly snugly.

Sprinkle the vinegar over them, season with salt and pepper and tuck in the thyme sprigs so they don't float. Pour enough olive oil over the onions to cover them.

Roast in a preheated 160°C (315°F) oven for about 1 hour, until the onions collapse.

Serve the confit onions with sausages and mashed potatoes, and keep the oil in the fridge for up to a month to use in dressings or other dishes.

enough potato onions (or shallots) to cover the base of a casserole dish

a sprinkling of white wine vinegar

thyme sprigs

enough olive oil to cover the onions

Leek

ALLIUM AMPELOPRASUM

Leeks are another plant that I never seem to start on time. For the plump, show-winning leeks I desire, I'd need to sow seed in November and plant the seedlings in trenches in January — and then, as my dreamt-of, show-winning leeks grew, I'd pull earth into the trenches to cover them and blanch the stems, creating the long, white shanks that produce that wonderful flavour.

Sadly, I'm too busy for all of that palaver. If I had a looser soil that responded well to digging, and some minions to aid me, I'd love to try, but for now I'm very content with my perennial leeks.

Perennial leeks are a bit of a weed. Each plant produces a bulb that multiplies underground, along with little nut-like structures that often remain in the soil when you harvest — a useful trait if you've carefully selected your planting site, as you'll have an unending source of leeks that can be dug at will through the cool months, and magnificent, towering heads of pale purple flowers in summer.

If you've not been so careful and built your greenhouse above a clump while it was dormant, as we did, you'll never be rid of them, as they'll keep shooting year after year... but it does help attract bees into the greenhouse to pollinate the cucumbers, I guess.

If you do unearth those pesky small bulbils, they can be planted in autumn, rather than starting leeks from seed, and they will produce edible-sized leeks over winter. You can plant them singly in your annual vegetable garden, then hill earth up around them as you would conventional leeks, for a similar, if smaller, result. If you harvest them before they go dormant for the summer, they won't have the chance to form bulbils and permanently move into your garden.

When I'm propagating them for my plant nursery, I drop all of the trimmings into large pots and, in winter, tip the pots out, shake off the soil and reap a very low-labour crop of baby leeks, which are luxurious when trimmed and laid in a baking tray under roasting joints of chicken.

Clumps left *in situ* in perennial or ornamental beds can be dug as needed; if left undisturbed, in mid-summer they will form scapes topped with flower buds, sheathed in charming, pointed paper hats that the plants slowly shed, revealing huge pompom allium flowers. Bees and chefs alike love the flowers — bees for the nectar, and chefs to break them into little onion-flavoured floret garnishes.

If you don't fancy eating them, the towering pompom flowers dry beautifully and last for months in a vase... because we still want the house to look nice, but who wants to head out to pick flowers when the apocalypse is on?

Their cousin Russian garlic — also known as elephant garlic — is another cultivar of *Allium ampeloprasum* grown for its massive garlic-scented bulbs, but it too produces little woody bulbils that persist and ensure a never-ending supply of food, and of towering, majestic flowers.

Alliaceae

43

Spring herb omelette

In early spring I take my basket and smallest, sharpest set of secateurs, and trim sprigs of the most tender growth from our chives, parsley, French tarragon and chervil. The leaves are stout, sappy and sweet, and the chives a darker green than they will be when they're in full growth. A lesson learned painfully is never to carelessly take a basket of that precious harvest with you into the chicken coop. The moment you slip your hand under a hen to retrieve a warm egg, the rest of the flock will have emptied your basket, for they are as hungry for spring greens as you. That same hunger has seen our hens gorge on spent winter crops of kale, lettuce, chard and cabbage, making those first spring eggs the most golden of the year.

Once safely in the kitchen, I set aside the prettiest sprigs of each herb. This is a ritual dish, the harbinger of a new season, and a portent of the parade of flavours to come as the season warms, so beauty is of prime importance.

The rest of the herbs I chop as finely as I can, aiming for a tablespoon of chopped herbs and two eggs per person.

Now comes the important part. Overcooked omelettes are a crime, so tending to your pan, to avoid over- or undercooking, is vital. Turn off the radio, have the bread sitting in the toaster, your plates and coffee already organised, and everyone shooed out of the kitchen.

My favourite omelette pan is an enamelled cast-iron beauty from our local tip shop. Yellow on the outside and white inside, as though it was

This is a ritual dish, the harbinger of a new season, and a portent of the parade of flavours to come as the season warms, so beauty is of prime importance.

made to cook eggs, it's a pan that keeps a gentle, consistent heat and easily releases the egg — which is vital, or you'll end up with a crust stuck in your pan, rather than an edge of buttery crispness on your omelette.

Put your chosen pan on to warm; you want it to melt a teaspoon-sized knob of butter and begin to foam within a few seconds. Gently break up two eggs in a bowl using a pair of chopsticks, to help you resist the urge to overbeat. Fold in half your finely chopped fresh herbs, a little grating of pecorino if you fancy it, a grind or two of pepper and a big pinch of flaky sea salt.

Roll the knob of butter as it melts, to distribute it evenly. Pour in your eggs and repeat the movement, rolling the pan so the egg spreads over the surface. Push down the lever on your toaster, then use your chopsticks to scrape the egg as it sets, gently pulling in from the edge of the pan to the centre, allowing the raw egg to pour into the voids you create.

When you have a pile of almost cooked egg in the centre of your pan (if you're a runny-omelette eater, you can add your reserved herbs and skip this next step) carefully flip it, throwing a touch more butter into the pan, lifting the skirt of the egg to let the melted butter flow under, then top it with the remaining chopped herbs.

Fold your omelette over and slide it onto hot buttered toast that, with good luck or good practice, will have just popped up from the toaster. A whisper of mustard on the toast can be lovely too. Grate on a dusting of pecorino and top with the pretty sprigs you saved at the beginning.

46

Chives

ALLIUM SCHOENOPRASUM

There is a misty softness to common chives. A slightly hazy coating on the leaves, a dusky translucence in the sheaths that hold the emerging flower heads, and in the open flowers the gentlest tones of rose and violet, perfect for the soft light of early spring.

Once I grew a row of them along the path to the chicken coop for beauty's sake alone, until we adopted a dog whose shortcuts tracked excitedly through every bed in our house garden.

Now, though that sweet, rambunctious pooch has passed, I harvest chives from along the front of my greenhouse, where they grow prettily and safely, away from bouncing paws.

In early spring I watch for their emergence from winter dormancy, along with French tarragon and tender new shoots of overwintered parsley and chervil. Hens, hatched the summer before, will lay their first little pullet's eggs and I'll prepare one of the most exciting dishes of my culinary year.

Winter is a time of stasis. Plants established during summer and autumn don't grow a lot. The cabbage hearts and cauliflower curds may swell a little; kale and turnips begin to bolt to seed, producing tender flower buds that we eat as rapini, but losing their hearts and no longer producing new leaves; our root crops wait underground for a gardener with a fork to tear them from their cold slumber… but they are soon finished, leaving us aching for new flavours after long weeks of living on greens, apples and pears.

The earliest plants to move in spring are the perennial herbs, their first precious shoots unimaginably tender, flavourful and sweet. Because they are so tiny early in the season, and because they must be harvested judiciously — they are of course seeking the sunlight that will fuel the plant's new season of growth as it emerges from dormancy — you'll never find them anywhere other than on the plates of gardeners.

I could have put my spring omelette recipe in the daisy section with the juicy, tongue-tingling tarragon, or in the umbels chapter with the essential parsley and delicate chervil, but it's the stout, deep green, peppery-savoury chives that I love the most in early spring.

Pop a clump of chives in any decent soil or garden container. Give them a bit of sun — or a lot, they don't mind. Feed them occasionally with a seaweed solution and a side dressing of compost. Don't let them dry out while they're in active growth — although, if you do, they'll perk right back up when you tend to them again. Year after year they'll reward you in spring with the stout first shoots I prize, then generous bunches of chives, and delicious and pretty flowers through late spring and early summer that are just the thing scattered on creamy new potato salads or herby dips. Then, after they've flowered, cut them back hard and you'll enjoy a second flush of green growth well into autumn.

All the other onions

A tiny orange native bee lives in our garden. It builds its home in dry, hollow plant stems and feasts upon nectar and pollen. On warm summer days I see them in their dozens in our garlic chives, enjoying the flowers, and popping out of the woody stems of improperly tidied weeds. It is a privilege born of gardening near Kunanyi (Mount Wellington) that wild creatures find homes and food among our crops.

The succession of onion flowers through the warm months welcomes all manner of winged things — bees, butterflies and beetles. Slender common chives are the first, garlic chives follow, then the pompom flowers of leek and elephant garlic. Spring onions, if left unharvested, form heads of translucent white flowers that are sappy, spicy and sweet when broken into florets and scattered over savoury dishes. There are also flavoursome and decorative alliums tucked into ornamental gardens the world over.

Siberian chives, *Allium nutans*, is one of those. Its blue–lilac flowers are glorious when planted in drifts. It tolerates poor soil and haphazard watering, but thrives in cool and damp gardens. Its fleshy, strappy leaves are used as you would chives, and its flowers make salads sparkle. The romantically named 'Bridal Lace' form of Naples garlic, *Allium neapolitanum*, is a Mediterranean species that would have been enjoyed for its edible flowers, leaves and bulbs long before anyone planted it in a flowering border.

'Society Garlic', *Tulbaghia violacea*, named because its garlic scent is said not to taint your breath — so you remain fit to mingle after eating it — is a South African native, but is so pretty and so happy in southern Australia that local councils plant it on traffic roundabouts, where you are just as likely to find a chef on a garnish-harvest mission as you are a butterfly seeking its nectar. The dusky pale-pink flowers are honey and onion flavoured, and its strappy leaves have become an essential ingredient in the butter my mum uses on her garlic bread.

Those same chefs scavenge roadsides and cemeteries for **three-cornered leek**, *Allium triquetrum*, a delicious — but terribly invasive — allium that has heads of the prettiest, sweetly flavoured white flowers, tender edible greens and tiny onion-like bulbs. It's easily identified by slicing a stem in cross-section to reveal its triangular shape. But never invite it into your garden, or it will take over and make lawn-mowing forever pungent. It is one of those edible plants in my 'pavement plant' mind map; it's a good one to know if my gentle apocalypse comes to pass, and you find yourself with your foraging basket on your arm, making do with the bounty around you.

Alliaceae

49

Amaranthaceae

Botanical classification got in my way. I thought this was to be a chapter about the goosefoot family, Chenopodiaceae. The name came from the Greek *chen* ('goose') and *pod* ('foot') — much as snails are gastropods, from *gastro* ('stomach') and *pod* ('foot'), as their stomach sits on their foot. That botanical family held the much-loved food items beets, chard, spinach and quinoa, and I'd composed tracts in my mind telling you about how magenta spreen, *Chenopodium giganteum* — a South American leafy green with crystalline, electric-pink cells on the undersides of its leaves — was the plant I thought most suited to the epithet, having the most goosefoot-shaped leaves. But I was thwarted when I found the goosefoot family had been subsumed into a larger one, Amaranthaceae, joining with amaranth, samphire and their cousins following a reclassification.

Botanists are constantly reviewing and changing the classifications of plants — simplifying, correcting and using new technology to place plants where they belong. I can hear you crying out that all this Latin is baffling, why not use common names? And often that is fine, but if you're delving into more obscure areas of edible plants, or communicating across cultural and language barriers, it's vital to know that you have the right plant — and binomial Latin names *do* have the distinct advantage of being pretty much universal.

Chenopodium album, a very useful goosefoot, is called 'fat hen' here in Lutruwita (Tasmania), and lamb's quarters elsewhere — which may make sense here as my chickens refuse to eat it... which, in turn, makes me wonder if lambs do. What I call silverbeet you may know as chard or Swiss chard, but *Beta vulgaris* subsp. *vulgaris,* Cicla group will be understood by plant nerds anywhere. This precise language is vital for biosecurity, international knowledge sharing and science. Saltbush in Tasmania is usually *Atriplex cinerea*, but in arid Australia it's *Atriplex nummularia* — and the two are often conflated in recipes and gardening advice, when they need slightly different treatment in both kitchens and gardens.

Whatever their names, and be they tied together by molecular classification or their likeness to the feet of fowl, this group of plants provides wonderful quantities of edible and nutritious leaves, grains, seasonings and medicines, and are also among the toughest plants you'll come across.

Beetroot

BETA VULGARIS SUBSP. VULGARIS (CONDITIVA GROUP)

The path was well trodden: early-twenties me and my friends, pre-gaming with cheap lambrusco at our flat while we glued on eyelashes, swapped jewellery and fixed each other's hair, before tottering on our ridiculous shoes to follow our favourite bands between bars until we landed at our noisy, wild, weekend home.

Bypassing the ground-floor bar where tradies and regulars nursed beers, we headed straight upstairs to sticky floors, pounding bass, cigarette smoke, and the most excellent late-nineties fashion Hobart could summon. On the top floor we'd sip raspberry vodkas and pretend we were cool enough to get into the hardcore techno, before succumbing to our simpler selves and heading downstairs to Syrup where the eighties music was pumping and we could dance around our handbags until our 4 a.m. taxi home.

One Saturday I learned the sticky dance floors were mopped and covered with chairs and tables, the windows flung open to let the nightclub fug escape, and our disco became a restaurant.

My friend Jo Cook is an incredible chef, and like all good cooks she finds the best ingredients and lets them shine. By night she was managing a nightclub that for us was the heart of our hometown; by day she was practising her craft in the kitchen, and she was bloody good at it.

Ordering Jo's duck and beetroot risotto made me feel daring and exotic. We children of the 1980s had only ever eaten over-sweet, vinegary beets from tins, and this bright pink dish of well-seasoned, creamy rice, earthy sweet beetroot, rich savoury duck and salty pecorino introduced me to one of the loves of my life.

When I eat beetroot I feel nourished. That colour speaks to my soul of plant chemicals that will feed the blood. The earthy flavour is grounding, and it has just the right amount of sweetness and succulence to make for excellent eating.

Beetroot and I have had our hiccups along the road to love. Early in my gardening life, I dug out a patch of earth and sowed a row of golden beets. No compost and very inattentive watering made for tiny withered-looking things, but I was determined to eat them. I sliced them finely and tossed them in a sweet, vinegary dressing, and they were awful. The slow growth of the stressed plants caused a build-up of oxalic acid that would have been harmless had I cooked them, but as we ate them raw it burned our mouths and throats and made me leave beets alone for a while.

I'm guessing it was a TV cooking show that rekindled my love. Watching someone like Maggie Beer or Jamie Oliver rubbing the skins from roasted beetroot with joyful sensuality and pink-stained fingers made me forget my burned mouth and try again. Now I love it — so much so that even a slice of the tinned stuff on a hamburger gives a nostalgic satisfaction. Beetroot makes the best 'sauerkraut', and my friend Kylie prepares a beautiful dip of raw grated beets with lots of mint, but roasted beetroot is my favourite by far. Roasting beets concentrates all their best qualities and dispels my fears of mouth-burn. It's almost as though beets were designed for roasting, for their skins to slip off with glorious ease.

Over the seasons we've begun to master the art of actually growing beets. They love a humus-rich soil, but too much nitrogen — poultry manure, rich fresh compost, or sowing after a nitrogen-fixing crop of peas or beans — can cause your beets to put energy into their greens, which are delicious, but not the crop we're chasing. Growing them in a plot that has previously held leafy greens or broccoli will mean that those hungry plants have used up a lot of the available nitrogen, making conditions perfect for root crops such as beets. They also like plenty of room in which to grow plump and sweet.

Beetroot and chard have conglomerate seeds — clusters of three or more seeds that will germinate in little clumps. I've found that each beet will push its neighbours out of the way and make its own space, but if you've sown your patch too densely, none will thrive.

Once they've germinated, thin the seedlings so they're about 5–10 cm (2–4 inches) apart, saving those thinnings to toss into a salad. Keep the seedlings well weeded and watered, and in 6–8 weeks you'll have a harvest. If you sow in late summer or early autumn, your beets will store in the ground well into winter.

Beets come in a veritable rainbow of colours and I've tried every one I can find.

I think the white ones are fine; neutral and sweet, possibly good as companions for other mild flavours. My plant friend Lindy used to describe her white beet seedlings as being excellent for people who don't want to stain their pant suits, and they definitely do have this advantage for those who wear white!

'Chioggia' beets have a similar flavour neutrality, their ridiculously beautiful concentric circles of pink and white in their flesh making them poster children for the heirloom vegetable movement, but they, too, lack the earthy oomph I crave.

Golden beets are better — rich, sweet and earthy, and beloved because they don't overwhelm other foods with either their juice or flavour. But overwhelm me, I say! Stain my hands, clothes and tea towels with your magnificent lurid juices. Feed my blood and nourish me.

I love 'Detroit Dark Red', 'Bull's Blood' and their maroon-fleshed ilk. There is even a variety, 'Cylindra', which grows long, deep, dark red roots, convenient for slicing and pickling, for a home-spun version of the childhood favourite.

Or avoid the vinegar and simply roast the youngest, sweetest beetroot you can find — and I guarantee you'll be sneaking back for more. And remember that the smallest beets aren't always the sweetest. If I'm choosing beetroot from the same row in my garden, or from the same producer at a farmers' market, the biggest ones will be those that grew the fastest. Perhaps they had a little more space in the row, or they landed in a richer spot of soil and grew more quickly — but they'll be the sweetest and most tender of the bunch.

Eat your beets!

Once you've roasted your beetroots (see opposite), there are myriad ways to enjoy them.

You can whiz the beets, onion, garlic and oily juices and purée it all into a **wonderful dip**, perhaps with a little thick yoghurt; you may need to season it with a little extra salt, as beets are so sweet.

For a **cheat's borscht**, purée the beets, add them to a rich stock, season with plenty of salt and pepper, simmer for 20 minutes and top with sour cream and a snip of chives.

Add the hot, peeled roasted beets to a **warm vegetable salad**, perhaps made with roasted carrots, pumpkin and red onion, for a spike of succulent sweetness, or let them cool, cut into bite-sized pieces and make a **chilled beetroot salad** with spinach and a fresh milky cheese, dressed with a vinaigrette made with the pan juices and a splash of red wine vinegar.

Or, embrace nostalgia with **quick-pickled beets**. Peel the beets and leave to cool, then slice and pack into sterilised jars. Boil together two parts malt or cider vinegar and one part brown sugar, with a teaspoon of salt, a few bay leaves or thyme, oregano or rosemary sprigs, a blade of mace, a few shards of cinnamon bark, a pinch of chilli flakes and perhaps a few black peppercorns. Let the solution sit for 10 minutes, then pour it over the beetroot, making sure the slices are submerged and there are no air bubbles. Seal while warm and store in a cool, dark place for up to a month. Once you've opened a jar for a perfect hamburger with the lot, it will keep in the fridge for up to a week.

Roasted beets

Roasting is the easiest way to prepare beetroot for the table, to enjoy their savoury succulence in salads, soups, dips and pickles with barely any effort. If roasted beets are sitting in my fridge, I'll often find myself snacking on a sneaky slice or two between meals, leaving tell-tale pink-fingered stains about the house.

Trim the leaves and stalks off the beets. (If they're nice, pop them aside to add to your next soup or batch of braised greens; in any case, it's always good practice to take the tops from root vegetables before storing them, even if you intend to eat the tops.)

Scrub the beets well, paying extra attention to the seams of little roots at the bottom where grit can hide. Place in a lidded baking dish with the onion and garlic, then anoint with olive oil, using your hands to ensure an even coating. Tuck the herb sprigs in and season well with salt and pepper.

Pop the lid on and bake for 45 minutes, or until the beets offer no resistance when poked with the tip of a sharp knife.

Allow to cool a little, then gently squeeze the beetroot skins — they should release easily. Squeeze out the pulp from the tender heads of garlic, then set aside with the roasted onion quarters. Drain any of the herby, oniony olive oil and pan juices into a bowl; I like to lean my baking dish against a cutting board and leave it for a little while, so the oil and sticky beetroot and onion juices can pool in a corner, to capture as much juicy goodness as possible.

The rest is up to you.

4 fist-sized <u>beetroot</u>, with leaves attached; make sure they're similar in size, so they cook evenly

1 large red or brown <u>onion</u>, quartered, or 2–3 shallots

1–2 <u>garlic</u> bulbs

<u>olive oil</u>, for drizzling

3–4 fresh <u>thyme</u> or oregano sprigs

Amaranthaceae

Spinach

SPINACIA OLERACEA

For all its ubiquitousness, spinach is a tricky crop to grow. Beloved by snails and slugs, it will bolt to seed at the whisper of a climatic challenge, and will yellow and wither if the soil is not to its liking. But my children adore it, so we persevere: if other gardeners grow lush, plump bunches, surely we can?

Spinach is a crop that needs the gentle shoulders of the seasons to begin life, that little space where the weather is gentle — bold but not scalding sunshine, cool but not icy air. Plants for winter harvest should be sown when autumn is just beginning to falter. Spinach seeds won't germinate well in warm soil, so coolness is vital. Get that timing right and your plants will flourish in the waning days of autumn and give you a bountiful harvest through winter. Your autumn-sown plants will respond to the lengthening days of late winter and begin to run to seed, so if you'd like a harvest in spring, sow more spinach seeds from late winter until very early spring. If you have cool, well-composted soil, you can sow staggered plantings for a continued harvest in all but the coldest months, but I prefer to let each plant have its season and work with less fickle plants when conditions are more challenging.

In the late 1990s — the joyous spring of my relationship with my now husband, co-parent and co-farmer, Matt — we were both doing apprenticeships, which made for rather tight purse strings. Our favourite haunt was a budget-friendly, mostly vegetarian, little neighbourhood restaurant tucked under a row of terrace houses. The owner was a creative force and a palpable presence in the restaurant. No poorly prepared dish would leave the kitchen on her watch, and her menu was heavy with nourishing vegetable dishes. Tables were beautifully set, our stingy BYO bottles were kept cool, and everything was delicious. You could go there on payday and feast, or venture in when the wallet was lighter, share a plate of bread, dips and vegetables with a friend, and still leave feeling sated.

Sadly, nothing perfect ever lasts. One evening, in the way of many young, broke adults playing at sophistication, we'd booked in for a date night, ready to enjoy our favourite food, an extravagant $15 chardonnay tucked under Matt's arm while he held the door for me... but as soon as I stepped through, I saw that our cosy little haven had changed.

We were seated by an earnest young waiter, clad in a very formal ruffle-fronted shirt, complete with a rakishly sideways bow tie, who took our wine. The decor was the same, but one glance at the specials board made me wary. One dish was laboriously described as 'Fish wrapped in paper and baked in the oven'; another included a description of the frying pan used in its creation.

The menu we were handed featured the same dishes we'd seen on past visits, so I chose my favourite — the honey brown mushrooms, which for me

were novel, exotic fare when I'd only ever had tinned champignons, white supermarket buttons, or fat field mushrooms foraged on holidays. On previous visits the mushrooms were whimsically presented on a plate filled with a rich tomato sugo, a circle of tiny spinach leaves laid out like the petals of a flower, in the middle of which sat a large honey brown mushroom, filled with a stuffing of spinach, garlic, pine nuts and cheese. As with all the dishes there, the vegetables shone. The dome of rich, green spinach at the heart of the mushroom was enough to swell the biceps of a dozen Popeyes.

On this visit, however, I received a plate of mushrooms that had been mistakenly cooked in honey instead of the 'honey brown' variety that were, at best, difficult to eat. We struggled through our awkward dinner, pretending to like the oaky chardonnay, too newly minted as a couple to voice our feelings directly, when we noticed the dinner music — a Crowded House CD — was stuck in a loop, with Neil Finn singing 'Something so strong... Something so strong' ad nauseam, until neither of us could stand it. When we paid the bill and asked for the rest of our bottle of wine, the waiter bent happily to retrieve our cork — from the garbage bin.

Uncapped bottle in hand, we wandered home, conveniently past a 24-hour kebab shop, and mourned the loss of a favourite haunt.

Those spinach-stuffed mushrooms were once such a hearty, whimsical and delicious meal. While I can never recapture the feeling of being a young, newly-in-love couple, wandering our city at night, I can try to relive those heady days by cooking the dish we loved so much.

Spinach-stuffed brown mushrooms

Preheat your oven to 180°C (350°F). Oil a large baking tray.

Wash the spinach well. Choose 24 of the prettiest small leaves and set them aside, then roughly chop the rest. Remove the stems from the mushrooms and finely chop, setting the caps aside on the baking tray, gill side up.

Warm the olive oil in a large saucepan over medium heat. Sauté the onion for about 5 minutes, until softened, then add the garlic and cook until fragrant. Toss in the chopped mushroom stems, then the spinach. Cook until just wilted, then set aside to cool. Add the herbs, lemon zest, walnuts and parmesan. Season with salt and plenty of black pepper and mix well to combine. Gently fold the cottage cheese through.

Evenly divide the spinach mixture among the mushroom cups, pushing it out to the edges. Top with the cheddar and bake for 30 minutes.

Tomato sauce: While the mushrooms are baking, rinse out the frying pan and sauté the onion in the olive oil over medium heat until softened. Add the garlic. Squeeze the bay leaves to bruise them and add them to the pan as well. Cook for a minute or two, until fragrant, then stir in the passata. Season with salt and pepper and simmer until thickened. Check the seasoning and add a little more salt if needed.

Spoon the tomato sauce into six warm deep plates or broad, shallow bowls. Arrange four of the reserved spinach leaves around each bowl, one at each point of the compass so they sit like flower petals once you lay a mushroom in the middle of each bowl. Serve hot.

Kitsch perhaps, but very delicious and quite pretty. Serve with plenty of buttered bread and an unblemished Crowded House CD.

Serves 6

3 bunches of English spinach

6 large brown mushrooms

2 tablespoons olive oil

1 onion, diced

4 garlic cloves

1 tablespoon fresh dill

1 tablespoon fresh oregano

1 teaspoon lemon zest

50 g (1¾ oz) walnuts, finely chopped

⅓ cup (30 g) grated parmesan

200 g (7 oz) cottage cheese

⅓ cup (30 g) grated cheddar

TOMATO SAUCE

1 small onion, finely diced

1 tablespoon olive oil

3 garlic cloves, crushed or finely chopped

2 fresh bay leaves

700 ml (24 fl oz) tomato passata (puréed tomatoes)

Silverbeet

BETA VULGARIS SUBSP. VULGARIS (CICLA GROUP)

There is a metallic taste in silverbeet that I crave. Perhaps it's the microbes that have a direct line from my gut to my brain that are screaming out for greens, or maybe it's a strong association with nourishment stemming from comforting childhood meals, a feeling that lingered when, as an impoverished young adult, I lived on silverbeet and steamed rice for a time.

Silverbeet and beetroot have a common ancestor, sea beet, *Beta vulgaris* subsp. *maritima,* a wild cousin that has colonised the banks of Timtumili Minanya (the River Derwent), where I grew up. Often as a youngster I was tempted to take a bunch home for my mum when I saw it growing wild by the beach on my walks. Now I'm glad I didn't. Leafy green vegetables are such wonderful accumulators of minerals that the ones on the shore of our beloved but abused river have likely taken up harmful quantities of lead and zinc from when the river was used as a dumping ground for smelter waste. Those living near the sea adjacent to the old zinc works are still advised not to grow greens in the existing soil where sea spray has contaminated the soil with these heavy metals.

But if you spy sea beet growing wild in a clean coastal area, it makes a beautiful, nutritious, pre-salted leafy green that responds wonderfully to braising. Silverbeet thrives as easily as its tough ancestor, wanting only reasonable soil with some nice compost, possibly a lick of boron, and regular, deep watering. Often you'll find it self-seeding in the corner near the compost heap, needing nothing from you, just waiting there to keep you well fed.

There isn't much you can't do with silverbeet. The shredded stems thrown into salted boiling water for a minute or so, before being joined by the young green leaves for a minute or two more, then drained and dressed with butter, lemon, salt and pepper, is a complete meal for me. Some buttered toast on the side, a dollop of good, thick yoghurt, a sprinkle of chilli and it's even better.

My mum wraps the leaves around a stuffing made with seasoned minced meat and rice, then bakes them in a rich tomato sauce. Matt is a spanakopita fan, an abundance of chard making for a rich, green filling, while my daughters adore the mini versions — triangles of filo pastry stuffed with chard, feta and parmesan, flavoured with lemon zest, a little nutmeg and pepper, and brushed with lots of butter before baking.

There is a metallic taste in silverbeet that I crave.

I remember the heady days of living in my first flat, independence and the empty wallet of an apprentice hairdresser sitting uncomfortably together, finally having the freedom to do anything at all... but very little cash to do it with.

Silverbeet was always there to sustain me through my questionable budgeting choices — free when I raided Mum's garden on visits home, or bought cheaply from the greengrocer, giving me a nutrient-dense meal in minutes after achingly long days on my feet.

My salon job saw an endless parade of fellow stylists moving from interstate and between salons, working the same ridiculous hours. New friends every month or two, all ending their days weary, in need of nourishment and cheap champagne. As a mother hen, even at 18, I would invite the most hungry and tired ones over. They'd supply the bubbles and I'd cook. One day, one of them brought his boyfriend — an *actual* chef — along to cook for us, and I reddened with embarrassment opening my meagre fridge and pantry to him. But he found the chard, dug butter and cheese from the fridge, and dijon mustard, flour and breadcrumbs from the pantry, and pinched some of our awful champagne — and then, like the loaves and fishes, he prepared a warming, satisfying meal for us, while we took off our platform boots and stretched our tired feet.

My larder is fuller now, but I still think of that chef every time I make this rich and comforting dish.

Amaranthaceae

Silverbeet stem gratin with lemony silverbeet greens

The crumbs are the most coveted part of this dish. I love using breadcrumbs made from a loaf of pumpkin sourdough; sometimes I'll even add lemon zest, paprika or parsley when I'm blitzing the bread to bits, depending on my whim, or what's in the pantry.

I've learned, through a few ugly mistakes, that silverbeet stems can turn grey if they're left standing after they've been sliced or even blanched, so don't prepare them too far ahead of adding them to the sauce and baking the gratin.

Preheat your oven to 190°C (375°F).

Crumbs: Melt the butter in a small saucepan, add the garlic and let it warm for a moment. Stir the breadcrumbs through, remove from the heat and allow to cool, then stir in the grated cheese. Set aside for the topping.

Warm the stock in another small saucepan. Squeeze the bay leaves to bruise them, then add them to the stock and let them infuse for a while. Stir in the cream and keep warm.

Melt the butter over medium heat. Add the onion and cook for about 5 minutes, until tender and translucent. Sprinkle the flour over and cook, stirring, for a minute or two, while the flour cooks out, to help prevent your white sauce becoming lumpy when you add the cream. Whisk in the cream mixture a little at a time, discarding the bay leaves, until the sauce is smooth. Season generously with salt and black pepper (chard stems love extra salt).

Serves 4

¼ cup (60 ml) strong, flavoursome stock

2 fresh bay leaves

½ cup (125 ml) single (pure) cream

30 g (1 oz) butter

1 small onion, finely diced

1 tablespoon plain (all-purpose) flour

1 bunch of silverbeet (Swiss chard), about 800 g (1 lb 12 oz)

FOR THE CRUMBS

15 g (½ oz) butter

2 garlic cloves, crushed and finely chopped

½ cup (60 g) coarse dried breadcrumbs

½ cup (50 g) grated gruyere

FOR THE GREENS

20 g (¾ oz) butter

juice and grated zest of ½ lemon

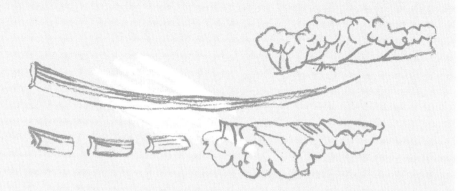

Meanwhile, bring a large saucepan of salted water to the boil, and set a colander in the sink.

Strip the green leaves from the white stems and veins of your silverbeet. (I hold the stem in one hand, sort of fold the greens to the centre, pinch them where they join the white part and tear both sides at once from the bottom. It's fast once you get the knack of it.) Slice the stems into 2 cm (¾ inch) lengths, and set the greens aside for braising later.

Tip the chard stems into the boiling water, cook for just a couple of minutes, then pour into your colander and drain well. They can hold a lot of water, which will dilute your creamy sauce, so press down on them with a bowl to remove as much liquid as possible. Tip them back into the pan and stir the creamy sauce through, mixing well.

Transfer to a shallow ceramic baking dish. Top with the crumb mixture and bake for 20 minutes, or until you see the edges bubbling and a lovely brown crust on the topping.

Meanwhile, roughly chop the reserved silverbeet greens. Put a steamer over a pot of simmering water and add the greens. Melt the butter and whisk in the lemon juice, lemon zest, sea salt and plenty of black pepper. After 5 minutes or so, when the greens are tender, pop them in a warm bowl and pour the lemon butter over.

Enjoy the lemony greens as a bright, fresh contrast to those salty, creamy stems.

To have weeds fit for a restaurant garnish, you have to pick them when they're young and tender.

Fat hen

CHENOPODIUM ALBUM

One of the cleverest of edible weeds, fat hen produces a spectrum of seeds clothed in various coatings, designed to survive in the soil for differing periods of time — some seeds ripen almost naked, fall to the soil and germinate with no trouble, while other seeds mature in a state of dormancy and wait for triggers in the environment to awaken them. The parent plant hedges its bets this way, its seeds germinating over several years, in differing conditions, ensuring the best chance of becoming a grandparent to thousands of fat hen babies.

While this may be excellent for the plant, it is not so excellent for me when my spring-sown carrots, one week free of weeds, are smothered by fat hen the next. Early in our growing-for-chefs business, we made the mistake of allowing weeds to seed so that we could harvest them for restaurants. As deliciously thrifty as selling edible 'weeds' as high-end food sounds, it was wildly impractical. To have weeds fit for a restaurant garnish, you have to pick them when they're young and tender — and that meant spending hours on our knees, in the dirt, plucking tiny tips of chickweed, *Stellaria media,* shepherd's purse, *Capsella bursa-pastoris,* sheep sorrel, *Rumex acetosella,* and fat hen. Our backs suffered, and the weed seed bank in our soil grew vast. The fat hen in particular, with its wily spectrum of seed dormancy, is unbeatable — but for all that, I still love it.

Fat hen produces useful quantities of tender leaves that are terrific in salads when picked in the first flush of youth, and older leaves that are excellent cooked as you would spinach. Its edible seeds are an ancient human food, found in the stomachs of people preserved in bogs, and in charred and preserved granaries from the first century CE. Occasionally I relive those heady on-hands-and-knees days, or imagine myself a skilled nonna, and I take my knife and basket to the field and gather weeds for the Lutruwita (Tasmanian) version of the Greek *hortopita*, or wild greens pie.

Amaranthaceae

Fat hen pie

This is delicious served with even more greens. A crisp lettuce salad on the side makes a beautiful contrast to the rich darkness of the wild greens. Some sweet, spicy, tart tomato chutney is also vital.

Wash your chosen greens well and drain them. Wild greens can be fiddly to prepare, but it's important to remove any fibrous stems and wash out all the grit. To make chopping them a little easier, gather all the small greens into a bundle and roll them tightly into a sausage inside a big leaf, such as a large chard or collard leaf. Then you can finely slice the leaves in bulk with ease, eliminating any tough stems you may have missed.

Most recipes for wild greens involve boiling then draining them. This may have advantages if your harvest is a little gritty, and perhaps removes some oxalates, but I cringe at all that beautiful, nutrient-rich water going down the drain — so I prefer to cook them in their own juices with a splash of water, broth or wine to help them along.

Warm the olive oil in a large saucepan and sauté the onion over medium heat for about 5 minutes, until softened. Add the garlic and cook until fragrant. Turn up the heat for a moment, allow the pan to warm — and just before things start to brown, tip in your greens and jam the lid on to trap the hiss of steam, giving your pan a shake to move things about.

Serves 4

500 g (1 lb 2 oz) <u>mixed greens</u> — such as fat hen, nettle, chickweed, mallow, shepherd's purse, young plantago leaves, sheep sorrel, wild radish greens, chard, collards, kale

2 tablespoons <u>olive oil</u>

1 large <u>onion</u>, diced

5 <u>garlic</u> cloves, crushed

a handful of finely chopped fresh <u>herbs</u> — a mix of hard herbs such as rosemary, thyme or oregano, and soft herbs such as fennel fronds, parsley or dill

a splash of <u>stock, white wine or water</u> — about ¼ cup (60 ml), depending on how long you braise and how succulent your greens are

<u>melted butter</u>, for brushing

12 <u>filo pastry</u> sheets, thawed if frozen

¼ cup (35 g) crumbled <u>feta</u> or labneh (optional)

Once the steam has settled, remove the lid. Stir in your hard herbs, season with salt and pepper and add the stock. Cook over medium–low heat for about 30 minutes, stirring now and then, and checking there is just enough liquid to stop the greens sticking — without letting them stew, or your pie will be soggy. Wild greens benefit from slow, tender care, so stir, moisten and tend your greens, tasting as you go, and enjoy the transformation. When you're happy with them, cook them a little longer without adding any liquid, to dry them a little. Remove from the heat, add your soft herbs and allow to cool.

Preheat your oven to 180°C (350°F). Brush a 1 litre baking dish with melted butter.

Working with one sheet of pastry at a time, and covering the rest with a damp tea towel so they don't dry out and become brittle, lay a sheet of pastry on the bench and brush lightly with melted butter. Place another sheet on top, brush with butter again and repeat until you have six layers. Lay the whole thing over your dish and gently press it into the corners, taking care to fold and wrinkle the pastry, rather than tear it.

Gently spoon in the cooled greens. Dot with the feta or labneh, if using, then butter another six pastry layers and place over your pie. Brush with extra butter and tuck down any edges that might catch and burn.

Bake for 30 minutes, until the centre is hot and the top crisp and golden.

Serve fresh from the oven. Any leftovers are wonderful eaten cold the next day.

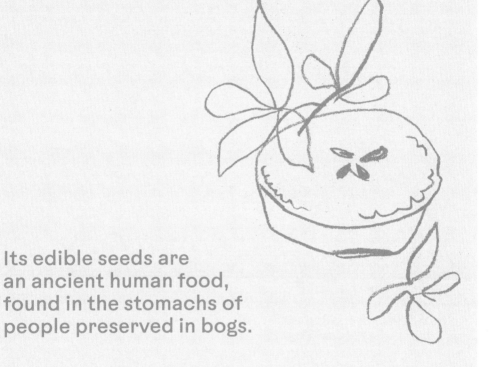

Its edible seeds are
an ancient human food,
found in the stomachs of
people preserved in bogs.

Goosefeet & glassworts

In the face of an uncertain future, the plants of the amaranth family are worthy of our attention. Many are able to survive a wide range of climatic challenges, while providing us with edible roots and stems, nutritious greens and protein-rich seeds — often bearing several of these gifts on the same plant… and they look magnificent while they're doing it! It may be difficult to see, superficially, the similarities between the goose foot-shaped leaves of sea orache, *Atriplex prostrata*, an edible introduced coastal weed species, and the fleshy beaded stems of its distant glasswort cousin, samphire, *Sarcocornia quinqueflora*, but the two share the common trait of toughness and stand strong in the face of tide, storm and sea.

A jar filled with the seeds of the **quinoa** plant, *Chenopodium quinoa*, holds a prime position in my pantry. Quinoa is a 'pseudo cereal' — a seed produced by a plant that isn't a grass, but whose seeds are used in the same way as those of the grass grains barley, wheat, rye and their ilk. It is lighter on the stomach than rice and quicker to cook, and is a wonderful accompaniment to curries and braises. I use the cooled leftovers in salads or fritters; they're also brilliant warmed and served with cinnamon, honey and yoghurt for breakfast. I source ours from a beautiful farm, Kindred Organics, here in Lutruwita (Tasmania), and on seeing their success growing it in our climate, then reading of quinoa greens being grown as a specialty salad crop, I thought it would be a worthy experiment for our garden.

Quinoa is best sown in spring and, all going well, germinates quickly. Within a month the leaves — almost indistinguishable from those of its relative, fat hen — can be harvested for salads or for cooking. By late summer, the plants will be plump with seed, ready to dry, thresh and winnow for the pantry. Our little experiment yielded many nutty salads, but we needed the bed space to begin our winter crops, so growing our own quinoa seeds for the pantry will have to wait for another season.

Their high protein, mineral and fibre levels have seen quinoa seeds become a darling of the superfood movement. With escalating demand, the price has also risen, putting this nutritious staple out of the reach of many people in Bolivia and Peru who have been eating it for millennia. Under Spanish colonisation, the cultivation of many indigenous food plants, including quinoa, was forbidden, so it is only due to the fortitude of its traditional keepers that we have access to this wonderful food. I often wonder if we should be paying an intellectual property levy on foods that have a direct lineage to the people who have held the seeds and traditions under such hardships. Maybe some of my wonderful, local quinoa could help the people who have historically tended it be able to afford it themselves.

I'm yet to delve into **leaf amaranth**, *Amaranthus* spp., beyond one beautiful red-leafed form that pops up unbidden every summer in my greenhouse and from there finds its way to our salad bowl. We did once grow some grain amaranth, my daughters having enjoyed a bag of puffed grains that they'd bought. I grew, harvested, dried and threshed it; then scorched it every time I tried to 'pop' the tiny seeds in my kitchen.

Good King Henry, *Chenopodium bonus-henricus,* is a perennial plant whose spring shoots are eaten like spinach. **Magenta spreen**, *Chenopodium giganteum,* is taking over our garden, much as its fat hen cousin has, germinating like hairs on a cat's back every spring in our fields, but stubbornly refusing to do the same in my nursery pots, making it difficult to share its blessings with other growers. It grows a metre or more tall, has grey-green leaves with hot pink undersides, makes a refreshing salad green and vivid garnish when young, and produces plentiful larger leaves for cooking until killed by cold soil in autumn.

Huauzontle, *Chenopodium nuttaliae,* is grown for its flower buds, harvested in heads like broccoli, which are traditionally — and wonderfully — prepared by pressing fresh, soft cheese into them before they are battered and deep-fried.

Another stunning and useful volunteer in our garden is **orache** or **mountain spinach**, *Atriplex hortensis.* It, too, germinates in spring, and is a frost-killed annual. There are myriad varieties, from 'Green Velvet' to 'Purple' and shades in between. They grow into tall, branched plants, and each provides months of picking if you pinch out the spinach-like tips as they form. Young leaves are tender raw, the older ones cook beautifully, and I love to drop the purple leaves into a clear broth for a stunning pink soup. The red varieties are beloved by ornamental gardeners as they grow tall, grand flower spikes, covered in thousands of disc-shaped seeds, at the end of the season.

Many plants in the amaranth family are halophytes — plants adapted to survive in saline conditions. This makes them ideal for an uncertain future, able to produce food in areas degraded by salinity and to remediate the soil. **Samphire** or **glasswort**, *Sarcocornia quinqueflora*, and **seablite**, *Suaeda australis,* along with **coastal saltbushes**, *Atriplex* spp. and others, grow naturally in salt marshes, and can be delicious if picked at the right stage of growth. Our southern-hemisphere samphire has a woody core that I think northern species lack, meaning only tiny tips of new growth are easily eaten. They tend to grow where shorebirds nest, so we only ever gather a little — and only when we can see clearly what's near our feet, lest we crack a tiny, camouflaged egg.

Apiaceae

THE UMBEL FAMILY

On still summer days, when my head is full and I need perspective, I wander through the umbels. In the thick of summer, carrots, coriander, fennel and their brethren burst into growth, sprouting towering flower spikes, their heads made up of a fascination of tiny flowers, arranged in circles upon circles, collaborating and merging their tininess together into grand, round umbels that are magnets to the greatest diversity of creatures in our garden.

Miniature orange-striped orb-weaver spiders risk predation from foraging wrens by perching on the highest flowers in hopes of trapping alighting insects. Native jewel beetles, decorated in impossible shades of metallic turquoise and orange, ramble among the umbels feasting on nectar and pollen. Slug-like hoverfly larvae inch slow paths along stems, feasting on plump, succulent aphids, and the tiniest of wasps forage alongside fat bumblebees. There is always a creature I've never seen before. And it is then that I am most strongly reminded that our garden is part of an ecosystem, and the wonderment — the utter magic of such diversity responding to plants we've sown and nurtured — grounds me.

We are fortunate to live near a vast forest, our days witness to a parade of scaled, feathered, furred and segmented creatures, but even among seemingly barren cityscapes, if you find an umbel in flower on a warm day, you'll likely find a miniature community supported by its shelter, its carbohydrate-rich nectar, and its protein-laden pollen.

It is not only birds, spiders and insects who benefit from the bounty of umbels. The Apiaceae family is incredibly diverse in both culinary and botanical gifts. Most would be familiar with the family's namesake genus, *Apium*, which takes in *Apium graveolens* — celery and celeriac — as well as the sea celeries *Apium prostratum*, *Apium insulare* and *Apium annuum*, which are important culturally significant plants to the Palawa here in Lutruwita (Tasmania), and to Aboriginal people throughout Australia. Carrots and parsnips are staples in most kitchens, parsley is indispensable, dill graces gravlax and pickles everywhere, and coriander leaves, seeds and roots are vital ingredients in many cuisines. Caraway and cumin find their way into most spice racks, angelica into many liquor cabinets, while lovage, aniseed and fennel are once-adored flavours finding their way back into common usage.

It is not a family to be trifled with, however. Increasing populations of hemlock are scrambling through the gullies and roadsides of Lutruwita (Tasmania). I once saw a young chef's Instagram post proudly displaying his foraged 'wild parsnip'; the red-purple splotches on the stems were a literal dead giveaway, so I called him and we prevented his fate echoing that of Socrates. There are other toxic species, too. I'm yet to meet water dropworts and false hemlocks in Lutruwita, but these grow merrily elsewhere, so always be extremely sure of your identification before eating any new plants gathered in the wild.

Parsnip

PASTINACA SATIVA

I'd always taken parsnips for granted. My mum has a miraculous touch with her roasts, making sure every piece of potato, pumpkin and parsnip has a crisp crust of caramelised meat juice on it, but it wasn't until we stopped at a little roadside vegetable stand that a new appreciation for parsnips dawned on me. A farmer with the most glorious hands — fingers large from hard work, veined with dirt-stained cracks — took our money while telling us about the heavy frosts he'd had, and how the parsnips we were buying would be sweeter than any we'd tasted. They were also massive, the plump stem ends as big as my palm.

I learned two lessons from him. The first was that small vegetables aren't always the best. In early spring, or at the beginning of a harvest, this may be true. Tiny vegetables pulled in the first flush of youth are sweet and tender — but as the crop matures, the plants in the best soil, with the most space, are the ones that grow faster, fatter and sweeter.

The second lesson, and my favourite, is that cold weather signals plants to convert starch into various sugars that, in the hands of a skilled cook, can be coaxed to form Mum's golden caramel crust with a creamy, fragrant inside that has everyone forgetting their manners and racing to serve themselves the brownest pieces.

Those behemoth, frost-sweetened parsnips came home with us and are still on my mind twenty years later. Whether the parsnips were so different, or it was the story, the farmer's beautiful hands, or Mum's culinary magic, those wondrous memories linger.

For all its hardy robustness, parsnip can be fickle in the garden. Planning is the biggest problem new gardeners have. How, in the wild abundance of summer — when zucchini are coming out of your ears, you're tying up tomatoes seemingly every five minutes, and dinner is as easy as boiling pasta and quickly pounding a pesto — do you turn your mind to frosty winter harvests and cosy feasts? To enjoy those enormous frosted parsnips in July you have to sow them, in our cool-temperate southern-hemisphere conditions, in January or February. This leads to the challenge of keeping the seeds moist, and preventing tiny emerging plants from being scorched to death in the heat of summer.

However, a simple trick or two will assist. The first is to choose a plot in your garden that has carried a hungry crop previously. If you've cut down a broccoli, chard or kale crop, that bed would be perfect. Too much nitrogen or freshly applied compost and your precious root crops won't bother to burrow down into the cool, deep soil, seeking nutrients. Instead, they'll lazily send out roots into the easy, shallow soil, giving you forked crops that you'll curse as soon as you've got them in the sink for scrubbing or peeling.

The next most important thing is using fresh seed. Parsnip seeds don't keep well. If I'm not using them immediately, I'll make sure they're perfectly dry, seal them in two layers of zip-lock bags, to keep out any moisture, and store them in the fridge, throwing the seeds in my compost bin after the second year. If you've got an older batch of seeds you're determined to use, you can germination-test them by popping a few seeds on a damp paper towel, sealing it up and leaving it in a warm place for around three weeks. If nothing happens by then, you're best off to compost the seeds, buy more and save yourself the heartbreak. It's a test worth doing with all your saved seeds — the perfect winter garden task that helps you plan your spring and summer garden.

And here's where I am, once again, going to be annoying. Many of you will have had parsnips bolt to glorious, golden flower. You may think, 'Well, I have a source of fresh seeds right here!' But plants that freely run to seed will likely produce children that do the same. If you want to save your own fresh seeds, lift the plumpest dozen parsnips and tuck them into a corner of the garden, where they'll live out their life cycle and produce copious seeds for you and your neighbourhood. (This also applies to carrots, beets and other vegies — so long as there are no near relatives flowering nearby.)

Sow fresh seeds into a weed-free garden bed, spacing them every centimetre (half an inch) to allow for failures, in rows about 30 cm (12 inches) apart. After sowing, water deeply to settle the soil around your seeds. If you're not a vigilant waterer, you can then lay planks over your drills, or weigh a piece of permeable cloth over the bed to keep conditions humid and favourable for wee germinating plants. Be sure to lift the covers to check for shoots, and remove them as soon as the first plants emerge. Pluck out the excess seedlings, so your parsnips are about 5–7.5 cm (2–3 inches) apart, and get back to your summer chores now you have something to look forward to in winter.

Apiaceae

Mum's magic roast vegetables

My nephew Felix really loves his gran's roast vegetables, and I have to agree Mum's technique is unbeatable. It does create more washing up than other methods, but it ensures the vegetables produce an all-over golden crust flavoured with the precious, delicious brown bits absorbed from their roasting companions.

Mum will likely have had a joint of meat in the oven, slow-cooking for a few hours, but the roasted vegies can also easily be prepared as a stand-alone meal. Mum turns the oven up and tucks potato, pumpkin and parsnip around whatever meat she's roasting that day. If the entire family horde is descending, she'll pop an extra tray of vegetables on, baking them with some of the dripping reserved from other meals and stored in the fridge.

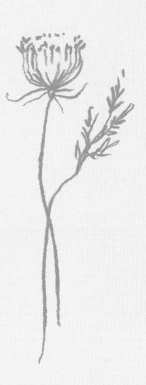

The vegetables are first roasted in their trays for half an hour or so — 30 minutes will do for parsnips alone; potatoes need a little longer and can be given a head start. The excess fat is then drained back into the dripping pot, and the vegetables are turned and roasted for another little while. When they're fork-tender, Mum removes the joint she's roasted, rests it on a carving tray, wrapped to keep warm, on the back of the stove.

The magic is in the finishing: the roasted vegetables are spread on a metal cake rack, with a tray underneath to catch the drips, and returned to a high oven, where they obtain a transcendent level of browned crispness while the meat rests, and while we prepare some greens and make gravy from the pan juices.

When the horticultural, seasonal and culinary stars align, crisp, creamy, savoury, aromatic and sweet parsnip, shared with special people, is what true love tastes like.

Carrots

DAUCUS CAROTA

Living on an island off an island is both a gift and a curse when you're a gardener. The gift, which ironically is also the curse, is isolation.

It protects us from pests and diseases, and from noxious weeds that haven't yet been introduced. To reap the rewards of this gift, we follow excellent biosecurity laws in Australia, but their administrative burden means that only horticultural and agricultural businesses with the economic scale to absorb the costs can bring certain seeds and plants into the country — and then, on top of that, sits another layer of regulations to bring things across Bass Strait to Lutruwita (Tasmania).

I am thrilled that we don't bite into apricots to find seething masses of fruit fly larvae — thank you, Bass Strait — and nor do I want to send onion smut into my friend's gardens hidden among seedlings, but it is painful to browse through a seed catalogue and find a treasure you'd love to grow and taste... only to learn that it's unwelcome in Lutruwita, or that it may play host to a devastating organism.

Once I fell in love with a carrot. We'd grown every cultivar we could lay our hands on. 'Lunar White' carrots were skinny and prone to bolting, and quickly fell from our sowing list. 'Amsterdam' grew quickly and made an excellent field snack when wiped on your jeans and eaten seconds from the earth, but needed to be gently levered from the soil or their crisp, fragile roots snapped off and went to waste underground. 'Paris Market' became a firm favourite, tolerant of shallow soil, maturing quickly and filling the air with a heady carrot perfume when pulled from the earth, but it is unforgiving of irregular watering — miss a hot day and the skin hardens, only to split when the carrot drinks beyond the limits of its drought-tightened skin when you next turn on the hose. We've grown purple carrots that are beautiful and delicious, but whose green tops snap off when tugged, making them difficult to harvest and impossible to bunch for market.

There are the fat French 'Royal Chantenay', staple, sturdy 'Kuroda', and long-keeping 'Autumn King'. But the carrot that has most won my heart is the lovely 'Jaune du Doubs', from France — plump, golden and dense, with a creamy texture when roasted. It is crisp and sweet when harvested small as a salad carrot, but comes into its own when overwintered.

The soil here is heavy, often becoming waterlogged and icy in winter. Our mountainside garden receives a few harsh, sparkling frosts each season, and only the hardiest root vegetables survive without turning to foetid mush underground. Our carrot friend Jaune is perfect. Slow, cool, growing conditions create a finer texture and deeper flavour, and stimulate plants to store their

Apiaceae

carbohydrates as sugars, so Jaune becomes even more delicious as the cold months continue. Harvesting in winter can be miserable — prising vegetables from muddy, clinging, cold soil on bitter days gives me chilblains, and washing them in icy water doesn't help either.

There was a beautiful restaurant in an old car showroom in Nipaluna (Hobart) named Franklin. The chefs were a dream to work with, often taking whatever we harvested on trust alone, knowing that with their alchemic skills, and our fondness for good produce, anything that entered their kitchen would become delicious.

On one of those icy days I'd had a particularly miserable harvest. Freezing rain blew under the hood of my raincoat, stinging my face. I'd run out of dry socks and lost feeling in my hands and feet as I drove my fork into the ground, gently pulling particularly hefty Jaune du Doubs carrots from their beds. I washed and packed them, along with cabbages, kale, turnips and other wintry veg, put on some almost-dry socks from by the fire and drove our harvest to the Franklin restaurant.

As I carted my heavy crates into the kitchen's cool room, I was met by a chef holding a fork. On the tines of Jack Donohoe's fork was a Jaune du Doubs carrot we'd brought in the week before. As I thawed my fingers by the wood-fired Scotch oven at the heart of their kitchen, Jack told me they'd brushed the carrots with butter, wrapped them in hay and slipped them into the slowly cooling oven after a long day baking bread and braising meats, where they sat in the oven's last gentle warmth becoming tender, snug in their blanket of almost-smouldering hay. The skin was a late-sunset gold, and the flesh inside, cooked so gently, was headily sweet, tempered by the salty smokiness from the butter and hay.

It seems a small thing, a mouthful of carrot, but the time Jack took to acknowledge the grower as part of the process was a magical act of generosity. The spell he cast made the rest of that icy winter's harvests a little warmer. Every time I sunk my fork through a crust of frost to prise more golden carrots from the soil I thought of that carrot, snug in its nest of hay in the warm oven.

Disastrously, just after Jack showed me how wonderful these golden French carrots could taste, a new disease threat was identified, and carrot seeds could no longer travel from France to Lutruwita without expensive testing. But all was not lost. Resisting the urge to eat the last of our crop, we pulled the best ones from their rows, removed the tops and planted them elsewhere to set seed, as I did with our parsnips (see page 75), and they grew beautifully, thrusting up their glorious umbel heads the following spring.

Carrot flowers are lacy, magnificent things, forming heads of tiny flowers, those circles within circles characteristic of their family, as big as your hand. The white flowers give way to immature green seeds, which in turn ripen to brown, becoming spiny, and the heads curl in upon themselves like closing fists, holding the seeds until conditions are right. When it's time for the seed to disperse, the whole head unfurls, scattering its spiny seeds to be carried and spread, stuck in the feathers or fur of passing critters, or snipped and popped into a paper bag by me, to continue growing season upon season.

Jack's hay-roasted carrots

At home, I can't replicate the smoky flavour imparted by a Scotch oven, but I have figured out that lush winter clover, if harvested and gently dried, imparts a subtle vanilla flavour to your carrot skins. Your hay is best gathered from a corner of a garden you're acquainted with — unless you have access to an unsprayed field. Urban dwellers without access to clean paddocks can still slow-cook their carrots to burnished beauty; just tuck some baking parchment around them to keep the skins moist and trap the magical aromas.

If you have a wood-fired pizza oven, pop the carrots in after you've cooked your pizzas and they will roast perfectly as the oven cools — or, use your electric oven and slow-cook other dishes while your carrots are sitting in there for a few hours.

Preheat your oven to 150°C (300°F). Melt some butter in a frying pan — enough to generously coat your carrots in. Roll your carrots in the butter and season generously with salt. Pack them snugly, top to tail, into the nest you've made, folding the ends of the hay over the top. Pop the lid on to keep it all contained.

Transfer to the oven and leave to gently roast for a few hours. If things are looking smoky, you can take the lid off during that time and sprinkle on a little water, or leave the lid a little ajar if it's too damp — ideally your carrots will be a little burnished on top when they're done.

Best served by a smiling, generous friend feeding you from a fork by a wood oven on a freezing winter's day, and also excellent with herby braised French lentils cooked in the same slow oven.

hay (make sure it's food grade)

carrots — choose chunky slow-grown ones, not slender, crisp spring carrots with tops

butter

Apiaceae

81

Parsley

PETROSELINUM CRISPUM

Every winter a ragtag bunch of small-scale farmers gathers in a small town, which could be anywhere in Australia, to talk shop — about growing food, caring for land or preparing our favourite produce. It's an event we all treasure, that gives producers — people who often work in isolation — a strong, warm sense of community. A conundrum often raised among us is how to get our customers to eat vegetables and herbs as we do, in vast quantities, and in every meal of the day. Many words of wisdom have come from these agrarian gatherings, but Fraser Bayley's simple pronouncement below about keeping fresh parsley to hand seems to me an excellent way for all of us to add more greens to our diet.

Eggs on toast, cheese sandwiches, mashed potato, salads, soups and sauces — there are few savoury meals that don't benefit from a scattering of parsley. I would go even further and suggest that parsley is a vegetable — or, at the very least, a salad green. I weep to see tiny leaves picked from bunches and scattered sparingly as a meagre garnish. Put a whole bunch, or even two, in your tabouleh. Pile gremolata onto your braises by the spoonful. Chop vast quantities to fold into an omelette, or use the tenderest leaves from the centre of the plant as the greens in a salad.

Parsley is a biennial plant, meaning it spends its first year after germination establishing leaves, strong stems and roots, ready to produce seeds in its second year — although every gardener knows that a stressed plant will laugh at such conventions.

'You neglected to water me or allowed me to become waterlogged? Subjected me to a tiny pot where my adventuring roots became cramped? I might die — I must produce seeds before succumbing to your torture!'

'Every kitchen should have a vase of parsley on the bench.'

Fraser Bayley, *Old Mill Road Biofarm, Moruya*

Stressed like this, your biennial plant may become annual. Don't be tempted to salvage the situation by saving seeds from plants that bolt early. You want to select for plants that have grit and longevity, beautiful flavour and disease resistance — so, pull out that stressed, bolted parsley and pop it in the stockpot before it sets seed. Bide your time and wait for your best plants to flower, as they're the ones whose progeny you want.

When given adequate water, reasonable soil and plenty of sun when it's cooler — and a dash of shade is great when it's hot — your parsley will grow for months. Plants tucked into the ground in late summer and autumn produce well into the following summer, by which time the ones you planted in spring are ready to take their place. I take care to harvest the outer leaves, allowing the inner ones to produce future harvests, but sometimes the succulent young leaves are too tempting — perfect used raw, they are magnificently sap-sweet.

Well-grown parsley stems are delicious, too. Chopped finely across the grain, they add a wonderful bite to salads. Often people turn their noses up at curly parsley, thinking it only fit to decorate a butcher's cabinet or a retro plate of devilled eggs, but I love its density and slightly earthy flavour, especially when used with mountains of mint in a tabouleh.

There is also a variety, Hamburg parsley, bred for its carrot-like roots. While it is delicious, it is slow to germinate and slow to grow, so has fallen from favour in our survival-of-the-fittest garden, but it remains on my list of things to grow. One day I'll master it.

Cheesy puffs, a family tradition

Is it a vegetable, is it a herb? A caveat here. Mum thinks this recipe has too much parsley. I think it's delicious, so add parsley to your taste. Corn kernels, chives, bacon and feta are also welcome additions.

I'm not sure where Mum found this recipe, written in biro in the front of a school-fundraiser cookbook from the 1970s. It takes moments to put together and makes lunchboxes, picnics and snacks satisfying. When I moved out of home, my sister Katie gave me a magnificent gift — a ring binder in which she'd compiled all of our family recipes. As well as being useful, it is a time capsule of 90s clip art, and every time I make these cheesy puffs, I wonder why she put the recipe inside a cartoon television and I smile.

Preheat your oven to 200°C (400°F). Generously butter a small cupcake tray; I use an old-fashioned Willow jelly cake tray, with shallow rounded cups.

Warm the olive oil in a frying pan. Sauté the onion over medium heat for about 5 minutes, until softened. Add the garlic and cook for a minute or two, until fragrant. Set aside to cool.

Place the parsley, cheese and flour in a bowl. Working quickly and lightly, as you would when making muffins, mix together using your fingers so the cheese isn't compressed.

Add the sautéed onion and milky egg mixture and stir quickly to combine — don't overmix. I like to use the blade of a butter knife and turn my bowl as I work, to scrape the dry ingredients through the wet — it's almost impossible to overwork a dough or pastry with a narrow blade.

Spoon the batter into your cupcake tray, but don't overfill, as it will puff up. Bake for about 20 minutes, or until the puffs are golden and spring back when pressed.

Serve hot with plenty of butter, or allow to cool and pack in your lunchbox. Just the thing when there's no bread for sandwiches.

Makes 24

1–2 tablespoons olive oil

1 onion, diced

1–2 garlic cloves, crushed

1 bunch of parsley, finely chopped

1 cup (100 g) grated cheese (an excellent way to use those awkward stubs of cheese in the fridge)

185 g (6½ oz/1 heaped cup) self-raising flour

1 egg, cracked into a 250 ml (1 cup) measure and beaten, then filled to the brim with milk

Coriander

CORIANDRUM SATIVUM

If you are one of those people who find coriander leaves taste like soap, I feel for you. Perhaps you're lucky enough to still enjoy the seeds as a spice, as some coriander haters do?

I am, without doubt, a coriander addict. Its sweet pungent flavour brightens soups, curries, salads and noodle dishes. I adore it by the handful in tomato salads — but it has to be the right coriander.

I strongly suspect that many food aversions stem from having only had access to badly grown, improperly stored or poorly prepared food, and although there is said to be a genetic component to coriander hatred, I wonder if some have only met the limp, pale coriander that has lost all of its vigour and life force and tastes flat and ugly. The coriander I live for is crisp. The thick, succulent stems will snap at the slightest touch, and the leaves shimmer with life. If the wan stuff is all you can get, use the outer tired leaves, stems and the roots to make a curry paste, and hopefully you'll find some brighter, fresher leaves at the centre of the bunch.

Far more fickle than parsley, coriander is another of those bolting plants and will begin to flower if it notices days lengthening, or if it in any way fears imminent death. Those flowers are things of the utmost beauty — small, white and rounded at the centre of the flower head, becoming lacier and developing little petals towards their outside edges. They are captivating. I once noticed a bee carrying pale purple pollen, and followed it as it gathered nectar and that very purple pollen from coriander plants.

Then there's the seeds. Green, immature coriander seeds, pounded to a paste with a little salt to help bruise them, are a lovely way to start a simple fish curry. Add some ginger, green chilli and garlic to your mortar and pound again. Fry the paste just a little, add some sliced shallots and fry some more. Pour in coconut milk and then, as it comes to a simmer, add your fish. Simmer until just cooked, season with a little fish sauce and a squeeze of lime, ladle over steamed rice and finish with plenty of fresh coriander leaves. Of course, adding aromatics such as lime leaves, galangal and cumin will make for a more complex-flavoured meal, but sometimes it is wonderful to simply let one pure flavour lead and really get to know that particular plant's peculiar gifts, so you can put it to its very best use in other dishes.

Next in the coriander harvest comes the mature, ripe seeds to dry for your pantry. It's a mild spice and, as always, fresh locally grown seeds will have the best flavour. They ripen sequentially along the stem, so if you want to maximise your yield, it's best to snip ripe umbels every week or so and dry them in an airy — but not hot — place. If you dry your herbs and spices too quickly, you can lose the volatile oils that make them so delicious.

Apiaceae

Skirret

SIUM SISARUM

My dear friend Lindy Campbell ran a nursery, Island Herbs, in the town of Snug, south of Hobart, which was the source of many of my very favourite plants. Not only was Lindy growing the biggest collection of conventional and obscure herbs, dye plants, fruits and vegetables in Lutruwita (Tasmania), but she freely shared her vast knowledge and experience with customers. When I first began growing for chefs, I'd visit her seeking foods that the chefs and I hadn't met yet. One day she took me to the back of the nursery where she stored excess plants and sold me a seemingly unpromising tray of knobbly-rooted little seedlings.

Trustingly, I took them home and potted them, planting a few out of curiosity, then went inside to read about them. The literature spoke of a plant with bitter skin and a woody core, a native of China that travelled the Silk Road, becoming a popular staple in medieval Europe for its hardiness, perennial nature and all manner of medicinal virtues, but was eventually usurped by the more productive parsnip, with the advent of potatoes sounding its death knell.

As I watched my skirrets grow, I was first impressed by their edible greens — sweet, young spring shoots that make an excellent addition to a broth. Then I admired their lush green foliage and the masses of white, lacy flowers that danced elegantly in summer breezes. It wasn't until winter, after a series of good frosts made the plant tops die back to withered brown skeletons, that I dug it up and realised what a wonderful vegetable it is.

When you unearth your first skirret, you may think it ugly, looking for all the world like a mass of long white grubs. You'll curse as heavy winter soil makes it difficult to keep the plump, crisp roots attached to the plant — the fat, bulbous ends of the roots are my favourite part, and the most likely to snap off in icy clay. You'll stick your fingers into freezing mud, wiggling every precious root loose, then apply a forceful blast of the hose to your hard-won harvest, revealing clean white roots. Those edible roots are easily snipped from the crowns of the plants — crowns that you can divide and replant right away for an ever-increasing perpetual crop.

Patient gardeners can also grow skirret from seeds. They require a period of cold to make them think they've endured winter and awoken into a gentle spring. You can sow seeds directly in the garden in autumn, but know that they're slow and unreliable germinators, and will likely be swamped by weeds or forgotten before you see them. A better strategy for gardeners in cool climates is to sow into seedling trays, covering the seeds with about 1 cm (½ inch) of seed-raising mix and allowing Mother Nature to have her way with them. If your winters are warm, you can pop your seeds on damp paper towel, seal them in a jar and let them chill until very early spring, when you can sow them into seed trays. You won't get much to eat after your first summer, but every season after that, as your crowns mature, you'll have a generous supply with minimal effort.

Once harvested, take the roots into the kitchen. You can roast them as my mother does, with her parsnip technique on page 76 (accounting for their smaller size and taking care not to burn them), and you'll enjoy a sweet vegetable — like parsnip, but not at all like parsnip. Sugary in a good way and creamy inside. Or sell it to a chef and you'll learn a plethora of delicious preparations. I've eaten it gently poached in smoked eel broth, served barely cooked in a warm salad with other unusual root crops, and used in the most luxurious buttery, creamy purée.

There are obscure and beautiful corners of the internet and online skirret forums devoted to the improvement of the crop. I'm told that the lack of cores in the strain of skirret roots my friend Lindy sold to me is unusual and very desirable, so I've sent wee packs of our seed to parts of the world with laxer quarantine laws than ours. There is also a rare pink-rooted strain that I'd give my eye teeth for.

Another wonderful corner of the web is devoted to historic recipes. As institutions scan and digitise texts, you can read wonderfully confusing recipes where medieval scribes have used the letter *f* for *s* and thrown an extra *e* merrily about to confuse modern readers. The one that entices me the most for its decadent richness is a pie filled with skirrets, dates, chestnuts, candied oranges, sugar, butter, salt and lots of bone marrow. After being baked for a while, the lid is prised off, in case it's not yet rich enough, and a custard is poured in before the pie is returned to the oven to finish cooking.

Apiaceae

Skirret & bone marrow pie

While our modern sensibilities may baulk at the idea of root vegetables, lard and marrow in a dessert, the creamy sweetness of skirret spiked with the tart–bitter peel and the warm spices makes for a comforting, rich sweet. We did find, though, that the traditional medieval addition of dates — and custard poured in after cooking — made it a little too rich for our tastes!

I suspect this pie would work just as well with parsnips, oca or even fruit such as quinces, apples and pears, if you can't get hold of skirret.

This recipe uses a 20 cm (8 inch) pie dish. While there's greater chance of success using a springform tin, it's far more fun to use a pie dolly: a turned wooden mould you lift the pastry around to shape the pie, as I imagine medieval cooks would have done. You could also make smaller pies; just reduce the baking time accordingly.

Preheat your oven to 180°C (350°F). Using a small sharp knife, cut a cross in the pointy end of each chestnut. Spread them on a baking tray and roast for 20 minutes. (Make sure you pop an extra handful in the oven for snacking on, as it's impossible to resist the scent of roasted chestnuts.) Remove from the oven and leave to cool briefly. Turn the oven off for a while; you'll need to reheat it later to bake your pie.

As soon as the chestnuts are cool enough to handle, peel away the hard outer shells, and make sure you remove the inner skin — gently squeeze the shelled chestnuts and you'll find the skin lifts away from the nut easily. Simmer them in a pot of salted water for 5 minutes to make them yielding and tender, then drain and roughly chop into chunks no bigger than 1 cm (½ inch). Set aside.

Gather your scrubbed skirrets and drop them into a pot of boiling water for just 30 seconds; any longer and they'll be too soft to handle.

Serves 10

350 g (12 oz) <u>chestnuts</u>, to yield 250 g (9 oz) peeled

200 g (7 oz) <u>skirrets</u>, scrubbed

125 g (4½ oz) <u>bone marrow</u> (from 2 marrow bones); ask your butcher to extract it for you

50 g (1¾ oz) dried <u>breadcrumbs</u>

50 g (1¾ oz) candied <u>orange</u> peel

30 g (1 oz) dark <u>brown sugar</u>

1 teaspoon <u>sea salt</u>

2 teaspoons ground <u>ginger</u>

1 teaspoon ground <u>cinnamon</u>

½ teaspoon ground <u>nutmeg</u>

8 whole cloves, or ½ teaspoon ground <u>cloves</u>

50 g (1¾ oz) butter

LARD PASTRY

450 g (1 lb) plain (all purpose) <u>flour</u>, plus extra for dusting

200 g (7 oz) plain wholemeal <u>rye flour</u>

125 g (4½ oz) <u>lard</u>

300 ml (10½ fl oz) <u>water</u>

½ teaspoon <u>sea salt</u>

1 <u>egg</u>, beaten with a splash of water and a pinch of salt

89

Drain, then cool under a cold running tap. Peel them by inserting the tip of a paring knife under the translucent skin and running it down the length of each root, slicing and lifting the skin as you go. The skin should peel away easily, but this is fiddly work — you may need those spare chestnuts and a pitcher of wine or mead, or jug of ale, to fortify yourself! Cut the skirrets into 5 cm (2 inch) lengths.

Cut the marrow into 1 cm (½ inch) cubes. Set aside.

In a bowl, mix together the breadcrumbs, candied orange, sugar, salt and spices. Dice the butter and set aside.

<u>Lard pastry:</u> Sift the two flours together into a large bowl. Put the lard, water and salt in a saucepan and heat to a simmer.

Pour the hot liquid into the flour and mix well, using the blade of a knife. When the dough comes together and is cool enough to handle, turn out onto a floured bench and knead for a minute or two, until combined. Set aside one-third of the dough in a bowl for the pie lid, then cover and keep it warm at the back of the stove until you're ready to use it, as lard pastry hardens and becomes unworkable if it cools.

Roll out the pastry to 5–8 mm (¼–⅜ inch) thick — if you're using a springform tin you can make it on the thinner side, but go thicker for a moulded pie, as the pastry will need extra engineering strength to remain upright.

Ease the pastry into your springform tin, letting some pastry flop over the edges, to ensure the sides stay up as the pastry cools. (Or, lift the pastry around your pie dolly; any straight-sided vessel can work as a dolly — I secured a piece of baking paper around the base of a bowl with a rubber band and it worked very well.) Put your pastry case in your non-medieval fridge and have a cup of mead while you give it 10 minutes to harden before you begin filling.

Reheat your oven to 180°C (350°F).

When filling the pie, I like to work in layers, with enough of each ingredient in each layer to barely cover the one below. I think the absorbent chestnuts are a good first layer, followed by the skirret, the marrow, then a generous dusting of your spiced breadcrumb mixture.

Repeat the filling layers until your pie is full, or you're out of ingredients. Gently press down to firm the filling, but don't compact too much — you want each slice to come out whole, not with crumbly ingredients spilling out everywhere. Dot the butter evenly around the filling.

Roll out the remaining pastry and cut a lid to fit. Trim the excess pastry edges from around your pie, place the lid on top and pinch the lid and sides together to seal. Cut a cross in the centre of the pie and lift the pastry outwards, to form a hole to allow steam to escape.

If you like you can leave things there, but the oven's on, the mead is running through your veins and there's spare pastry, so live a little! You could shape a fluted pastry funnel to tuck into the hole in the centre of the pie. Or weave tiny strips of pastry to create a pattern for the top of the pie — rabbits, braids, love hearts... (Any spare pastry freezes beautifully in a sealed container for another day.)

Brush your egg wash all over your pie for a pretty, glossy result.

Bake for 1 hour, if you've made one large pie, or 30–40 minutes for smaller pies. The pastry should be a lovely, burnished brown; any bits that are browning too quickly can be covered with foil during baking. (If you're unsure it's done, the pie is cooked when the centre reaches 80°C/175°F on a meat thermometer.)

Cool and chill for easy slicing, although the pie is also lovely eaten warm with cream.

Other wondrous umbels

With delicious seeds, roots, stems, flowers and leaves that are eaten raw, cooked, dried, candied or even infused into exotic liqueurs, the gifts of the Apiaceae family are celebrated in every culinary tradition.

Celery, *Apium graveolens,* one of the most common umbels, sadly sits on my not-yet-mastered list. It's best sown in very early spring and planted out as soon as possible, so it can enjoy the cooler conditions of late spring and early summer. To stop it becoming tough and stringy or bolting to seed, it needs fertile soil and consistent watering, and it loves stable weather — a trifecta I'm yet to achieve. While I'm learning how to grow tender, pale green heads, I make use of Chinese leaf celery and par-cel — both varieties of cutting celery that are harvested leaf by leaf, rather than in whole heads, giving you ample flavour for your mirepoix for months from a single, easily grown planting. Its slower-growing cousin celeriac, *Apium graveolens* var. *rapaceum*, offers a mild celery flavour and delicious nuttiness in its fleshy, dense root — which is the main prize — but it too has bountiful, celery-scented greens that will round out the flavour of soups and braises beautifully. Like its cousin parsnip, it demands forethought from the gardener. The tiny seeds must be sown in spring; I find it easiest to start them in pots and plant them out in January to grow plump, ready for winter harvest.

Caraway, *Carum carvi*, is spectacularly easy to grow, and well worth the time. Each plant will grow to half a metre or more and, in its second year — hello, biennial plants! — will produce handfuls of minty, delicious seeds. If you think you don't like caraway, I'd urge you to taste it fresh, as it little resembles the dusty intensity of some shop-bought stuff. The plants also self-seed, bringing copious beneficial insects to your garden, and you can harvest the roots of plump seedlings when the leaves wither in autumn. They taste a little like tiny, creamy parsnips.

We've grown tiny crops of aniseed, *Pimpinella anisum*, and used the precious harvest to make sweet biscuits; the plain sweetness of shortbread is the perfect vehicle for learning the taste of new sweet spices. Equally tiny crops of cumin, *Cuminum cyminum* — which only grows a few inches high in our cool-temperate garden before flowering, seeding and giving up — have flavoured roast potatoes, another neutral and delicious medium with which to explore flavour.

When I introduce a new plant to someone, they'll often nibble or smell it, deciding in that moment whether they like it or not. If you chewed on raw cumin seeds, I doubt you'd think them at all worthy of growing or cooking with, but there isn't a spice — bar pepper, perhaps — that I reach for more often in my kitchen. Find a context, a proper way of preparing a plant, and try it several times to give it a fair chance before throwing it by the culinary and horticultural wayside. Often, given time, aversions can become addictions.

Anise herbs took me a long time to love. As a child, liquorice was a flavour I'd tolerate in order to eat the sugar it came with — the chocolate around a liquorice bullet, or the sugary rainbow tiles between the black layers of a liquorice allsort.

Apiaceae

My *oma* would suck on pucks of hard Dutch salted liquorice, which had no redeeming sugar... and if a Black Cat liquorice was included in our twenty-cent bags of mixed lollies, we'd generously give it to our mum.

Given this intolerance that I'd learned so early, **chervil**, *Anthriscus cerefolium*, and **sweet cicely**, *Myrrhis odorata*, took me a while to understand: the scent and flavour I'd always associated with sweetness was meant to be included with chives and parsley, in savoury meals? But, by taking my own advice and continuing to cook and eat, I've become addicted to the first shoots of these sweet herbs every spring — the perfect refresher for a palate worn by a long winter of brassicas and bitter greens.

Chervil is a tiny, delicate annual herb that can be sown and established in autumn. It's a gamble whether or not these late-sown plants will bolt or harbour early hordes of aphids when spring comes, but if you're lucky you'll have healthy plants that throw magical, tender shoots of incomparable sweetness before the rest of your garden wakes from winter. Seeds sown in early spring are more reliable, but you will have to wait for them to grow.

Sweet cicely, on the other hand, is a perennial. Growing through the warm months, sleeping winter away, then heralding the coming spring by sending sweet, delicately furry stems skyward, it is my absolute favourite harbinger to send to chefs in town — a delicious, bright banner announcing 'Spring is here!'. Later in the season, as the plants grow taller, cocktail-makers love its hollow, anise-flavoured stems, which make perfect, edible drinking straws. The sweetness of cicely is taken full advantage of when cooking with astringent, sour foods like gooseberries, rhubarb and sour cherries, meaning you can use less sugar in your baking or cocktails. The lacy flowers carry the same flavour — and the unripe green seeds are like eating candy.

Another perennial umbelliferous harbinger of spring is **lovage**, *Levisticum officinale*. Its stout, celery-like foliage has a flavour like celery, parsley and chicken stock cubes — hence its German nickname, 'Maggi herb'. Young leaves add beautiful savouriness to salads and green sauces, while older leaves, as you may have guessed, are perfect for filling in the savoury note sometimes missing in stocks. The waxy yellow flowers are a beautiful, flavoursome garnish, the roots can be used if you need a lovage hit in winter while the plant is dormant, and the seeds have long been used as a spice. It is strong and should be used sparingly while you get to know it, but once you've made friends you'll want to keep a plant by the door so you can nip out whenever you need some delicious stock powder flavour in your life.

Dill, *Anethum graveolens*, is another strongly flavoured herb, one I don't find myself reaching for often, apart from using it in a big batch of green sauce, or as a garnish for blinis. But I can't make pickles without the seeds. Their bright, earthy, resinous flavour is locked in a tasty memory with briny, tangy gherkins, and never shall they be separated.

We grow a wonderful collection of Eastern Apiaceae. **Ashitaba**, *Angelica keiskei*, is an uncommon Japanese herb that produces succulent young shoots that are wonderful dropped into a broth or salad of shiitake mushrooms, soy sauce and soba noodles. I use **minari**, *Oenanthe javanica*,

Later in the season, as the sweet cicely plants grow taller, cocktail-makers love its hollow, anise-flavoured stems.

and **mitsuba**, *Cryptotaenia japonica,* in similar ways — minari being a robust, bountiful herb, perfect in that damp corner of your garden where other plants might struggle, while mitsuba slips right into the ornamental garden — especially if you seek out the red-leafed form — and its delicate parsley flavour is beautiful with other gentle dishes such as the silky, savoury, Japanese egg custard *chawanmushi*, or in a simple dashi broth.

For me, the absent apiaceous elephant in this room is **fennel**, *Foeniculum vulgare*. It's a plant I struggle to grow — often bolting to seed, giving me the gifts of sweet fronds, glorious gold flowers and wonderfully spicy digestive seeds, but not the plump, sweet-savoury bulbs I love. It's a matter of timing, I think. I should be tucking seedlings that have suffered no flower-inducing stresses into yielding, fertile soil in early autumn. Luckily there's always another season to learn something new. For now I'll enjoy the seeds that I first learned to love when local farmer Matthew Evans brought his Fat Pig Farm pork and fennel sausages to the Nipaluna (Hobart) farmers' market where we both sold produce. Fennel's bright, clean flavour and digestive properties make it the perfect complement to unctuously rich pork sausages.

Apiaceae is a vast and delicious, but sometimes deadly, family — and we've barely scratched the surface here. Back in the 1990s, no cafe cake was complete without leathery angelica leaves beside a pile of cream and an unripe strawberry half, so I was in awe when I met the actually delicious culinary **angelica**, *Angelica archangelica*, that lends its sweetness to roast rhubarb, and its vivid green to chartreuse and candied angelica stems. There is a plant called **turnip-rooted chervil**, *Chaerophyllum bulbosum,* that I grew once and must again, for its delicately flavoured, sweet, fine-textured roots, each around the size of a ping pong ball. A chunk of **asafoetida**, *Ferula assa-foetida,* resin has lived in my spice cabinet for years, being occasionally grated into a curry, and someone has finally imported its seed into Australia, so perhaps I'll soon be able to taste resin that is less than a decade old.

Even in the depths of winter I'll find a self-sown carrot in a forgotten corner holding its umbel of fuzzy seeds squeezed tightly closed, waiting for the warm, drier days of spring to unfurl and scatter its progeny far and wide. While it's cold, that clenched fist of seeds also holds sleeping ladybirds and other tiny creatures waiting too for warmer weather, so they can fly forth and sip nectar from those swaying summer umbels.

Asteraceae

The first daisies that come to my mind are the little white lawn daisies, *Bellis perennis*, that I made crowns with as a child. Splitting the stems with the edge of my thumbnail, plucking another bloom and sliding it through the slit on the first flower's stem until the bulk of the head locked it in place, repeated until a circlet of twenty or more was complete. Afternoons in the sun that lasted forever, filled with incidental meditations on those fine, white petals — ending with everyone adorned in daisy chains, and all the children with green-stained thumbnails. You can eat lawn daisies and their leaves, although there's little besides novelty to recommend them, but I love them because they survive with grace, like most in this family. Mow them, subject them to drought, play soccer right on top of them and they just keep growing their joyful little flowers.

What appears at first glance to be a single daisy flower is actually many flowers; tiny florets are bundled into a disc, working together to form a whole that may be more attractive to pollinators, or might be more efficient for the plant to produce. Surrounding the tiny florets that make up the disc are ray florets that most of us would see as petals, but are elongated, modified flowers. Many daisies have seeds that blow in the wind on tiny parachutes, to grow miles from their parents; others have underground parts that can survive for years in the one place, tolerating drought and frost and bursting to life when conditions improve. Others, like sunflowers, produce large seeds that are too heavy to blow anywhere — although I do like the idea of sunflower seeds growing dandelion parachutes and blowing into austere McMansion gardens, sprouting against their dreary, grey-rendered fences to cheer them up.

I've not made use of my sunflowers for their edible qualities, unless you count feeding them to chickens then eating the eggs, but we grow them every year for their ability to attract pollinators, create quick summer windbreaks and produce biomass for mulch and compost materials. We've also had delightful success using them as supports for climbing bean plants. Their flower structure mirrors perfectly the little lawn daisy, with a compound head of hundreds of tiny flowers surrounded by the beautiful golden ray florets.

Globe artichoke

CYNARA CARDUNCULUS

Even if I couldn't eat them, I would grow artichokes just for the perfect shade of violet in their flowers. They are the grandest of vegetable plants; I think my landscape design friends would call them 'architectural'. At the first glimmer of spring, they shoot forth huge silver swords of leaves that gather into glorious, jagged grey mounds in the blink of an eye. Then comes the culinary prize — huge, towering spikes of flower buds. After the first plump buds are picked, side shoots form, growing buds of ever-diminishing size as the poor plant fights against greedy humans thwarting its chance to flower and propagate itself. As both the plant's reserves and the gardener's appetites weary, a bud or two will be left to mature, and flowers of the most impossible shade of purply blue will open, summoning every bee in the neighbourhood to dine. Sometimes, if there's been good summer rain, a second flush of buds will grow — the perfect ingredient for warm evening barbecues. As the warm weather wanes, the tired old leaves are trimmed and add precious volume to autumn compost heaps. Later, just before things warm again in early spring, three-year-old plants can be dug, brutally split with a sharp spade and replanted, ready to begin the generous, magnificent cycle again.

When we pile artichoke buds on our market stall table, the cooks who know swoop in and gather them up, clutching them to their breasts like precious babes in arms. Those who don't yet know wrinkle their noses, mystified as to why you would buy a vegetable that requires trimming down to a third of its size and having its hairy choke removed, dipping in acidulated water as it's prepared — and then, upon being cooked, ending up as a small amount of greyish leaves and a little heart.

I remember the disappointment when first suffering that labour for little yield, my hands not knowing the work, and only a line-drawing in a book to guide me. Then my dear friend Natalie came along. Natalie grasps life with both hands, and treats her food the same way. Her mother taught her to choose tight young artichoke buds — they shouldn't 'give' when you squeeze them — and she cooked them whole, in a pressure cooker, taking away the work of trimming. She'd serve the artichokes with home-made mayonnaise and everyone would tear in.

I don't have a pressure cooker, so I put a pot of salted water on to boil, perhaps with a few bay leaves, peppercorns, halved garlic cloves and a few lemon slices to scent the water. I trim the spines from the tips of the heads, then pull away the oldest leaves from the outside, leaving a few centimetres — a good inch — of stem on, before boiling them until tender; around ten minutes should do, and a knife should pierce the thickest part easily. Then you simply drain them, grab a pile of napkins, little bowls of salt and olive oil — or make aioli — and find a big bowl to contain all the mess you're about to make.

Eating with your hands and teeth is a sensual pleasure. Think of sucking the meat from crab legs, spitting cherry pits from a porch, or shelling walnuts at a table with friends. Sharing a bowl of boiled artichokes is a delight like that. Done right, it will feel like a seduction — you have to be tender and work for the prize. The outer leaves hold little reward, but you'll still pull them from the bud, dip them in the olive oil and scrape the tender bit from the base with your front teeth. As you work towards the centre, each leaf will yield a little more food than the last. When you're down to the most tender, paper-thin inner leaves, you have to slow for a second, unfurl them, pick up a spoon and gently ease out the inedible choke — the central part of the flower bud that, if unpicked, would have opened to form the purple disc floret of the artichoke flower. Then you'll be left with the heart, the meatiest, inner part of the artichoke. Now you should grab what's left of your olive oil, pour it on and sprinkle with salt. If your artichoke is large, you can pick up a knife and fork... or just continue using your hands and complete your feast.

If you're dining in company that requires less abandon, or if you just fancy adding other classic flavours to your artichokes, the following easy — but smashingly delicious! — preparation method may suit your needs.

After all of that sensual, rich eating, you may need a little something to settle your stomach. The cynarin that creates the bitterness of artichoke leaves, and sweetens your wine, can be used to great effect, aiding digestion when taken as a tea or liqueur. For those who love bitter flavours, a tea made from the youngest leaves of artichoke plants, shredded and dried, is a delight.

Asteraceae

Stuffed globe artichokes

Preheat your oven to 200°C (400°F). Mix all the stuffing ingredients together in a bowl.

Using a sharp serrated knife, trim the top of the artichoke leaves, just above where the inner leaves begin to look pale. Trim the stems, so the bases will sit flat.

Now sit each artichoke on a cutting board and hit it. I like to put another cutting board on top and whack that, but if you have big hands or small artichokes, and you've removed any spines, you can use your fist. The idea is to loosen the leaves so you can work your way in, first to remove any feathery chokes, then to work the stuffing in between them.

Put the artichokes in a lidded ceramic or earthenware baking dish that just fits them. If the stalks you trimmed off are tender, you can tuck them in around the heads, as they have a morsel of flesh that's well worth eating in their core. Push a little of the stuffing into each artichoke leaf, being a bit more generous with the centre. If the stuffing overflows, all the better — the oily breadcrumbs will become crisp and delicious. Sprinkle some cheddar on top of each artichoke.

Pour some stock into the baking dish, about 2.5 cm (1 inch) deep, top up with a little wine and season to taste; keep the tide low, so the crumbs don't float away, and tuck the bay leaves among the artichokes. Pop the lid on.

Bake for 30 minutes, then remove the lid and bake for another 20 minutes until the crumbs become crisp and golden.

Serve with a green salad, and plenty of good bread to mop up the juices. And a drier wine than you'd usually serve, as artichokes contain cynarin, a compound that can trick tastebuds into thinking other foods taste unusually sweet.

Serves 4

4 plump, fresh globe artichokes

50 g (1¾ oz) cheddar

1½–2 cups (375–500 ml) good chicken stock

a splash of savoury white wine

salt, to taste

2–3 fresh bay leaves

STUFFING

50 g (1¾ oz) stale sourdough breadcrumbs

50 g (1¾ oz) pecorino, grated

2 tablespoons olive oil

1 tablespoon finely chopped parsley

1 tablespoon finely chopped fresh thyme, rosemary, oregano and/or lovage

2–3 garlic cloves, crushed

zest of 1 lemon

Radicchio

CICHORIUM INTYBUS

An enormous sulphur-crested cockatoo called Barry terrorised our neighbourhood. A discarded pet, he straddled a dangerous line — wild and wise enough to survive in the wild, but with no fear of humans, and a massive, vicious beak. He'd cruise the skies above us screaming 'Barry, Barry!', landing occasionally to destroy something. A vine I'd raised from a seed, then nurtured for ten years until it grew around my front gate, was bitten off at ground level. Neighbours had precious pots knocked from shelves, and all the kids went inside when he descended, fearing for their tender fingers.

Barry's reign of terror was during a beautiful time for our business. A restaurant called Garagistes had opened in Nipaluna (Hobart), and under the guidance of chef Luke Burgess we explored the boundaries of culinary horticulture, harvesting weeds and flowers and growing every edible plant we could find. I even found myself commissioned to make table decorations for a special dinner one evening with a visiting chef, nervously unpacking cases of local handmade tableware from Ben and Peta Richardson's Ridgeline Pottery to fill with wintry beauty from my garden. At the time, all vestiges of autumn were long past. The palette the garden offered was green, green and green, but occasional splashes of burgundy broke the scene — cheery heads of radicchio, their hearts glowing like winter roses.

On the day of my restaurant adornment, I looked to the rows I'd direct-seeded with radicchio, taking tiny plants that had grown at the base of their bossier siblings and hadn't had the chance to shine. I gathered moss from under my nursery benches, and branches of lichen-covered hawthorn and red rosehips from a roadside hedgerow. Every bit of colour was precious. I am no florist, but I hoped my biophilia and the inspiration from my bonsai and miniature landscape-creating mentor Will Fletcher would enable me to create something worthy of Ben's vessels.

I sow radicchio around the summer solstice in seedling trays, and plant into the garden in February so they can fatten through the warm months for winter harvest. The finest radicchio in Italy are grown through summer — lifted from the ground, their roots tucked into vats of flowing spring water, which stimulates growth and triggers the plants to develop dense, delicious heads. Having no flowing spring, we harvest our radicchio straight from the field, their leaves sheltering and blanching the hearts, although sometimes we pull up the outer leaves and tie them closed with string, protecting the hearts from the light to brighten their vivid colours. Our cold mountain air and winter rains make the plants grow bittersweet, plump and dense, perfect for harvest until mid-spring, when their thoughts turn to flowering, and their hearts loosen and raise tall spikes of daisy flowers in the gentlest shades of sky blue.

Asteraceae

Most radicchios are named
for the region in which they
were originally cultivated.

Radicchio's diversity and beauty is astonishing, from Castelfranco's iceberg lettuce-like leaves, flecked and marbled with red, to the long, lance-shaped, spectacular deep-maroon, white-veined leaves of Tardivo. Most radicchios are named for the region in which they were originally cultivated, and each has its own unique, traditional preparation methods — whether braised or grilled, or used in salads, pasta fillings, soups or stews.

Mid-winter is when we eat for warmth. Potatoes, pasta, cured meats — satisfying but heavy things that can leave us feeling sluggish and weary. If you nibble radicchio slowly you'll feel an instant rush of saliva, an excellent beginning to a meal and a wonderful foil for heavy foods, as it has long been thought that bitter flavours stimulate bile, making all of that wintry food more digestible.

I was first introduced to radicchio in a salad containing orange, the sweetness of the orange enhancing the radicchio's bitterness, making it the worst of first meetings for me. Now, having trodden a gentler path to acquaintance — first eating it braised with onions, where cooking soothes the bitterness, then shredded and allowed to wilt on a warm plate under a resting pork chop, then dressed as a salad with walnuts and fennel — I'm addicted. As with coffee, dark chocolate or beer, once the craving for bitterness seeps into your being it is there to stay.

For those who haven't yet converted, radicchio has a sweeter chicory cousin, escarole, *Cichorium endivia*, which is crisp and only mildly bitter, a leafy salad green that is more substantial than lettuce and is perfect eaten cooked or raw.

On the day Barry brought his terror to my door I was working outside, mindful that the cool weather would keep my tiny, rosy radicchio plants vibrant, and tucked moss, pebbles and thorny, wintry branches carefully into place, finally 'planting' the radicchios just-so. I was almost finished, feeling optimistic and satisfied, after being creatively overwhelmed, hating what I'd made halfway through, persevering, then finally feeling I'd achieved something beautiful. Just a few more branches to tuck in and I could whisk my piece of the country away to soften a city restaurant — when a whirring of wings and an awful cry of 'Barry!' assailed me from above.

He landed, that beautiful and awful creature, the fault of whoever thought it was a good idea to cage such a beast, make it unaccustomed to the wild, then set it free in a world that didn't suit it. So, although I thought him beautiful, I felt anger and fear when he landed next to my day's work and opened that terrible beak.

A beak, sharp and strong enough to rip pine cones from a tree and tear out the seeds, began to pluck those precious radicchios, tiny hawthorn berries and red rosehips. He had no fear of me. I'd once seen a child's finger horribly bitten by a cockatoo. All alone, I yelled, waved my hands and watched the destruction, quickly ferrying my broken work to my car.

I grabbed the spare, unused branches, moss and tiny plants and sat in the car, safely away from Barry and his terrifying maw, and began to cry.

It wasn't how I'd planned to appear to the fancy Belgian chef in my favourite kitchen, red-eyed and with my miniature gardens in disarray, so I drove a safe distance from Barry and repaired the damage by the roadside. When I finally delivered my brambly, mossy little gardens, I was content: Ben and Peta's vessels, brightened by the earthy radicchio roses, sung together in that perfect restaurant.

I returned home, swept the carnage from my work area and was resting with a restorative glass, when my friend Sue, who happened to be dining at the restaurant, sent me a message — she'd felt so at home in that beautiful setting, and so pleased with our produce, that midway through the meal, echoing Barry, she'd plucked a radicchio from her table decoration and begun to eat it.

Asteraceae

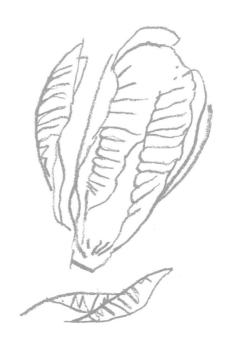

French tarragon

ARTEMISIA DRACUNCULUS

You could be forgiven, after reading about radicchio just now, for thinking that daisies are bitter, only for palates whose pleasures lurk on the dark side — but then there's French tarragon, in all its tingling, dazzling sweetness.

Chances are you've met her bolder cousins. You may have seen my nit-picking ilk at greengrocers, tut-tutting by the herb shelf at bunches of Mexican tarragon, *Tagetes lucida*, or Russian tarragon, *Artemisia dracunculoides*, packaged for sale as tarragon. Sure, they're both wonderful herbs. Mexican tarragon has a pure anise flavour and makes the richest, sweetest herbal tea, while Russian tarragon is vigorous and herbaceous, perfect to use by the fistful — the young, tender leaves used raw or briefly cooked, and older leaves added to soups or stews.

But neither of these wonderful herbs gives you the same tingle on the tongue as true French tarragon. Nor do they have the same gentle anise-but-not-too-anise flavour. And I find the dumbing-down of botanical nomenclature and varieties a shame. If you've gone to the trouble of making a subtle, savoury cream sauce recipe that asks for French tarragon, only to hit it with the strong sweetness or green herbaceous character of the other two tarragons, you may decide you don't like true French tarragon — without ever having actually tasted it. As young French and Russian tarragon plants can appear similar, when I've lost labels on my nursery plants I've found myself nibbling my way through the seedling pots, waiting for the tingle before labelling them again, to be absolutely sure no imposters pass my gate.

French tarragon is a magical plant, historically reputed to cure snake bite. (A tiger snake curled itself around the potted tarragon near my back door last summer, perhaps pointing toward its own remedy?) But I wouldn't depend on tarragon's medicinal efficacy — anti-venom will most certainly work better. The word 'dragon' makes up part of its Latin name, and there is something of the serpent in its ropey, twining, underground rhizomes. A herbaceous perennial, it is dormant in the cold months, with little woody material visible above ground while it sleeps — and from the sleeping rootstock a miraculous whole new top shoots every spring. It has a reputation for being difficult to grow, but given the right conditions it is easy and hardy, and for gardeners who like to be in control, its spreading rhizomes can prove a little too vigorous.

Mark your new plant with a stake so you know where to look with your slug-hunting torch at night.

Plant it in spring or early summer in deep, freely draining soil with plenty of compost and all the sunshine you can give it, and it will never look back. Slugs and snails adore it, so you could safely attribute most failures to them, particularly if you plant it while dormant, as they will graze every tiny shoot that attempts to grow almost before it breaks the surface of the soil. So, mark your new plant with a stake so you know where to look with your slug-hunting torch at night (my favourite gastropod control method), and so other gardeners in your household don't mistake your sleeping plant for a dead one and pull it out.

After a long winter diet, the first sprigs of French tarragon will awaken your tastebuds. It's a difficult sensation to describe — numbing, cooling and tingling all at once, while your mouth is full of a sappy, savoury, anise flavour. If you use your tarragon in cooked dishes, the sensation is reduced, but the flavour remains. We Euro-centric chefs use French tarragon and enjoy the sensation with eggy or creamy foods, but the compound that makes us tingle is the same one found in the Brazilian toothache plant, *Spilanthes acmella*, and Sichuan and sansho peppers, *Zanthoxylum* spp., that are commonly, and deliciously, eaten with chilli to give a hot/cold/numb party in your mouth. Perhaps an experiment with French tarragon and something spicy is in order?

But, back to tradition. In our home, the first tarragon of the season is always used in an almost ceremonial spring omelette (page 44) with chives, parsley and chervil. I adore it for its ability to ease the richness of a cream sauce, and we also mix it with butter, lemon and salt and tuck it by the handful under the skin of a plump chicken before it goes in the oven.

We are a home divided along a strong culinary line. On one side lies my husband Matt and our eldest daughter, on the other our youngest and I. Around the dinner table, I watch as the various items on our plates disappear. Matt and Elsie devour their pasta, potatoes, meats and savoury elements first, while Heidi and I eat mounds of greens and salad, pouring on extra vinegary or citrusy dressings as we go. We all clear our plates, but the line of preference is clear. Sometimes, as the primary cook, it is hard for me to lean in to what palates that aren't mine desire. And that's where our dear tarragon comes in. A cream sauce to please the rich, savoury eaters, leavened with the bright freshness of tarragon, a little lemon and a dash of mustard, and both sides of the table are equally happy.

New potatoes with French tarragon cream sauce

A boiled egg or two on the side turns this simple dish into a complete meal for me. It's also wonderful alongside cured meats and pickles for a perfect low-effort, late spring dinner.

Wash your potatoes, put them in a pot of cool, salted water and bring to the boil. Leave to simmer for 20 minutes, or until just tender.

Meanwhile, make your sauce. In a frying pan, warm the grapeseed oil over medium heat and slowly cook the shallots for 5–7 minutes, until softened and just beginning to colour. Pour in the vermouth, letting it lift all the tasty shallot brownings from the bottom of the pan. Stir in the cream, letting it simmer for 2–3 minutes until it thickens. Add the tarragon and remove from the heat.

Test your potatoes; they're done when a skewer meets the faintest resistance. Drain them, place in a warmed serving dish, drizzle with a little olive oil and season with salt.

Pour the sauce over, garnish with extra tarragon sprigs and serve.

Serves 4

600 g (1 lb 5 oz) new potatoes, so young that their skins slip off easily under the tap

1 tablespoon grapeseed oil

2 shallots or potato onions, finely chopped

50 ml (1¾ fl oz) vermouth

150 ml (5½ fl oz) single (pure) cream

1 tablespoon finely chopped fresh tarragon, plus extra for garnishing

olive oil, for drizzling

Lettuce

LACTUCA SATIVA

The most refreshing of vegetables, lettuce finds its way into our kitchen a few times a week, usually mixed with other tender raw greens and dressed with a simple vinaigrette of cider vinegar and olive oil. I read once that salad dressings are helpful for nutrient absorption — that some nutrients are soluble in acids, others in fats, so a dressed salad makes them more available to your body. It certainly makes salads more delicious!

A misleading metric is often used when talking about nutrition. Nutrient density — the amount of a mineral, vitamin or beneficial compound in a given ingredient — is a valuable measure, but comparing kale and lettuce is like comparing the proverbial oranges and apples. I can eat half a cos lettuce in a sitting, but I'd find the same weight of kale overwhelming. And when somebody told me that thyme has more iron per gram than kale, I wondered how one would eat a serving of thyme.

I'm not a nutritionist, but I understand that in lettuce, exposure to the sun affects nutrient density — and the greener, or redder, the leaves are, the more beneficial compounds you're ingesting. So, don't be overzealous when stripping the sun-greened outer leaves from your lettuces, but at the same time don't discard the delights of those pale, crisp hearts.

With the vast array of heirloom and modern lettuce varieties available now, offering a plethora of flavours and textures, this subtle vegetable can never be accused of being boring.

We grew up eating crunchy iceberg lettuce, varied only by the dressing — French, lemon and pepper, or a splash of mayo from a bottle. Years later, I ate with unabashed joy when a local chef, our friend David Moyle, daringly placed a wedge of it, simply dressed and seasoned with seaweed, on our restaurant table. I was even happier when the fairy godfather of small-scale vegetable growing in southern Lutruwita (Tasmania), Tony Scherer, began to grow them for market. His icebergs were a deeper green than any I'd seen before, and had such a wonderful minerally flavour that you had to be early to nab one from the market stall.

On a family trip to France with my in-laws, and a babe at my breast, I was gobsmacked by the range of lettuces I'd not seen before — even in the *hypermarchés* — and quickly fell in love with butterheads, which looked like small, velvety icebergs. I had no idea what I'd bought at one mind-boggling supermarket until, back at our rented abode, I washed it and noticed its yielding texture. I dressed it simply with white wine vinegar, salt and olive oil, and we ate it in the garden, its silky tenderness a revelation after a lifetime of crunchy lettuces.

Asteraceae

Once we began our own market garden, the real exploration began. 'Amish Deer Tongue' forms tiny, almost cos-like heads that are tender and full of flavour. 'Butternut' (also called 'Buttercrunch') is a traditional green butterhead that, when grown in compost-rich soil, sings with flavour. I grow pots of 'Ricciolina', a little loose-leaf variety, by my back door so we can pop out and grab a leaf or two for a sandwich any time. There are thousands of lettuces — crisp or tender, tiny or huge, sweet, plain or bitter — and just as many ways to eat them.

We feast on salads of whole, shredded or torn leaves, with simple or creamy dressings. We fill lettuce cups with all manner of things and even revisit my high-school cooking lesson when our teacher terrified us by giving us lettuce, frozen peas, butter, seasonings and a chicken stock cube. Cooked lettuce? That seemed weird and unpalatable, but we did as we were instructed and made a cleansing, satisfying pea and lettuce soup — an excellent way to use up those outer leaves.

Celtuce — also called wosun, or stem lettuce — was another astonishing new vegetable. In its early stage of growth it looks just like a cos lettuce, with green, spear-shaped leaves standing upright, but as it matures a solid core forms, a stem that can grow as plump as your wrist — and that is the prize. We pull away the leaves, keeping the older ones for cooking, or for the chickens, and peel the tougher skin from the stems to reveal translucent, pearly-green centres about 20 cm (8 inches) long. They are nutty and sweet when eaten raw, if you've picked them young enough, beautiful when sliced and quickly pickled with soy and rice vinegar in the fridge for an hour before dinner, and wonderful stir-fried with ginger, garlic, soy sauce and sesame oil.

The cooking that brings out the savouriness in celtuce is equally excellent with cos lettuces. We grow a variety called 'Little Gem', a diminutive cos that's perfect for one or two people. On lazy summer days when I don't want to go inside, I'll light a little fire to heat up our outdoor grill, on which we'll cook all manner of things. Marinated slabs of zucchini; cobs of corn in their husks with slices of cold, salted butter wrapped inside; burgers and sausages from our excellent local butcher or a friend's farm — anything goes. When our protein, buttery or marinated vegetables are nearly done, I drizzle cos lettuce halves with a little oil, sprinkle with salt and put them on the grill, cut side down. I let them cook for a minute or two, just long enough to get some smoky grill marks, but still remain crisp. Then I'll flip them over, making a raft of them on the grill plate, and pile whatever tasty thing I've been barbecuing on top to rest. Depending on the heat of the fire, I might rake the coals away, or otherwise turn the heat down, and let the juices of my sausages or zucchini run into the lettuces for a few minutes, filling their hearts with savoury goodness that is released when you cut through their gently yielding crispness. You could also cook the lettuces on a barbecue, or the stovetop, but I find the flavour of smoke and coals is well worth the effort.

Daisy
Roots, rhizomes & tubers

Before we knew better, we hired a rotary hoe — a noisy, powerful machine that made short work of turning our old chook run into vegetable rows. We thought that patch of earth was barren. The chickens had eaten every bit of vegetation, so we'd moved them to a bigger paddock, where they'd never run out of greens, but our birds had only skimmed the surface. Lurking under the soil were two vigorous, persistent plants that we will never now be rid of.

It turns out that rotary-hoeing dormant Jerusalem artichokes, *Helianthus tuberosus*, and comfrey propagates them, and both are almost ineradicable once established. So each winter we dig, selling comfrey crowns to gardeners, with caveats about their persistence — and Jerusalem artichokes to cooks for their succulent, creamy rhizomes, preparing ourselves before market for the inevitable, relentless 'fartichoke' jokes we know we'll hear all day long. The sugar in Jerusalem artichokes is called inulin and is beloved by our gut bacteria, but indigestible by humans. Perhaps I don't eat enough of them, or my gut bugs are relaxed, or my theory about frosted artichokes being gentler on the digestion is true, but I've never suffered from the side effects our customers love to joke about. Roasted in a hot oven and seasoned well, they are delicious, and if you grow them yourself, you'll not find more calories for less labour than these wonderful vegetables.

Their cousin yacon, *Smallanthus sonchifolius*, is less common in Australian gardens. Their underground parts look similar, but a different structure is eaten. A rhizome is an underground stem that can spread, with eyes or nodes capable of growing new shoots and roots, and it is this knobbly structure of the Jerusalem artichoke that is eaten. Yacon produces rhizomes that look like artichokes, but the prize is actually the succulent storage tubers attached to them — teardrop-shaped organs in which the yacon stores its resources to fuel next season's growth. Yacon tubers are crisp and juicy, and have a simple sweetness from the same sugar, inulin, as their cousin. We harvest and wash them and leave them in the sun to cure for a few days, which is said to make them sweeter and more digestible. Then we scrub them, julienne them and toss them in a salty, spicy, sour dressing — as you would jicama — or roast them, chopped in large chunks, in a ridiculously hot oven so all that sweetness will caramelise, and the interior will stay crisp and sweet rather than turn mushy. I've heard of people making syrup from yacon as a substitute for maple syrup, but so far I haven't found the patience to juice and simmer them. They're another of the plants I'd grow even if I couldn't eat them, just to admire their large velvet leaves in dusky shades of green and purple that grow from the dormant rhizomes each summer.

Asteraceae

One summer I sowed burdock, *Arctium lappa*, also known as gobo. It grew like the weed it is, fast and lush. I was excited to taste its roots, and to send them into town to the chefs we supplied. We pulled away the leaves that had died back for the winter, and began to carefully dig, and dig; I'd read that we mustn't wound the roots, or the weeping sap would lessen the eating quality. By the time we'd extracted two roots, each about 60 cm (2 feet) long, we began talking about our hourly fee. If we were to charge ourselves out at the base horticulture rate, these two roots would be worth sixty dollars a kilo — not even including the time to grow, tend and deliver them, or all the other costs of doing business. I read about methods to make harvesting them easier, including laying sheets of corrugated iron diagonally in garden beds and training the roots along the corrugations. Instead, we decided to leave gobo cultivation to those with lighter soils than ours.

Scorzonera, *Scorzonera hispanica*, proved a similar, although not quite as low-yielding, proposition. The brown–black roots are also harvested in winter, and are also brittle and difficult to lift without damage. The sap they exude if wounded is very sticky — and once harvested, this same sap is equally messy in the kitchen. We learned to scrub the roots well, then boil them for a few minutes before peeling: voilà — no sticky hands, peeler, cutting board and bench! You can then finish cooking them in any way you desire. Their earthy, sweet, nutty flavour is best enjoyed with little added, so boiling in salted water until barely tender then finishing in a pan with butter, salt and pepper is ideal.

Salsify, *Tragopogon porrifolius,* is the easiest of the root daisies to grow and prepare — and, if you neglect to harvest in winter, the spring shoots are an exquisite green vegetable. Best sown in mid-summer, the first leaves look like grass, and I suspect many gardeners have pulled them out, thinking them weeds. In winter, preferably after a few frosts, the roots are dug out much more easily than burdock and scorzonera, and not as prone to snapping or weeping milky sap. Once in the kitchen it's a versatile vegetable, making creamy, nutty purées, and also beautiful roasted or poached in flavoured broths. If left in the ground, the plant will shoot and run to seed in spring, making the root woody and inedible, but the tender flower stalks, if picked before the flowers fully form, are magnificent. Sappy and with a unique sweetness, I love to roll them in a little pan of butter with some salt until they're warm, add a few drops of water to generate steam, quickly jam the lid on to trap the steam, and give them a minute or two to become tender. I'd grow salsify for these sweet shoots alone. If you leave the plants even longer, they'll produce beautiful pinkish purple flowers and giant shimmery dandelion-like seed heads. Here in Lutruwita (Tasmania) they can seed into dry grasslands, so if you're anywhere near wild areas you should snip off the seed heads and pop them away for sowing next summer.

The seeds of all of these plants are best sown fresh. They won't germinate at all if left in the seed cupboard too long. If in doubt you can fold a few in damp paper towel and place in a sealed container for a week to ten days. If you don't see any action after that time, you can safely assume it's time to buy fresh seeds.

The seeds of all of these plants are best sown fresh. They won't germinate at all if left in the seed cupboard for too long.

113

Crazy daisies

We have a family meal that we call Mongolian hotpot. I don't think it has anything at all to do with Mongolia, but once a family meal gets a name it sticks. On the table we have plates heaving with vegetables, mushrooms, meats and noodles, as well as a simmering pot of broth, and a little brass basket with a long handle for each person to submerge and cook whatever morsel takes their fancy. I spend most of the meal filling my poaching basket with shungiku and immersing it in the broth for just a moment before eating.

Shungiku, *Glebionis coronaria*, is also known as *tung ho*, chrysanthemum greens and chop suey greens. The flavour is difficult to describe — floral, herbaceous and, once you get a taste for it, addictive. A Japanese customer once told me she hated it because it reminded her of being sick. When she was ill her mother would cook a huge bowl of shungiku and make her eat it, steaming hot and doused with lemon juice. After recounting her story, she bought a bunch anyway; I love to think of people remembering family when they eat the food we grow.

On the other side of the flavour spectrum from the gently savoury shungiku lie the bitter daisies. **Tansy, wormwoods, costmary** and **yarrow** have all found their way into liqueurs, herbal remedies and spring dishes in just about every culinary tradition. Bitter tansy, *Tanacetum vulgare*, is used for pancakes. Mochi is made with Japanese wormwood, *Artemisia princeps*. Costmary, *Tanacetum balsamita*, is an ingredient in bitter ales. Yarrow, *Achillea millefolium*, features in the wonderful herbal tea 'YEP' — yarrow, elderflower and peppermint — that I drink to soothe colds and hopefully lessen their severity. Many of these bitter herbs contain toxic compounds and should be used with care, although their powerful flavours deter consumption of large volumes. Absinthe wormwood, *Artemisia absinthium*, grows easily in the garden, but given its reputation, I'd approach preparing drinks with the utmost caution.

German chamomile, *Matricaria chamomilla*, self-seeded in my back garden. Each head produced hundreds of dust-like seeds so tiny they blew into every sliver of a crack in the concrete, meaning I'm never without chamomile tea, and hoverflies never lack for nectar. Chamomile tea has a bad reputation of tasting as its seeds look — dusty — but freshly harvested a.   ed with care, it has a gentle, floral, slightly resinous sweetness, nothing at a. ..e the flavour you'll get from a supermarket tea bag.

Calendula, *Calendula officinalis*, is an equally free self-seeder that flowers all winter, and all summer. We scatter the petals on salads for colour and cheer in the depths of winter when, with no tomatoes, our green salads need a lift. In summer, the marigolds (*Tagetes* spp.) that we grow to attract beneficial insects also find their way to the salad bowl, their gold, orange and burgundy petals impossible to resist.

There are many, many more edible daisies, but I'll leave you with the most electrifying: *Acmella oleracea*, known variously as the **buzz button**, toothache plant, electric daisy, Sichuan button, spilanthes, paracress and jambu. It is a

magnificent plant, in temperate gardens best sown in late spring and enjoyed through summer. It gets around 10 cm (4 inch) tall, spreading a little, and produces tender 2 cm (¾ inch) long leaves and round daisy heads that are gold at the edges, with a red eye in the centre, and lacking the ray florets or petals that most other daisies possess. Pop a leaf in your mouth and it will tingle, disconcertingly so — but chop fresh leaves with chilli, add salt and lime juice, and you have an addictive condiment that will make your saliva flow, in a good way, enhancing the taste of whatever you're eating it with.

Brassicaceae

CABBAGE FAMILY

It may seem surprising for a garden in the foothills of a mountain, in the cool south of Lutruwita (Tasmania), to find that winter is a time of plenty. Summer and autumn pass with their bright red tomatoes, warm-orange pumpkins and golden ears of corn... and then, in winter, we embrace the cold and relish the bounty of the brassicas.

Rib-sticking colcannon, made with mashed potatoes and cream, is saved from being too rich by the sweet pieces of braised cabbage and leek folded through. Hearty minestrone, heavy with beans, tomatoes and herbs, finds an even deeper flavour when shredded Tuscan kale is added to the pot. And when we need relief from all that warm, heavy winter food, the crisp flesh of kohlrabi, radish and turnip comes to clear the fug away.

Some brassicas — cabbages, brussels sprouts and collard greens — require forethought, sowing and planting in the height of summer so they can mature before winter slows their growth. Others, like rocket and radishes, can be grown for most of the year; we only take a break from sowing them in June and July, and they mature in a few short weeks.

The brassicas are a family with branches on every thawed continent, and a long history of humans in every region working, selecting, cross-breeding, cooking and tasting to produce versions that suit their local climate, soil and culinary traditions.

Broccoli

BRASSICA OLERACEA VAR. ITALICA

My love story with broccoli began with difficulty, as it does for most children.

It wasn't that I hated it. Mum was an excellent cook, but before her Chinese cookery classes, and before we learned that broccoli only needs a lick of steam or a flash in the wok, it was often the last item on our plates near the end of the meal. Not nearly as maligned as boiled pumpkin or brussels sprouts, it still held little appeal to our young palates when cooked to a bland shade of khaki.

But Mum learned fast. She was soon dropping broccoli into a hot pan with her beautiful cashew and chicken stir-fry, right near the end — after the carrots, but before the snow peas — so everything arrived on our plates perfectly cooked, and luminously, appetisingly bright. Sometimes she'd pop it on top of a boiling pot of new potatoes just before they were done and jam the lid on, giving the broccoli a quick sauna in the potatoes' steam, just enough to make it tender — then she'd drain the water away and douse the whole lot in butter, salt and pepper. Enough to make my teenage appetite reach for the broccoli first.

This joyful foray into broccoli's delights wasn't to last.

When the first head of broccoli my parents grew was carried proudly into the kitchen, I remember being astounded by the sweetness and full flavour of our freshly harvested head after years of eating only supermarket ones. All was going swimmingly at the table — until my sister discovered half a caterpillar in her forkful of broccoli. I'm not sure she ever recovered.

Living in my first flat, frugality was the order of the day. I began to question why I was paying by the kilo for this chunky head of vegetable, eating only the tiny florets and throwing the rest in the bin. I began, meal after meal, to work my way down the stalk, learning as I ate that the flavour of the succulent stems was actually better than the flower buds. In one last flash of daring I pared back the base of the stalk — normally too woody for consumption — and found inside a translucent, crisp heart that tasted incredible raw, and brilliant after a quick flash in a hot pan. My love affair with broccoli was back on track, any thoughts of half-eaten caterpillars forgotten.

Our love story had a few more challenging twists to navigate when we moved onto the land we now farm at Neika, twenty minutes' drive from Nipaluna (Hobart), in the foothills of Kunanyi (Mount Wellington). The first time I grew broccoli, the seedlings flourished. A tiny pair of heart-shaped leaves was followed by stout, leathery green leaves with a waxy, glaucous coating that held beads of dew like crystals. After a month or two, the uppermost of these began to curl in on themselves; when I parted them I saw the beginnings of a tiny broccoli head, and my heart sang. I went out most days to admire their lengthening leaves, plumping stems and, finally, swelling buds. I could almost taste the first harvest. One morning, just days from harvest, on my way to

Brassicaceae

feed the hens, I noticed something was terribly wrong. Overnight, a dastardly possum had raggedly torn the tops off every single broccoli plant.

But I was not going to let this ruin our relationship. I was told a man named Ron knew just how to 'keep the buggers out'. After a week of watching Ron work like a driven man, taking him numerous cups of sweet milky tea, and picking up his cigarette butts of an evening, we had a fortress. Ron had laid wire that would keep rabbits from digging underneath, fine, stout netting to stop pademelons squeezing through, and on top, strands of hotwires with outriggers to stop the dreaded and wily possums climbing over. Invigorated and filled with bravado, I planted a whole row of broccoli. By then we'd begun working with chefs and I'd taken a deep dive into seed catalogues.

I planted 'Spigariello', an earthy-flavoured Italian beauty that produces thick, willowy shoots that carry curly tendrils of leaves with them, making the bunched stems look like something from under the sea. 'Purple Sprouting' broccoli went in — a variety that needs to go through a cycle of shortening days in autumn and the lengthening ones of spring to trigger flowering, so the harvest doesn't occur until well into spring, which is wonderful for extending your harvest. We also planted 'Di Ciccio', another Italian heirloom that grows traditional fat heads — but after the initial harvest, throws succulent broccolini for weeks.

While Ron's fence kept out the furred marauders, and we'd since learned to plant when the bulk of the equally damaging cabbage white butterflies were gone in autumn, we hadn't counted on things with feathers. The love story was about to take another sad turn.

It was early winter. Our newly fenced rows were thriving. The plants were up to knee height, with some growing still to do before their heads plumped up. Outside our fence, the grass was grazed to nothing as wallabies, pademelons and native hens — known locally as 'turbo chooks' — competed for diminishing autumn food. Native hens are flightless birds, the size of a skinny chicken.

They earned their turbo nickname for their ability to run, fast. We loved watching them raise their young on our dam every spring, and that particular year had been a good one for us, because there were many turbo-chook teenagers hanging about, stoushing for territory.

Little did we know that as well as running fast, turbo chooks can climb. One tragic morning we awoke to find that our new electric fence didn't bother them at all. They'd climbed right over it and denuded the entire end of our broccoli row, leaving ragged stumps where there'd been a luscious patch of green.

We went back to the drawing board, as farmers always do. We made the fence even higher and kept them out.

And ever since, the love between broccoli and me has remained strong.

From our own experiments and from talking with chefs and home cooks, we've begun to harvest, sell and eat broccoli leaves — which are easily as good as kale or collard greens. On the flipside, we also sell the impossibly sweet and wonderful spring shoots from our kale and cabbages as a kind of broccolini.

I sow my broccoli seeds in little pots every January in a netted plot to keep out the cabbage white butterflies that you'd be forgiven for admiring — white, fluttering beauties that will decimate your crop, and whose caterpillar progeny might traumatise your little sister. Look beneath the leaves of any unprotected brassica in the height of summer and you'll likely find a minute clutch of their glossy yellow eggs — or the plump green caterpillars that hatch from them — but luckily for us they can't survive in the cool of autumn and winter.

We top our beds with compost, seaweed meal, and whatever minerals our soil tests tell us we need, then we broadfork to loosen the subsoil and let a little of that delicious topping fall into the cracks the fork makes. On hands and knees, we tuck in our precious seedlings, giving each a space of 60 square centimetres to reach their full glory. Then we water them in, a vital step to stop the tiny feeding roots, wrenched from their snug pots, suffering transplant shock. We don't mulch broccoli beds initially. Slugs love broccoli, but they also love damp debris to hide in, so we mulch with straw once the plants are established. Every fortnight or so we make a little seaweed tea and wander the garden, spraying a magic elixir cloud that settles on the plant leaves and soil, feeding the microorganisms that feed the soil that feeds the plants that feed us. Some butterfly-egg squishing still happens, and we tolerate a little damage, having learned that without a pest, you have no predators to control them. Our garden plays host to all manner of carnivores who eat caterpillars and aphids — sometimes from the inside out.

It's not all smooth sailing. A flock of wood ducks arrives at random every few years, eating as much as they can before wheeling into the sky as we run at them, arms waving, shouting to wake the dead. And as for the grey cabbage aphid — the less we say about that undefeatable beast the better.

But a vegetable that responds to hard, bone-jarring frosts by becoming sweeter and more delicious, that yields florets, shoots, leaves, succulent stems and edible flowers, provides spring forage aplenty for the bees, and also happens to be very, very good for you, is worthy of all the love this mountainside farmer holds in her heart.

Charred broccoli with bacon vinaigrette

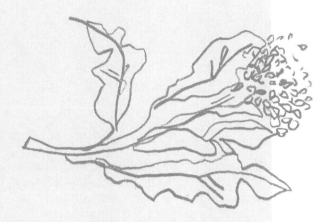

Instead of broccoli, you could use a bunch or two of broccolini. The leaves from broccoli plants, kale and other greens are also terrific cooked this way.

Choose a large frying pan with a lid, or one you can fit a dinner plate over. Add the oil and warm over medium heat, then add the diced bacon and cook slowly to let the fat render. When the bacon colours just a little, add the garlic and fry until it softens.

Scoop the bacon and garlic from the pan into a small saucepan, along with a tablespoon or so of the bacon fat, leaving a good film of the fat in the frying pan. Place the pan of bacon over low heat to keep warm.

Reheat your frying pan over high heat. While it warms, rinse your broccoli, shaking most of the water off. Drop it into the pan, standing back a little, as it will spatter and hiss furiously — which is what you want. (Sorry for the mess!) Turn it now and again for about 30 seconds, until you begin to see a little charring on the edges. Sprinkle on a tablespoon of water and quickly jam the lid on to trap the steam. Leave for 30 seconds, then turn the heat off and remove the lid.

Scoop the bacon from the saucepan with a slotted spoon and scatter it over the broccoli. Whisk the vinegar into the warm bacon fat, add salt and pepper to taste and pour over your broccoli.

Serves 4 as a side dish

a splash of <u>olive oil</u>

2 thick-cut slices of proper free-range, <u>smoky bacon</u> or speck, diced

5 <u>garlic</u> cloves, crushed

a head of <u>broccoli</u>, cut into long florets, the stem peeled and cut into batons

2 tablespoons <u>red wine vinegar</u>

Kale

BRASSICA OLERACEA VAR. ACEPHALA, BRASSICA NAPUS

Cult wellness has much to answer for, but no more heinous crime has been committed against a vegetable than that of putting kale in a smoothie.

The tragedy of our binary culture is that we're encouraged to have an opinion, to 'like' something or not, with no room for nuance or progress. Bad first experiences with foods can close minds to how wonderful they could be, and if we were to introduce a little curiosity and humility to the way we form opinions, we may give things a second chance. The first kale you tasted may have been grown in summer — not ideal for developing sweetness. It may have sat for a week in a cool store, swathed in plastic, and not been at its best when you bought it. Or what if we considered that maybe steaming kale in a puritan low-salt, low-fat manner, or blitzing it raw in a smoothie, didn't really give it a fair chance? And why, if it is truly so awful, would such an ancient vegetable still be in common and widespread culinary use?

The cringe away from the over-boiled vegetables of decades past led us to enjoy crisp carrots and bright green broccoli, but made us forget about braising — an almost alchemical conversion that can turn ingredients with coarse or harsh qualities into something unctuous, teasing out and balancing their flavours, and making them tender. And, in opposition to the conventional, nutritional thinking — that raw or steamed is always best — a long, slow cooking time can unlock nutrients not available to our bodies in raw or briefly cooked foods.

So, I ask you, can you please soften your preconceptions and give kale a chance?

My daughter Heidi loves kale. For as long as she's been aware of the seasons, she's noted the first frost with joy, telling us that the kale will be sweet, and tearing out to the garden to gather some. This is a child who eats everything. Despite my idealistic hopes of feeding my kids only local organic wholefoods, she has explored every culinary boundary and happily moves between her favourite whole spelt and broccoli salad to spending all her pocket money on chicken nuggets and sour straps. Her precocious love of kale is not a side effect of a childhood of deprivation, but of her good fortune in being able to eat the vegetable as it was intended — fresh from a winter garden and prepared with care.

That frost-sweetened kale comes in many varieties, all with their own qualities. Tuscan kale, also known as cavolo nero, is the most strongly flavoured, and best suited to being finely shredded and added to a minestrone or braising.

Braised kale

I love to begin my kale braise by warming lots of olive oil or bacon fat, say 2 tablespoons, in a deep frying pan. I add some finely sliced shallots or brown onion and cook gently until just translucent. Then I add lots of garlic; it is winter, after all, and we have to care for our immune system. Crush the garlic with the flat of your knife, peel, chop finely and add it to the pan, keeping the heat low so nothing burns.

Wash your kale and shake off most of the water, leaving it a little damp — the hiss of steam when you add it to the pan will help it collapse and meld with your oniony, garlicky oil. Shred it finely. Turn up the heat under your pan for a moment (so the damp kale won't cool it too much) and, when the onion starts to sizzle and jump a little in the oil, add your shredded kale. Turn it in the oil and pop the lid on, or sit a plate over the pan, to capture that first rush of steam. Remove the lid and let the steam evaporate for a moment. Add salt and pepper, letting your kale fry for a minute or two once the water has evaporated. This moment of frying will add a nutty, toasty note that will improve your braise no end.

Now add your liquid of choice, about ½ cup (125 ml) at a time. Chicken, vegetable or ham stock are wonderful, water is great, and a mild meat stock can be lovely too, but overwhelming if too strong. Then let it cook on low, stirring whenever you pass the kitchen, adding a little more stock or water as it evaporates.

Your braised kale will be good after 10 minutes, lovely after 20 minutes, and excellent, yielding to the tooth, completely digestible and delicious (if a little ugly) after 30 minutes. Adjust the seasoning to taste — extra pepper, smoked paprika, butter, some crispy cubes of speck or a squeeze of lemon are all perfect additions.

We eat it piled onto toast with fried eggs on top, or as a side dish to any family dinner.

Heidi's
kale salad

Wash your hands well. Pop the lemon juice, oil and salt in a jar, screw the lid on tight and shake until emulsified. Put your kale leaves in a big bowl, pour the dressing on and rub the dressing into them. You'll see a beautiful transformation as you work the dressing in and the cell walls in the leaves rupture, revealing a beautiful, luminous green.

Once the leaves have collapsed, and just before serving, sprinkle on some wakame, sesame seeds and chilli flakes and mix them through. If you're like Heidi, anoint with some Kewpie mayo... If you're like me, skip the mayo and sprinkle with more wakame, sesame seeds and chilli flakes.

Serves 4

1 tablespoon Meyer <u>lemon</u> juice, or your favourite vinegar or sour citrus

1 tablespoon cold-pressed <u>sesame oil</u>, or olive or grapeseed oil

a few generous pinches of <u>sea salt</u>

a generous bunch of tender, frost-sweetened <u>kale</u>, stems removed and torn into bite-sized pieces

<u>wakame flakes</u>

toasted <u>sesame seeds</u>

<u>espelette chilli</u> flakes, sweet paprika or similar, to taste

a squirt of <u>Kewpie mayo</u> (optional)

You don't have to cook the life out of all kale varieties. 'Russian' and 'Pentland Brig' kale grow tender and sweet in our winter garden, and Heidi has a keen eye for those as well. Gather leaves from near the centre of the plant for salads, as they'll be younger and more tender. Wash them well — you don't know what those wintry slugs have been getting up to on your leaves at night. Fold the leaf in two, holding the stem in one hand and the lower leafy part in the other, and strip the tender leaf from the stem. Once you get the knack of this, it's really fast and you have no waste at all. If you've paid for that kale and want all possible resistant fibre in your diet (go you!), just slice those stems across the grain, blanch and freeze them to add to your next pot of soup or vegetable curry.

My other daughter, Elsie, loves to add kale to her two-minute noodles — a nutritional compromise for sure.

We have a strange kale 'tree' of unknown parentage that lives in the garden near our kitchen, getting tatty from cabbage white caterpillars every summer, and turning on a new burst of growth in time for Elsie's winter noodle snacks. Supplementing this is a kale plant on the back veranda, growing in a 20 litre (5 gallon) pot (kale loves lots of space and compost) that Elsie barely has to step into the rain to harvest.

I have no doubt these naturally nutrient-seeking young humans have been primed and aimed in the right direction to feed themselves well, and that allowing some nutritional leeway gives them an easier, healthier relationship with food.

Cabbage

BRASSICA OLERACEA (CAPITATA GROUP)

Who would have thought this most common of vegetables would be so difficult to grow?

Gross feeders, susceptible to cabbage moth, snails, slugs, cutworms and grey cabbage aphids. Fickle enough to decide death is near and throw forth flower shoots at the slightest hint of stress, and greedy for space — each tight head, the size of a child's, is supported by vast leaves, spreading up to a metre, and provides only a single harvest, so they need a lot of room to grow.

But when you get it right — what a dream.

We begin our cabbage seedlings in late December (it's a difficult thing for the mind to ponder winter vegetables at the height of summer) in a netted fortress to ward off cabbage white butterflies. Each tiny seed is dropped singly into a potful of compost, minerals, sand and seaweed meal — a recipe designed to give enough food for germination and moderate growth, but not too much nitrogen, which would make for blousy, weak plants. The seedlings only take a week or so to emerge with their two tiny heart-shaped leaves, and another three or four weeks to be ready for planting out.

We like to plant them in the beds that have grown broad beans, peas or other legumes the previous season. We cut the bean plants to the ground, top the soil with seaweed meal, lime, blood and bone and some mineral fertilisers, and cover with a layer of compost to protect the soil while the brassica babies are growing. We tuck a seedling in every 60 cm (2 feet), staggering the rows in our beds so that every plant has as much room as possible to spread its voluminous foliage. We go out at night wearing head torches and carrying old plastic milk bottles and drop every slug, snail and cutworm we find into them. Every week in summer and autumn, or after rain, we apply a formulation of *Bacillus thuringiensis* — a soil-borne bacterium that paralyses only lepidopterous insects that ingest it, and doesn't affect other organisms. Through a combination of this treatment, helpful birds, predatory insects and old-fashioned caterpillar squishing, we make it through to early winter, when the first frosts and the plant's maturity see an end to all the rampant predation of summer. Many of my farmer friends use exclusion netting, which I struggle to keep in place in our windy garden. Every environment is unique, so I think it's vital to experiment to find the best path to success in your own garden.

A plump row of cabbages, ready at the beginning of winter, holds the promise of many nourishing meals to come, and makes some primal larder-stocking corner in my heart feel at peace. A happy cabbage plant will hold its head — so to speak — well into spring, sitting there patiently until a cook with a knife begins the harvest.

When I cut a cabbage plant I take it straight to our fence. Our garden perimeter is bounded by a chook run, and chickens have a voracious appetite for greens. Trimming a cabbage straight into the run summons the birds. Our rooster makes his gentle 'took took took' noise telling the hens there is a snack to be had, and the frenzy begins. Eating without hands — when your meal is a dinner plate-sized leaf, your head is only the size of a dessert spoon, and you're competing with twenty other birds — is a violent process. The hens grasp the huge leaves with their beaks, toss them about wildly to tear off large pieces, then throw back their heads, opening and closing their mouths as vast amounts of greenery disappear down their throats. I always find comfort in this spectacle, knowing that when I bring the eggs from those birds to the kitchen and beat their golden yolks, any cake, custard or ice cream I make with them is practically a vegetable dish — chock-full of all the nutrients those cabbage leaves have mined from the soil and magicked from sun, water and their underground bacterial and fungal allies.

Later in the season, as winter becomes spring, the calling of birds and bees can no longer be denied and thoughts of both animal and vegetable turn to reproduction, a tectonic cracking of tight cabbage hearts begins. The first time I saw it I was dismayed, thinking my crop was wasted, but one frosty morning, wandering the garden, I snapped a stem — wonky and distorted from having fought free of its tight head — and I ate it on the spot. It was, I think, the sweetest form of brassica: firstly sweetened by frost, and then by the plant throwing its entire investment of sugars into the final primal task of perpetuating itself.

We began to offer bunches of those willowy, broccoli-like stems to our friend Tom Westcott, the chef and co-owner of our favourite pub Tom McHugo's, who put them to use in all manner of broths, braises and salads. Later in the season the yellow flowers are a sweet, cabbagey delight for human mouths, and a bounty for the bees. Oddly, the honey we collect from our hives in brassica season, when the bees have harvested from kale, radish, cabbage, mustard and rocket, has none of the sulphurous funk or piquant spiciness we associate with brassicaceous vegetables, only a clean, rich sweetness; it is my favourite honey of all.

At the end of the season, we cut the cabbage plants as close to the soil as we can and let the vast root system that fed them feed the soil biome, and, in turn, feed our next crop. After the cabbages, we usually sow carrots or parsnips, which relish the search for nutrients in the soil the cabbages have greedily fed from, sending their roots down deep in search of their own food — a wonderful harnessing of the gifts of each plant to nourish the soil.

Calf's heart with herbs

We once kept pigs and had the local mobile butcher visit to dispatch and help us process them. On learning of our willingness to eat all but the squeal, the butcher — replete with meat and desirous of vegetables — began to message me with offers of offal and other bits his customers had no appetite for. We willingly traded livers, tails, cheeks and soup bones for vegetables, and one day a heart of cabbage was traded for the heart of a calf.

Despite my usual gameness, a heart was something new. This organ, representative of love, to me — literally the most visceral symbol of life — came into my hands oozingly fresh, even still slightly warm with the lifeblood of the animal who'd held it.

The poetry of 'a heart for a heart', and a commitment to not wasting a taken life, led to a deep dive into my cookbooks. I opened, trimmed and washed the heart, soaked it in salted milk overnight and washed it again, before making a stuffing with a huge bunch of fresh parsley, sage, lemon zest, garlic, some breadcrumbs and a little fatty bacon. Wrapping the heart around this, I sewed it shut with a butcher's needle, browned all sides in beef dripping — why waste beautiful, grass-fed fat? — and dropped it into a saucepan of chicken broth and herbs to simmer for a couple of hours.

What, you may well ask, other than the trade, does this have to do with cabbages? Rather a lot, I think.

Through the ages, the seasonal availability of foods has led to many beautiful synchronicities. The marriage of cabbage and heavy meats is just one of those. The best meals use piquancy to foil richness, sour to balance sweet, bitter to work with fatty. And what better thing to balance the almost overwhelming meatiness of a heart than the fizzy brightness of newly made sauerkraut, alongside soothing mashed potatoes.

Sauerkraut made simple

Once I went to a workshop run by fermentation guru Sandor Katz, where he shared his simple, permissive sauerkraut method of chopping or grating whatever vegetables you have to hand, massaging them in a bowl with salt until the juice runs, creating a brine, and the plant cells are beginning to break down, then tasting and adding more salt until it makes your mouth happy — you should be able to taste a nice amount of saltiness. It's a technique that has served me well.

I then like to flavour my salted shredded cabbage with a few peppercorns, dill seeds and bay leaves, but you can use whatever you like — fennel, lovage, juniper, chilli.

Bottle the cabbage mixture in clean, plump (but slim-necked) pickle jars, making sure it is packed down well, free of trapped air pockets, and completely submerged under its brine. I use tiny ceramic dishes that fit in the necks of the jars to weigh the mixture down.

I keep the jars on the kitchen bench, watching for the fizzing to begin, occasionally opening the jars to 'burp' them and check for any bits of cabbage poking above the brine, or any white, wrinkly kahm yeast that needs skimming from the surface. (The kahm yeast is harmless, but not delicious.)

After a few days of fizzing (the timing varies depending on the temperature of the kitchen, the sugars and natural yeasts on and in the vegetables, and how much salt was used), I begin to taste, looking for the amount of tang and funk I enjoy. When it's there I pop the lids on and keep the jars in the fridge for up to a year, although I enjoy it most within a month or two. I always use a clean utensil to take out what I need and push the remaining vegetables back under the brine before returning to the fridge.

In our home, this sour, salty, crunchy and occasionally thrillingly fizzy condiment graces everything from hot dogs to breakfast eggs, and serves as both vegetable and pickle — and just the thing to eat with a calf's heart.

Brassicaceae

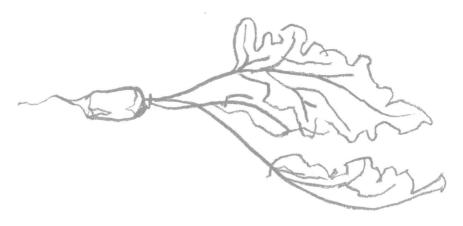

Radish

RAPHANUS SATIVUS

Elsie dreamed of having a cat. A feline companion who would love and understand her, and who she could have warrior adventures with, like the heroic cats in her favourite books. Though I dearly wanted to grant her deeply held childhood wish, where we live there is an abundance of marsupials who can become infected with a terrible parasite, *Toxoplasma gondii*, that blinds, stupefies and eventually kills susceptible animals, and lives part of its life cycle in cats. I couldn't trade beautiful endangered eastern barred bandicoots for a furry killer, so we settled on a pet that would be cute, could be left with friends if we went away, and might even earn her a few dollars.

With her hard-earned pocket money, Elsie bought a packet of radish seeds. We gave her a little patch of earth, which she raked, composted and sowed with those seeds, following our instructions to put her rows a hand-span apart, and her seeds two finger-widths from each other. She covered them lightly with soil and watered them in. A few short weeks later, the tiny red globes were ready for harvest and she proudly took them to market. She stayed and sold every last bunch... and finally her tiny investment in her new pet project had turned into enough money to buy a clutch of quails.

Then she went to see Grandpa Phil. The two of them raided his store of timber, took some of her radish takings to the hardware shop, and built a quail palace. It had a sliding roof, so no matter where the quails sat, they could never be quite safe from cuddles — and a dry spot for storing feed and fresh hay, so they'd always be warm and well fed. And to live in that new palace, after some time and misadventure we finally found a trio of Japanese quail, the most exquisite, plump, sweet birds — Snowy and the Mud Twins.

Buttery quail eggs & radishes

Radishes can be sweet or pungent, and the more stress they're under as they grow, the spicier their flavour. But a fleeting moment in a hot pan full of butter renders them sweet enough for the most sensitive palate.

Cook your quail eggs in gently boiling water for exactly 2 minutes. Drain them and drop them into iced water to stop them becoming hard-boiled. Peeling quail eggs is fiddly, and they are easily damaged. For perfect, mildly pickled eggs, I cool them after cooking, then submerge them in the vinegar and watch the magic happen — their beautiful brown spots will lift away and the shells will gently fizz as their calcium carbonate is dissolved by the vinegar. After half an hour, remove the eggs, rinse them and you'll only have a little membrane to peel off. By all means skip this step and peel them the old-fashioned way if you don't want to waste the vinegar. Set aside.

Wash your radishes and trim the tops. If the tops are green and lush, chop them coarsely and set aside. If your radishes are more than 2–3 cm (1 inch) in diameter, slice them in half.

Warm the butter in a frying pan over medium–high heat until it's just beginning to foam. Tip in the radishes, roll them about in the hot butter and add the thyme. If you've halved the radishes, be sure to let the flat surfaces brown a little in the butter. Season with salt and pepper. If you've reserved the radish tops, add them now to wilt for just a moment, then sprinkle with the fresh herbs.

Serve tumbled over hot, buttered toast.

Serves 2

6 quail eggs

½ cup (125 ml) vinegar, in a glass (optional)

1 bunch of the sweetest radishes you can find

50 g (1¾ oz) butter, plus extra for your toast

1 thyme sprig

1–2 teaspoons finely chopped chives, parsley, chervil or tarragon, or a mix

sourdough slices, sitting at attention in the toaster

At first things went swimmingly. The Mud Twins were hardy, productive layers and didn't mind the cuddles too much. But new laws came into place regulating the sale of eggs by smallholders — so Elsie joined the campaign for scale-appropriate rules. She was interviewed about her business on the local *Country Hour* radio show, and I like to think her eloquence helped win our battle.

Elsie's now-legal quail eggs flew off the market stall, so we bought Snowy a few more girls for his harem, and even hatched some of the tiny eggs in our incubator. But something changed in our sweet Snowy and he turned murderous. One morning his white feathers were stained red: he'd pecked one of the poor Mud Twins badly.

We banished Snowy to his own hutch, washed and dressed the hen quail's wounds, and she recovered. Sadly, without Snowy to keep his harem in check, they turned on each other, giving an awfully graphic illustration to the term 'hen pecked'. We eventually determined which hens got along with each other, and kept the girls in happy clutches — but Snowy could never be let back in with his harem.

Elsie had been saving her quail egg money, and after covering the cost of the feed, hay and egg cartons, she spent her remaining egg-earnings on her dream budgie, Pecorino.

Quail eggs are sweeter than chicken eggs, and a perfect bite-sized treat, so it seemed fitting to serve them with the radishes that funded them in the first place.

For perfect, mildly pickled eggs, cool them after cooking, then submerge them in vinegar and watch the magic happen.

Cauliflower

BRASSICA OLERACEA (BOTRYTIS GROUP)

We've only ever missed one restaurant harvest. It was when we were at the peak of our powers: young enough that our knees and spines breezed through harvest day, and old enough to know what we were doing and work like orderly machines.

We live 300 metres (1000 feet) above sea level near a mountain at a latitude of 43 degrees south, but for all that we receive surprisingly little snow. When we do, a hush envelops the neighbourhood. No cars, just bird calls, the snow softening their echoes. One July evening it began to snow, and didn't stop. I woke to that magical silence with my snow pants and coat already laid out in preparation for our harvest day. I pulled my layers on and went outside to an enchanting sight; be you seven or seventy, the delight of a rare snowfall makes us all children again.

It was beautiful. Every farmer will tell you that snow hides all their sins. I couldn't see a single weed, thrown-down tool or blown-away pot. Just the neat, repetitive mounds of our garden beds, with flitting robins and fairy wrens making everything magical. This also meant we couldn't see our vegetables.

That year we'd grown three kinds of cauliflower, and contrary to conventional farmer wisdom, we were thrilled at their muddled rates of maturity. A big problem for home gardeners is that seedlings from nurseries come in punnets of six or so plants. If you plant them all at once you'll find yourself with six enormous cauliflowers, which can be hard to use in a timely manner. An excellent strategy is to share seedlings with your neighbours and take turns buying punnets of lettuce, cauliflowers or spring onions and stagger them, for more sensible harvests. As market gardeners we want to extend our season too. And since our brassica planting window is tiny — a small interval between when the cabbage moths give our plants a break, and while the soil is still warm and the days long enough to make plants grow — the simplest way to stagger our harvest is by growing different varieties.

We grew 'Macerata Green', 'Sicilian Violet' and the white 'All Year Round' that year. Every week, different plants had grown curds fat enough for harvest, but through the thick blanket of snow there was no way to tell which to pick. There was also absolutely no chance of finding the radicchio, or even knowing which row the carrots were in.

So we rang our dear chef customers and apologised with sincere regret that we were letting them down, but with no regret at all for our unplanned holiday.

We tobogganed, used footprints in the snow to follow the wallaby tracks to find the gap in the fence they were squeezing through, and when we were chilled to the bone we knocked snow from the cauliflower row until we found a good, plump head, then took it inside for a warming cauliflower macaroni and cheese dinner.

We found a good, plump
head, then took it inside
for a warming cauliflower
mac and cheese dinner.

Cauliflower mac & cheese

Dozens of vegetables benefit from the savoury creaminess of a simple cheesy white sauce and crunchy breadcrumbs — but cauliflower is our family's favourite. I love the simplicity of putting a dish straight from the oven onto the table, and letting everyone help themselves.

Preheat your oven to 200°C (400°F).

Bring a large pot of salted water to the boil. Add the pasta and cook until it's only a little under-done, then add the cauliflower, put the lid on and let it boil for a minute more. Tip into a colander to drain.

Meanwhile, melt the butter in a saucepan large enough to hold the cauliflower and pasta later on. Gently cook the onion over medium heat until tender and translucent, then add the garlic and cook for a minute or two more, until fragrant.

Sprinkle the flour over the buttery alliums and stir for a minute or two, until you're sure the flour is cooked. Turn the heat down to medium–low and gradually begin to add your milk. If you're too hasty at this stage, the flour will cook into lumps that cling to the onion, so begin with about ½ cup (125 ml), stirring briskly with a wooden spatula, until it becomes quite thick. Add another ½ cup (125 ml), stirring well again until it thickens; it will be a little looser than the first addition. You might find it easiest to change to a whisk as you add the rest of the milk, ½ cup (125 ml) at a time, letting it almost come to a simmer.

Serves 4

250 g (9 oz) dried pasta, any short shape will do — penne, macaroni, shells

½ head of cauliflower, cut into bite-sized pieces, including the stems and pale inner leaves

60 g (2 oz) butter

1 small onion, finely diced

5 garlic cloves, crushed and chopped

2 tablespoons plain (all-purpose) flour

800 ml (28 fl oz) milk

3 teaspoons dijon mustard

70 g (2½ oz) pecorino, grated

140 g (5 oz) cheddar, grated

½ cup (60 g) coarse dried sourdough breadcrumbs

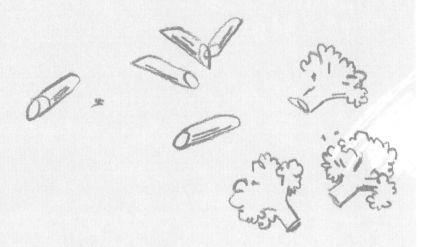

Finally, whisk in the mustard and season with salt and pepper, then whisk in the pecorino and half the cheddar. Taste your sauce: if anything, you want it a little too salty, because the pasta and sweet cauliflower will be crying out for extra salt.

Turn the heat off and tip in the cauliflower and pasta, folding them through the sauce, until combined into a cheesy, milky cloud. Pour it all into a baking dish and top with the breadcrumbs and remaining cheddar, sprinkling them evenly over the surface. (My daughter Heidi advocates for twice as much cheese at this point; I prefer a crusty, crumby topping — so adjust accordingly.)

Bake for 15 minutes, or until appetisingly crisp and browned on top.

Best served on a cold night after a bracing day, with a crunchy green salad.

TIP: This recipe uses half a cauliflower and half a packet of pasta, so is easily doubled; you can freeze half the cooked cauliflower and pasta (without the topping) for another day. When you're ready, just thaw it in the fridge, top with cheese and breadcrumbs and warm in the oven until piping hot and golden.

Turnips

BRASSICA RAPA (RAPIFERA GROUP), SWEDES,
BRASSICA NAPUS (NAPOBRASSICA GROUP),
TURNIP TOPS, BRASSICA RAPA (RUVO GROUP)

Turnips, like their radish cousins, come in many shapes, textures and forms. Japanese turnips mature in just a few weeks and have unparalleled sweetness. Children will eat the round, white globes like apples, and there is nothing more delightful to use on a platter of crudités. Classic French or Italian turnips, with their charming purple shoulders, can be used raw and sweet when young, or left to mature in the ground to be cooked in stews, or to provide sweet, light relief among heavier vegetables with your Sunday roast.

Their sturdy cousin the swede has a strong childhood taste memory for me; Mum served it peeled, boiled and roughly mashed, with melted butter and lots of pepper, which was somehow simultaneously starchy, filling and refreshing. A truly beautiful vegetable, swedes grow easily, but they do need a long time to mature. They store wonderfully well for whenever you have the stew pot on.

Cime di rapa (rapini), which translates from Italian as 'top of turnip', was a delicious and bountiful revelation for me. Rather than growing turnips for their underground parts, you sow cime di rapa's tiny seeds about 20 cm (8 inches) apart in autumn or early spring — and within a month you'll have bountiful turnip tops that look a little like miniature broccoli, but are more tender and bittersweet, with tiny yellow flowers to add whimsy to your dinner. It's at its best braised using the same method as the kale on page 125, but only for a few minutes, as it's a far more tender vegetable. It's traditionally served with orecchiette, garlic, anchovies, olive oil and seasoned toasted breadcrumbs.

We've made our own orecchiette a few times. Heidi is the master of pressing the little pieces of dough along the bench, forming them into beautifully rippled 'little ears' — but I always seem to make my dough too doughy, and the brightness of the cime di rapa is lost among my chewy pasta.

Trawling through my collection of old cookbooks, looking for inspiration for a dinner party, I found a recipe for passatelli — a pasta made of breadcrumbs and cooked in broth, which I decided would be beautiful spiked with the slightly bitter cime di rapa greens. Since I'd just bought a vintage, gold-rimmed set of crockery and crystal candlesticks, I took far too much trouble to make a clear broth, and to simmer my passatelli in salted water beforehand to keep my broth clear. This is entirely unnecessary, and every Nonna in the land will be shaking her head at me, but you have to follow your whims.

If, like me, you make breadcrumbs from random loaves (I can't bear to throw those beautiful sourdough ends away), you may want to practise this recipe *before* your dinner party, to work out the right amount of moisture to hold your bread together and still give you tender noodles — or are they dumplings? It took me a few goes to make them hold together and have a pleasing texture, and I'm grateful to my family for soldiering through my chewy or mushy failures.

Elegant thrift — before you begin

This is a dish of scavenged bones, cheese rinds, breadcrumbs and a vegetable that grows like a weed, but when prepared with care, it is sophisticated and perfectly delicious.

To prepare the **breadcrumbs** I thinly slice every stale piece of sourdough I find in my kitchen, let it dry until it's brittle, steal my daughter's smoothie maker to grind it, then leave the crumbs to dry completely before storing them in a jar. For this recipe a fine crumb is best, so I choose white or spelt loaves and trim the crusts from them before drying and grinding.

Broth is the same. I butcher my chickens and save the frames, fat and wing tips in the freezer until I have enough to fill my stockpot. I love to roast the bones with halved onions so that everything browns and makes a sticky, caramelly chicken and onion 'jam' on the roasting sheets that I work free from the baking trays with boiling water and a spatula. This brown, sticky stuff that hurried cooks may wantonly wash down the sink is the most flavoursome part of the broth, and if you're cleaning it from the trays anyhow, you may as well use it. I save rinds from parmesan and pecorino and add them to the stockpot as well.

Passatelli in broth with rapini

Scale this recipe up as required. I make one portion per person as a hearty main meal, or share it between two or three people as a starter.

If you're having a special dinner and want an astoundingly clear broth, you can freeze your strained chicken stock and let it thaw in the fridge through a sieve lined with muslin (cheesecloth). It's a ridiculous but immensely satisfying thing to do; there's no need for this step unless you're feeling fancy — the bright green rapini does look wonderfully luminous through a clear broth.

Passatelli: Find a potato ricer or passatelli press and insert the screen with the largest holes. Put the breadcrumbs, parmesan, butter and nutmeg on a clean kitchen bench or in a large, shallow bowl. Season with salt and pepper, gently work the ingredients together, then make a well in the centre. Crack your egg into the well and pull in the dry ingredients a little at a time to prevent a lumpy dough, and knead together. Some methods tell you to chill the dough for a couple of hours, but I find it can seize and become difficult to push through my potato ricer, so I put a wax wrap on my dough and let it rest at room temperature for half an hour.

Put a pot of salted water on to boil, a colander in the sink and a slotted spoon near the stove. Hold the potato ricer over your boiling water and put a tennis-ball-sized piece of dough

Serves 1
as a main meal

rapini (turnip and kale flower heads and leaves; cime di rapa), blanched in salted boiling water for a minute, then drained

PASSATELLI

30 g (1 oz) fine dried breadcrumbs

⅓ cup (30 g) finely grated parmesan

1 teaspoon softened butter

grated nutmeg

1 medium egg

BROTH

1 cup (250 ml) chicken stock per person for a main meal, less for a starter

inside. Push the dough through the colander and, when they're a couple of inches long, slice the noodles into the boiling water. (If the water isn't hot enough, the noodles can begin to soak it up and turn mushy before they cook, whereas briskly boiling water makes them cook quickly and remain firm.) As they float to the surface, which only takes a minute, scoop them from the water into your colander and repeat until they're all cooked.

If you're not particular about a clear broth you can skip the colander and slotted spoon and sensibly press the noodles straight into your boiling broth, for a more rustic but still delicious dish.

Add a serving of passatelli noodles to warmed soup bowls, along with a few stems of quickly blanched rapini. Ladle hot broth over and top with a little grated parmesan if you like.

Best served with soup spoons, cloth napkins and candelabras.

Mustard greens, choi & wombok

BRASSICA RAPA

There was a time when bagged salad mixes rocked our worlds. Tiny iron-tasting beet leaves sat alongside frilly purple lettuces and spoon-shaped choi leaves, and I'd pick through the salad bowl seeking out the most exciting greens I'd ever tasted — the mustard greens. Sharp, a little bitter, a little sweet, a little spicy, and nothing like the neutral crunch of the iceberg lettuce salads I was accustomed to. Leaves with flavour, what a revelation. Now I'm grateful those same mustard greens have colonised my garden.

Huge, spicy 'Osaka Purple' mustard self-seeds alongside a pale, sweet choi type, and the two make a perfect salad dressed with soy, Chinkiang vinegar and sesame oil. Matt sows little rows of 'Ruby Streaks' mustard — crisp, peppery, jagged-leaved little garnishes that seem to grow overnight and thrive in cool weather, giving our jaded winter bellies a fresh pick-me-up when they most need it. We once grew a fascinating stem mustard that looked like a giant brain. The swollen stem of the plant was the prize, and it was like crisp, appley mustard. I can't find the seeds anymore, but I love to buy it ready-pickled from our local Chinese grocer. Its mysterious savouriness is addictive.

Pak choi and bok choy are a little harder to grow. They need sowing in cool, well-composted soil and consistent moisture and weather to form the fleshy white petioles that we devour in hot noodle soups.

Wombok's crisp sweetness is brilliant raw, braised or fermented — is a fridge complete now without a pot of kimchi? It, too, loves cool soils and matures quickly if sown in early autumn or early spring.

And then there are mustard seeds. Wholegrain mustard makes a cheese toastie sublime, hot dogs aren't complete without a streak of yellow American mustard, and a Dijon-style mustard is in every white sauce I make, and many salad dressings as well. Every summer I preserve tomatoes in a version of kasundi, a spicy tomato pickle that uses copious amounts of mustard, giving it a savoury, warm, rounded flavour. I keep nearly empty jars of mustard in the fridge, add a little vinegar or lemon, salt and oil, shake vigorously, and enjoy the added benefits of a delicious no-waste mustard vinaigrette and an almost-clean jar to wash up.

So many important brassicas

Many cabbages are grown for their leaves, rather than their hearts, such as **collard greens**, *Brassica oleracea var. viridis*, from Southern American foodways, and **tronchuda**, *Brassica oleracea* (Tronchuda Group), a sweet, enormous leaf from Portugal that travelled from there to Brazil. I've grown many delicious African cultivars, too — generous tree cabbages that produce for multiple seasons as you pick your way up an ever-growing stem. There's even one that was found growing wild on a remote island off the north-west coast of Lutruwita (Tasmania) — remnants left behind by Chinese vegetable farmers who grew food there to supply sailors and sealers. It now grows happily in our mountain garden, looking tatty and near death every summer, then leaping into growth as the cool weather chases pests away.

Brussels sprouts are one person's pleasure and another's nightmare, but even the most stubborn haters can be turned around by sampling sprouts that have been halved, barely blanched in boiling water, drained well, then fried until crisp with little shards of bacon. They are a labour of love to grow — they must be planted here in January and protected from summer predators for months, in order to produce in winter. But as well as their main crop, the plants offer wonderful miniature cabbagey tops and big spoon-shaped leaves that are just as good to eat as the sprouts.

I couldn't live without the spicy brassicas. Thuggish **horseradish,** *Armoracia rusticana*, will take over your garden with its huge sword-shaped leaves, which are edible and quite good when young, and its thick, pungent roots. We try to only eat beef from farmers who work regeneratively, storing carbon in the soil, and our occasional steak, perfectly cooked, is served with a pile of freshly grated horseradish on the side. Mixing fresh horseradish with the resting juices from the meat is incredibly delicious. My mouth waters at the thought.

Wasabi, *Eutrema japonicum*, while a little more difficult to grow, isn't beyond the abilities of cool-climate gardeners who regularly water their plants. Its deep-green rippled, saucer-sized leaves are magnificent, and arching stems of white flowers dangle over them in spring. From early autumn you can lift three-year-old plants to harvest the stout, hot rhizome, and once you've hosed off your plant you'll find lots of plantlets have formed around the base of your old plant. You can re-pot these in good-quality potting soil, or plant them out in a cool part of the garden with morning sun or light shade. They won't thrive in warm, humid gardens, and many things love to eat them. The finest wasabi is irrigated with moving water from mountain streams, but to my palate the plants I gather from my shady garden and prepare within minutes of harvest are delicious enough — vibrant, complex and slightly sweet along with their beautiful heat — and the most pleasing shade of mossy pale green. The leaves make excellent wraps to hold all manner of snacks, and the leaf stems are crisp and spicy, making for a beautiful quick pickle that adds tang to our family nori roll nights.

That addictive brassica heat comes in salad form, too. **Wild rocket,** *Diplotaxis tenuifolia,* is a perennial plant I recommend to people who want to grow food in limited space or containers, as it produces vast amounts of greens in perpetuity from a single planting, and has pretty, sweetly honey-scented, yellow flowers. **Salad rocket,** *Eruca sativa,* is also a generous plant, and will self-seed, popping up here and there for whenever you want a salad. It will be spicier in summer and sweeter in winter, and earns a place in the ornamental garden with its moody red stems of black-veined, cream-coloured flowers that are also a beautiful garnish.

Watercress, *Nasturtium officinale,* is also easily grown. I sow it in pots, and sit them in trays of water that I regularly flush, as it loves to be wet, but not stagnant. **Salad cress,** *Lepidium sativum,* is wonderful when grown on the windowsill as sprouts. Sow it in the ground, let the leaves mature to around an inch long, and you'll be rewarded with a spicy, refreshing salad.

We'll end the brassicas on a high with one close to my heart, **kohlrabi,** *Brassica oleracea* (Gongylodes Group). With the crunch of an apple, the minerally deliciousness of kale without the bitterness, the sweetness of a frosted turnip, and leaves that you can eat, to top it all off — as well as charming alien good looks — it's an easy vegetable to love. The part you eat is a swollen stem that grows just above the ground, and when peeled and cut into matches it makes a brilliant salad. Dress it simply with a white wine vinaigrette and a little parsley, and it will sit happily alongside just about any meal.

Cucurbitaceae

Cucurbits are a plant family that know their own minds. Pumpkins will romp across your garden covering any plants, mislaid spades or slow-moving gardeners in their path. Cucumbers climb, and climb, and climb. I spend many happy hours encouraging their coiled, springy tendrils to venture up the trellises I've provided for them, discouraging them from swamping their pepper or basil neighbours with their clingy-lover habits. Mouse melons grow like crazy, their ivy-like foliage prettily covering a summer garden screen, but they, and only they, decide when it's time to fruit, frustratingly producing tiny male flowers for weeks before the female flower — whose pollinated, swollen ovary is the tangy, juicy mouthful I'm after — appears. And zucchini? Never a more generous plant was grown. I once had twenty kilos I couldn't use or sell, so I left them on the bonnet of my car in the shade near a busy path, right in the middle of town. I posted them on social media and left a big sign saying FREE ZUCCHINI! while I spent two hours wandering through the Tasmanian museum. Upon my return, the very same twenty kilos were still there. Thank goodness for friends with pigs.

The pumpkin family is a lavish one of almost 1000 species, occurring naturally on every continent apart from Antarctica — although the origins of many are murky, with some modern varieties having no known wild relatives, and others having migrated with people across ancient land bridges. While many wild species are toxic, humans in every corner of the globe have, over millennia, selected varieties to reduce the undesirable compounds wild plants developed to ward off pests.

And then the fun began. People selected for traits that suited their climates, their cuisine, their cultural ideals. Sweet, fragrant melons that were picked ripe and almost bursting with sugars reigned supreme in France. In Eastern Europe, hull-less pepita pumpkins are prized for the delicious oil pressed from their seeds. Hard-skinned winter squashes thrive all over North and South America — selected and bred for millennia in pre-Columbian civilisations and by modern gardeners today. The culinary diversity of zucchini found its zenith in Italy, while in Africa refreshing watermelons are bred for their water content, delicious sweetness and protein-rich seeds. There are luffas eaten young as a summer squash, or allowed to mature and ferment before their flesh is washed away, leaving behind a useful natural-fibre sponge. Other pumpkin varieties are grown primarily for their vitamin-laden greens and shoots. There are gourds grown for use as receptacles, instruments or decorations, and melons grown for seeds as snacks in China.

Cucumber

CUCUMIS SATIVUS (& SOMETIMES CUCUMIS MELO)

The world has not been my oyster. Trades like hairdressing and horticulture make for a modest purse, yet a childhood spent by rivers, beaches and lakes made me long for a trip to Larapuna (Bay of Fires) as much as an adventure to Paris. Add to that an early commitment to a home, a dog, a piece of land, a family and a farm, and you have a recipe for staying put.

While I still harbour dreams of going somewhere — anywhere — with gardens, fruits and vegetables that are different to here, and staying long enough to grow, cook and get to know them, for now I happily travel through the pages of books.

All of my favourite books have food as an anchor, a way for people to serve, care for and please one another. Food can act as a signifier of culture or status, climate or season, and as a gathering point — where better than around a table to bring your characters together and show their foibles and desires?

I've spent time in a North Korean military school with boys who eat only rice and kimchi they make themselves. I've suffered with a blind French girl, surviving on preserves with no way of knowing if she would get vinegary beans or sweet peaches when she opened each jar. And I've witnessed poor Esther Greenwood's greedy bliss turn to agony after she indulged in dodgy crab meat at a New York luncheon.

But this is a chapter about cucumbers. Japanese novelist Haruki Murakami always makes me hungry. His organised, if a little confused, protagonists prepare simple, fresh-sounding meals — always something crisp, always something savoury. In *Norwegian Wood*, Toro performs the most tender act of generosity, feeding cucumbers piece by piece, dipped in soy and wrapped in nori, to a dying man. A more perfect snack for the poorly and bed-bound I can't imagine — the appetite-arousing umami coupled with the bright freshness of the cucumber both soothing and stimulating. The foetid, oozing snozzcumbers in Roald Dahl's *The BFG* delighted me as a child; the schadenfreude the BFG enjoys as he forces the human-eaters to live on them seemed a perfect outcome. But my favourite cucumber-eating scene is from Tolstoy's *Anna Karenina*.

The depiction of food in the novel is as diverse as the characters. It's easy to empathise with Levin's reaction to Oblonsky's gluttony at a dinner that began with three dozen oysters, wine, soup and creamy turbot. How on earth could the man go on to eat the meat courses, let alone the fruit and cheese that followed? I felt far more pleasure reading of the simple dexterity of the *muzhik* — Russian peasant — who gathered and pocketed wild mushrooms without losing the rhythm of his scything, leaving poor Levin panting and sweating in wonder and envy. The two then shared a simple meal of bread and cheese while lying in the grass — a pleasure I know well — the enjoyment of simple food after a hard day's work easily rivalling the grandest of banquets.

After hundreds of pages of upheaval, grief and trauma, Tolstoy rewards our fortitude by taking us to Levin's apiary, where everyone seems to be healing and finding equilibrium. They feast on honey and cucumbers while waving away bees and wasps that are after their own share, gently prising bees from the comb and placing them on leaves to recover, tending with gentleness to the tiniest of creatures while discussing with seeming casualness battles and the deaths of soldiers. In Russia at that time of year there would have been no fresh cucumbers, so the ones the party enjoyed must have been pickled. I love imagining my way into a scenario like this, when the writing is done by a diligent author with deep knowledge behind the scene they've set. That thinking inevitably leads to research and wanderings in the backwoods of the internet, where I learned of cucumbers being pickled in hollowed-out pumpkins, or in wooden barrels submerged under the ice in rivers where the temperature remains constant.

When our book club decided to read *Anna Karenina*, I leapt at the chance to host our chat and prepare food to set the scene. Despite the novel's eight hundred or so pages, it still didn't allow me quite enough time to grow and pickle the cucumbers for our feast, so in an indulgent nod to that apiary scene, we had to settle for a honey cake made with honey from a hive not twenty metres from where we discussed the book — along with little potato dumplings, tiny pickled mushrooms and delicious mock-caviar made with eggplants and eaten with blini. It was of course no hardship, but in the spring following our gathering I dug through my seed stash and found a treasure.

'Bushy' is the name of an old-fashioned cucumber variety, said to have originated in a *dacha* — culturally important small-scale production gardens that still produce a significant proportion of Russia's food. Russia is vast and I'd love to know more about the region these plants are from, but they are, as their name suggests, low-growing, bushy vines that are hardy, even in cool summers. They produce excellent crops of short, bumpy cucumbers, best eaten small and pickled in brine, or allowed to grow a little plumper, then peeled and sliced into salads and sandwiches, or turned into a quick pickle for eating the same day.

We sow cucumbers in October, in little pots in the greenhouse. You can, if you have fewer slugs than we do, sow them directly in the garden when the soil temperature is around 18°C (65°F) and the threat of frost has passed, but there is no benefit in rushing the season and sowing cucumbers until it is warm. They'll only sulk and have more chance to attract pests before they begin to grow. All cucumbers benefit from having something to climb up — and even the judicious removal of a few growing stems. You can prune them as you would a tomato plant, taking away some vegetative growth to encourage more concentrated fruiting, but I leave my 'Bushy' plants to their own devices. This means I'm regularly pushing back vines to find fruit — miss one and your plant will put all of its resources into ripening it, to the detriment of further fruit set.

In the peak of summer, cucumbers form seemingly overnight. Catching them when they're small enough to pickle, but large enough to have formed some of the succulent seed cavity that gives a gherkin that satisfying inner squelch, is difficult. Ideally you'd gather and pickle the same day, but for efficiency's sake I pick over a few days, pinching the blossom from each one as I go, maximising the yield of fruit that is of similar size, and store them sealed in the fridge until pickling day.

Just when you think you have a handle on cucumbers — smooth-skinned, Lebanese types for salads; prickly gherkins for pickles; old-fashioned apple cucumbers for peeling and slicing onto thickly buttered bread and seasoning with salt and plenty of pepper; and even the exotic 'Poona Kheera' types from the cucumber's subcontinental cradle, served in a glorious coconut salad with curry leaf, mustard seeds and chilli — along come 'melon' cucumbers, from the genus *Cucumis melo*, rather than *Cucumis sativus*. Some of you may have met the pale, slender Armenian cucumbers, which I think are the most flavoursome variety available. We've also grown an Italian cultivar, 'Tortarello Barese', which is disturbingly furry when young — but wash away the fluff and you have a dense, tasty cucumber that's botanically a melon. One season I entered my greenhouse to the delightful scent of ripe rockmelon: under my cucumber trellis was an aromatic 'Tortarello Barese' cucumber that I'd missed during harvest. It was not very sweet, but entirely delicious.

Cucurbitaceae

153

Pickled gherkins

Seek out small cucumbers for this recipe. Admittedly, this can be challenging, and if you're buying them from a farmers' market, expect to pay a premium, given that the growers are forgoing a bigger yield for a smaller boutique one that is labour-intensive to harvest. Old-fashioned varieties, bred for pickling, that have remnants of spines and rough skin, are best as they have a lower water content than the more common Lebanese (short) types.

Wash the cucumbers, massaging to remove any small, black spines. Pinch any blossom ends off, as they can make your pickles soften if left on. If your cucumbers are more than 2–3 cm (1 inch) in diameter, you can cut them into batons and slice out a little of the seed cavity, leaving only firm flesh.

Layer the cucumbers in a large straight-sided jar or tall, narrow bowl, sprinkling each layer with salt as you go. I do this by feel, but be generous. Whole cucumbers will need more salt than cut ones, and you want to make sure there's a little salt clinging to most of the exposed surface. As you add each layer it will share the salt with the layer beneath.

When you're out of cucumbers, find a saucer that firmly fits the mouth of your vessel and place it on top. Pile as much weight on top of the saucer as you can safely manage — a tower of tinned food is ideal. Cover with a loosely draped tea towel and leave overnight.

Next morning, drain the brine from your jar and discard. Give your cucumbers a very thorough rinse. Drain well, spread them on clean tea towels and blot them dry, pressing quite firmly to extract as much water as possible.

Pour the boiling water into a bowl. Add the 160 g (5¾ oz) salt, spices and bay leaves and stir until the salt is dissolved. Pour in the cold filtered water.

Makes 8 x 500 ml (17 fl oz) jars

3 kg (6 lb 12 oz) small pickling cucumbers

160 g (5¾ oz) salt, plus extra for sprinkling over the cucumbers

2 cups (500 ml) boiling water

1 tablespoon fennel seeds

½ tablespoon coriander seeds

½ tablespoon yellow mustard seeds

½ tablespoon black peppercorns

16 fresh bay leaves

6 cups (1.5 litres) cold filtered water

fresh unsprayed grape, oak or currant leaves

Pack your gherkins tightly into a clean jar or fermenting crock, adding a few of the grape, oak or currant leaves as you go. Pour in the brine, including the spices and bay leaves, until the jar is two-thirds full, then tap it on the bench, tilting and rolling, to allow any air bubbles out. Then you can fill the jar until the gherkins are completely submerged. If you pack your gherkins tightly, you'll find you can jam them below the neck of the jar, making it easier to keep them submerged under the brine they ferment. I often pick twigs of bay leaves and tuck them into the neck of the jar to stop the cucumbers floating to the surface; a small condiment dish, or a glass jar with a little water inside, also makes an excellent pickle weight.

Cover your pickle jar with muslin (cheesecloth) and secure with string, or put the lid on your crock and pour boiled water in the seal. Then just wait.

Depending on the warmth of your kitchen, and which lovely yeasts and bacteria your ingredients have brought to the party, you'll start seeing bubbles within a day or two, but it may take three or four.

Keep an eye on the surface of your liquid, particularly if using muslin. Occasionally a white, matte skin forms on ferments. It's kahm yeast and is harmless, but can change the flavour of your pickles. If it appears, skim it off regularly, rinse any weights you're using and change your muslin for a clean piece. If any green, pink or fuzzy growth forms on the surface you should discard your pickles, sterilise everything and begin again.

After three or four weeks, the bubbles will have slowed and your bright green cucumbers will have transformed into moss-green gherkins. Drain them, reserving the brine, leaves and spices, and pack the gherkins into small, sterilised jars with their flavourings. Pour the reserved brine over the top, then seal and store in the fridge. Many American books suggest water-bath canning them at this stage, which will ensure shelf-stable pickles — but it will also kill all of the fun fizz and any beneficial bugs, so I leave that choice to you.

Read your Tolstoy and nibble on a pickle while imagining an agrarian utopia in Levin's apiary.

Pumpkin

CUCURBITA MAXIMA, CUCURBITA
PEPO, CUCURBITA MOSCHATA

When I first began growing food for a living, our family had a breadwinner in my husband Matt, which gave me the freedom to put my energy into building soil, trialling crops and learning my craft. Our children were finally at school five whole days a week, I had my dear friend Sam working with me on one of those days, and I had the boundless energy and freedom from aches and pains that is the young gardener's gift. I was fit, time rich, and free to explore every culinary and horticultural curiosity that came our way. (Why do we never know how good things are in the moment?)

A neighbour had stables that needed mucking out, so Sam and I forked manure and hay into our trailer. We layered it with all manner of weeds, rakings and prunings, into huge mounds that looked for all the world like a row of untidy Daleks in an unused corner of the garden.

The beauty of manure collected from a stable rather than paddocks is that horses don't hold their bladders overnight; they relieve themselves on the straw and manure at their feet. Urine is full of nitrogen — just the thing for powering the microbes that kick-start composting. The key to good compost is a ratio of around one-third green sappy things (for nitrogen) to two-thirds brown but not-too-woody things (for carbon), or your compost can become hot, anaerobic and stinky. The mix of carbon-rich, partly digested hay and grass in the manure, and nitrogen-rich, urine-soaked straw from the stable floor, can work well enough on its own, but it was lovely tossing in barrows full of sappy weeds and grass clippings as well as gum mulch. We'd raked the fallen leaves, twigs and bark from under our gum trees and run over it with our lawnmower to break it into smaller pieces and allow microbes to get to work on breaking it down. We turned bushfire-prevention rakings, that are too often burned as a waste product, into an excellent soil-building resource that gave our compost structure.

Gathering all of these 'waste' products, turning them every few days when the temperature in the middle of the pile reached around 60°C (140°F), and watching them turn into lush, brown compost was a delight. Sure, there was a lot of labour, and I'm not sure if my back would be up for the rigours of making such a volume by hand these days, but when it was finished we felt rich beyond measure.

A quick note on food safety

Both 'hot composting' and time are vital if you want to use compost — particularly a manure-based compost — on food plants you intend to eat raw. Around salad greens or low-growing fruiting plants such as tomatoes or beans, only use compost that has been aged for at least a year. Allowing your compost to reach a high temperature also helps kill any pathogens that may be present in animal manures.

By mid-October our heaps had broken down into chocolatey, worm-rich compost, with just enough residual microbial activity to keep the soil warm, and Sam and I gleefully popped in far too many pumpkin seedlings for the size of the garden we'd made.

The seedlings grew lush and triffid-like, swallowing the space we'd allowed them, and continuing onward. We checked their growth by pinching the tips from the tendrils — which can help to induce fruit set — and we used the tender tips, complete with their tiny immature pumpkins, fried with garlic and bound with eggs, to make omelettes that looked like they belonged in a fairy tale.

I'd read of pumpkin leaves having wonderful levels of vitamin A and being used in curries in parts of Africa, so we figured out how to strip the leaves of spines, the way you'd string a stem of celery, and we learned that the *Cucurbita moschata* cultivars — including butternut pumpkins and tromboncino squash — have the most tender leaves. After stripping, we spread each leaf with freshly ground peanut butter, rolled and secured them with toothpicks, immersed them in a spicy tomato curry and gently simmered them for half an hour. As strange as it sounds, it is delicious, and a wonderful way to eke a few more meals — and extra diversity — from your pumpkin patch.

It is a challenge to find the pre-Columbian stories of the North, South and Central American cultivars of pumpkin and winter squash, *Cucurbita maxima* and *C. pepo*, that we value so much in our gardens, larders and kitchens today, but it is vital to remember that before any of these seeds passed into the hands of colonisers, modern-day seed breeders, or to you in your home garden, they were shaped by the hands of countless seed-keepers who have set the genetic foundation for the foods we enjoy now.

We'd tucked in seedlings of 'Anna Swartz Hubbard' squash, an American heirloom that ripens to a rich, speckled green with an orange spot underneath. It's a difficult shape to describe — round at the bottom end, and domed like the top of an egg at the other. Anna, who bred the squash, had selected a wonderful strain for hard times. They improve, as many pumpkins do, with time in storage; the tough skin resists rotting, and the deep-orange flesh is among the fullest-flavoured you'll find.

'Oregon Homestead Sweet Meat' went in too, a more modern strain selected by Carol Deppe, famous among seed-savers for her work producing crops with the flavour and beauty of heirlooms, and the commercial practicality of modern cultivars. 'Oregon Homestead' is a rather normal-looking pumpkin, reminiscent of a 'Queensland Blue' with its smooth, grey skin, but inside you'll find a tiny seed cavity — meaning more bang for your pumpkin buck — and silky, flavoursome, deep-orange flesh. It's another excellent keeper, as are all the pumpkins and squash we grow on our farm — a necessity for those of us in cool climates, given that the time between pumpkin harvests is almost a whole year. Crops like these, which actually improve with storage, make for a much more diverse kitchen at lean times of year — an often overlooked aspect of seasonal eating.

We grew a few more delicate vines at the edge of the plot — exceptions to the long-keepers, but worth growing for their compact size.

'Uchiki Kuri' squash is a delicious, tear drop-shaped Japanese heirloom with beautiful, edible vibrant orange skin, the perfect size to feed four people. 'Delicata' and 'Tuffy Acorn' are two small squash varieties, both incredibly delicious — the Tuffy with a dry, starchy texture perfect for soaking up butter and tasting as though it has been infused with brown sugar, while the Delicata, when sliced and roasted at high temperature, crisps up — seeds, skin and all — giving you the nuttiest pumpkin snacks that taste like popcorn.

We also grew 'Tonda Padana', an Italian variety with floury flesh that makes excellent gnocchi, and a Mexican 'Tatume' squash that can be eaten young like zucchini, or left to develop a slightly stringy, moist flesh that absorbs flavours such as garlic, chilli and coriander and makes a wonderful taco filling. 'Kakai' was our final curiosity — an Austrian oilseed pumpkin whose hull-less seeds we ate raw and fresh, relishing their milky, nutty, pea-like flavour.

But for sheer size and productivity, the winner of them all was the 'Blue Hubbard' — a glorious prize that ultimately yielded a small domestic tragedy.

The Blue Hubbard winter squash vines laughed at our fences, rampaged down the driveway and over the chook house, thuggishly smothering other plants in our too-small but extremely fertile plot. Each vine grew three or more gigantic pear-shaped, blue-green fruit, which my daughters carted around like enormous dolls. With so many pumpkins, where to store them? Our property is home to many brushtail possums and bush rats who feast upon anything within reach… so our living room became a pumpkin cellar. Desk, dining table, kitchen bench and floor were covered in them. As autumn became winter, we sold, ate and gave them away until only the most awkward, thirteen-kilo behemoth remained. Too big for one family to get through, too hard to cut, and given strange looks by market-goers used to tame wedges of pumpkin, not huge, canoe-shaped hunks. And so this big Blue Hubbard remained on the kitchen table — until one day it decided it was leaving home. I'm not sure who bumped the table, but this massive squash suddenly rolled off, straight through the window — ending up in the front garden, split open, but luckily safely free of broken glass.

Soup and pumpkin scones were eaten for days, the excess roasted in olive oil and salt, passed through a food mill and frozen for the long-distant day when my family could face another pumpkin meal. I never did work out if the profit from that verdant pumpkin patch covered the cost of the glazier.

Delicata squash with butter, brown sugar, cumin & its own seeds

Delicata squash are unique, in that they have seeds and skin that, when cooked just-so, are nutty, delicious and edible in their entirety. If you substitute a pumpkin with larger seeds you'll still be able to crack them with your teeth and enjoy their insides, but the shells won't become crisp and edible as those from smaller squash.

This sweet, salty roasting method is perfect for any pumpkin, whether you can eat the seeds or not. If using larger big pumpkins, cut them into slices about 3 cm (1¼ inches) thick.

Preheat your oven to 190°C (375°F). Wash your squash and use a sharp knife to cut it in half lengthways. Scoop out the seeds, and the sticky, orange flesh around them, and place in a bowl.

Combine the remaining ingredients in a small bowl, squashing the sugar and spices into the butter.

Using your hands, spread half the butter mixture over all surfaces of the squash. The butter will be a bit uneven, but the warmth of the oven will distribute it for you. Lay the squash, cut side down, on a baking tray.

Add half the remaining butter mixture to the reserved squash innards, then spread them around the squash, into a flattened pile.

Serves 2

1 delicata squash

50 g (1¾ oz) butter

1 teaspoon dark brown or rapadura sugar

1 teaspoon cumin seeds, lightly toasted and coarsely ground

½ teaspoon espelette pepper or paprika

½ teaspoon sea salt

They improve,
as many pumpkins do,
with time in storage.

Roast for 10 minutes, then remove from the oven and mix your seeds around a bit, pulling the browning outer ones into the centre, and moving the less-cooked seeds to the outside to brown them up a bit.

Roast for another 10 minutes. Turn the squash over, then add the remaining butter to their cavities, and mix the seeds again. You want them to become crisp, and the flesh around them to become sticky and jammy.

Bake for a further 10 minutes, until the squash is tender. During this time, if your seeds are at risk of burning, just remove them from the tray and keep warm until the squash is done.

I found this recipe in a Mexican book years ago, so I often find myself serving this with soft tortillas, a salad and a tomatillo birria — a spiced tomatillo braise made with a slow-cooked joint of meat — as part of a Central American feast.

Topped with a few dollops
of goat's cheese, zucchini are
the tired gardener's friend.

Zucchini

CUCURBITA PEPO

He had the bluest eyes you've ever seen, enhanced by his private school blazer, and perhaps the added *frisson* of the forbidden... private school boy, public school girl — it could never happen.

It started on our shared bus ride home, with the Morrissey album tucked under the arm of a slim, pale, long-haired kid, who was being hassled by other private school boys over his taste in music. I'd like to say that one of us defended him, but we were all abashed by the bullies. Better to look away and stay out of it... and when we looked away, we looked at each other. I found myself alighting from the bus one stop early, when he invited me to walk the long way home with him, to look over his back fence at the canaries in his mum's garden. For the rest of that week we sat together on the bus and I developed a fateful crush on this Montague.

A few days later, Mum's elderly Dutch friends did us the 'favour' of delivering yet another box of giant marrows to our door. Mum did her best hollowing out those blimps, salting them, filling them with her brilliant bolognese sauce, sprinkling with cheese, then baking them until they miraculously became appetising. That evening we sat around the table, determined to do justice to her labour, when there was a knock at the door. It was the blue-eyed boy. Back in the 1980s, you didn't Snapchat from your bedroom with a potential beau. You invited them in to meet Mum and Dad — and nor did you leave the table until everyone had finished eating. And so he sat with us, waiting for me to finish. Imagine my agony, scooping out forkfuls, strings of melted cheese holding fast to the marrow on my plate as I brought each bite to my mouth, feeling his eyes on me as red sauce stuck to my lips and chin. The concept of first-date food — meals that don't stick to the face, the teeth, the breath — was an idea I felt keenly that evening. Meal finished, I made my escape, and as I walked our suburban streets with that boy, the family dog playing chaperone, we made plans for a first date.

I will never know if it was my red oily chin, the thought of visiting my home and being made to eat marrow, or the sheer fickleness of teenage hormones, but before that dreamed-for date could occur, my blue-eyed boy kissed another girl — a private school Capulet — at a party and my romantic hopes were dashed.

But the marrow have remained loyal.

They may be harder to fall in love with than cute boys on buses, but once you've learned the myriad ways to prepare and enjoy them, and the gifts that different varieties offer, your love for zucchini, marrow and summer squash will last a lifetime.

The first heirloom zucchini variety I grew was 'Romanesco', a gigantic plant with sharp, raspy spines and majestic buttercup-yellow flowers big enough to hold big spoonfuls of goat's cheese stuffing, but it's the fruit of this plant that is the game-changer.

If you've only eaten commercially grown, stored and shipped zucchini, you can be forgiven your loathing. The spongy texture, absence of flavour and the ludicrous lies you've been told about it being an excellent pasta substitute (I'm looking at you, zoodles) can all make for unappetising eating. The Romanesco, however, is a dense thing. Picked while young, it is tender and crisp, but even when left to mature a little longer, it is nutty, firm and succulent. Best of all, the fruit that gets missed, hiding under the massive leaves and ballooning out to marrow size, is still firm and tasty.

After Romanesco, we explored every other variety we could get our hands on. We've grown another Italian, 'Da Fiore', bred solely for its abundance of huge stuff-able flowers, and 'Ronde de Nice', a French variety producing compact round fruit, perfect for a small household that doesn't need foot-long zucchinis. A firm favourite in our garden and kitchen is the Lebanese type — small, grey fruit, best picked only a few inches long, and traditionally hollowed out, stuffed with a lamb and rice filling and baked in a rich tomato sauce.

Lately I've become more practical. As much as I adore Romanescos for their flamboyant flowers and terrific flavour, I've learned that on harvest day, lower yields — a gift for home gardeners who don't want to be swamped — actually make harder work for my market gardener's back, as I'm rewarded with fewer fruits for each bend to the plant, and their spiny leaves, while tolerable for the first few plants, become painful after you've bent to pick a crate full.

Another Italian, 'Striato d'Italia', joined our planting list, along with 'Cocozelle' and 'Mutabile', all delicious, finely textured and ridiculously productive varieties, and all with very few spines.

After a long summer day working in the garden you never feel like cooking, and zucchini are your best friends. Needing nothing more than to be sliced lengthways into finger-thick slabs, briefly marinated in a slurry of herbs, garlic, salt and olive oil, given a quick kiss by a hot pan or barbecue plate and topped with a few dollops of goat's cheese, they are the tired gardener's friend.

The friends you haven't met yet

The cucurbits that follow are nothing new to those fortunate enough to have found them on their childhood tables, but I relish the journey of discovery every time I meet a new plant. Each and every one of them is delicious once you've spent some time together, trawled books and the internet to find their stories, and, after much practice and patience, learned how to grow, harvest and cook them.

The most exuberant plant I've ever grown is the **chilacayote**. Native to Mexico, but apparently more frequently grown in the Andes, the chilacayote, fig leaf gourd, shark fin melon or *Cucurbita ficifolia* is a rampant vine that can be grown as a perennial in frost-free gardens. In our mountainside garden however, each plant spreads to cover a few square metres over the warmer months before succumbing to frost, so I dread to think what kind of world domination they'd achieve without a hard winter to keep them in check.

The fruit can be harvested from the moment it forms — it's like a summer squash or zucchini at that stage. But, let it grow a little plumper, say the size of a child's football, cut it into wedges and simmer it in your favourite broth until tender, then slice away the skin and return the gelatinous, stringy flesh to the soup, and you'll have something that is said to resemble shark's fin soup. Having never eaten shark fin, I can't confirm or deny such claims, but I can tell you that the tender, faintly sweet, translucent strands of melon flesh absorb the most delicate flavours beautifully, and the texture is like spaghetti squash and sweet potato noodles got married. Leave it on the plant even longer and it grows to the size of a party balloon. The skin hardens and is absolutely beautiful — a base of cream, netted with a bubbled fretwork of dark green and flecks of gold. It's so beautiful that you'll want to keep it rather than eating it — and the terrific news is that you can.

A ripe chilacayote — sometimes called angel hair melon at this stage — will sit happily on your kitchen shelf for at least two years, all the while becoming sweeter, and the strands in the flesh more defined. After your two-year wait, you take the fat melon, have the tallest person in the family (or the tiniest standing on a table) hold it above a swept hard floor — and drop it. (This is the safest way to crack any hard cucurbit. Many tough-skinned pumpkins and winter squash can be difficult to force a blade through, and while your pumpkin pieces may be wonkier, there'll be no bleeding palms!) Now gather up your shattered chunks, pick out any seeds you can find — these are traditionally dried and made into a toffee brittle — and place the chunks in a roasting tin, skin side down. Cover and bake slowly, for 45 minutes or so, until the flesh is easily teased away from the skin with a fork. Make a heavy syrup using brown or rapadura sugar, orange juice, cinnamon, allspice and maybe some pepper, enough to cover your melon strands. Simmer them gently in the syrup until the strands become translucent 'angel hairs'. You can dig straight in and serve it hot with ice cream, use it as a filling for sweet empanadas, or — like our friends at our favourite pub, Tom McHugo's — turn it into a mustard fruits–inspired conserve to enjoy with preserved meats.

Cucurbitaceae

Don't want your yard taken over by a rampant gourd? Can't wait two years to eat angel hair — and don't have a sweet tooth anyhow?

Caigua, *Cyclanthera pedata*, and achocha, *Cyclanthera brachystachya* — both known also as stuffing cucumbers, and with similar growing habits and culinary applications — could be for you. These are more delicate vines, growing up supports to at least two metres (six feet). The caigua has gorgeous palmate leaves that visitors to my garden, thinking themselves the first to make the joke, say remind them of marijuana — and although you can't smoke the leaves to any great effect, you can pick and eat the young tender leaves and shoots. The fruit of both species, when picked young, has the flavour of a cucumber. It can be eaten raw in salads, and is also great stir-fried or pickled. But I love them best when they're allowed to mature. When almost ripe, but still crisp and green, the fruit become hollow, and you can remove the black seeds and the fibrous membranes by cutting a slit down the centre and hooking them out with your finger. I then stuff them with a mixture of minced beef, chopped hard-boiled egg and raisins, along with a little garlic, cumin, salt and chilli, and bake them in a spicy tomato sauce. The stuffed caigua look like little elfin slippers, while the achocha are covered with tender green spines, making for a dramatic-looking but wonderfully wholesome dinner.

With a thousand members in the cucurbit family, I'm barely scratching the surface here, but for the cool-temperate garden these are all varieties that have proved reliable and productive. I've just sourced an Eastern European melon from an area with short summers like ours, so perhaps that will be added to my list in coming years, and I'm yet to try growing bitter gourds or winter melons. Every year I sprout a choko (or chayote) vine that grows wildly, but it always succumbs to frost before fruiting.

There is always a new friend to meet, and the cucurbit family will provide many.

167

Fabaceae

LEGUMES

Legumes feed both us and the soil in which they grow. They work in complex relationships with bacteria and fungi, which capture nitrogen from the air and convert it into a form the plants can use — and the plants reciprocate by sharing the carbohydrates they've made through photosynthesis with their underground allies, also providing a habitat for them within their roots. The bacteria lie dormant in the soil, awaiting the germination of a suitable host — then they begin their friendly invasion, entering the host plant via its tiny root hairs, and inducing the plant to produce the nodules in which they live. If you pull out any healthy leguminous plant — a pea, a wattle or prickly gorse bush — you'll find them, small creamy- or pinkish-coloured sacs you'd be forgiven for assuming were signs of disease.

We try to grow leguminous crops after root crops, and before leafy ones. Fruiting crops grown after legumes often produce copious amounts of leaf at the expense of the plump fruit we're after, and their stems can grow sappy, inviting sap-sucking pests such as aphids in for a meal. Root crops can also grow billowy tops susceptible to pests, and their roots may fork. Leafy crops, though, will lap up the nitrogen left by legumes, growing deep-green and thriving. With growing awareness of the carbon emissions associated with the production, transport and use of fertilisers, and with the finite nature of many of the inputs used in their manufacture, farm- or garden-produced fertility is becoming increasingly vital for food security.

Gardeners can assist the nitrogen-fixation process, if need be, by buying an inoculant of host-specific rhizobial (nodule forming) bacteria to aid new species of legumes in their fields. In a very unscientific trial, the only time I've grown a successful — and delicious! — edamame crop was when my seed supplier added a little sachet of inoculum to my order, which I sprinkled over the dampened seeds before sowing. That same crop of edamame was grazed by an invading wallaby, so perhaps the stress of a vicious pruning induced it to set a succulent crop of pods. Or, as soy beans had never graced our fields before,

these legumes would have had no relationship with the life in our soil, so it may have been the connection provided by that bag of black dust that made the difference. One agricultural advisory group suggests having at least twenty nodules on your broad bean roots two months after germination is a reasonable number. So off you go, find your trowel and do some garden science.

The ability to aid soil fertility for subsequent crops comes from the ecological niche legumes have evolved to occupy. Following disturbance, fire, erosion or other catastrophes, the seeds of legumes will germinate. Many have evolved with hard seed coats, perfect for plants who wait in the darkness of soil or leaf-litter for the fire that will crack that coat, or the flood that will make them swell and grow. Their gift for helping the barren become fertile makes them very easy to love.

Climbing beans, bush beans & runner beans

PHASEOLUS VULGARIS, PHASEOLUS COCCINEUS

Jack knew what he was about, trading the cow for those beans.

Never mind geese and golden eggs, a handful of dried beans will produce endless protein that you needn't get up early every morning to milk a cow for. Some tender, warm earth, a good drink of water upon planting, sunshine, something for them to climb upon — if that's what your variety needs — and gentle watering from sky or hose, and you'll feast on crisp snap beans and end the autumn with a larder full of protein-rich dried beans for soups, salads, purées, and for next year's sowing, and for the one after that, and so on, in perpetuity.

These beans, *Phaseolus vulgaris* and *Phaseolus coccineus*, are indigenous to Central, South and North America, and we owe a great debt of gratitude to the seed-keepers there who steward these plants and who, over millennia, have developed them into the delicious, practical and diverse forms we know today.

Bush beans sown into warm soil will begin producing about two months later. Their lives are short and sharp; after about three weeks of fruiting, the plants will tire and their productivity will wane. If you're growing dried beans this is an excellent outcome, as it makes for an efficient all-at-once harvest, and you can pull or cut whole plants. If you're growing them for fresh eating you can sow sequentially, planting a new batch every few weeks in the growing season for ongoing productivity. The beans will need regular and thorough picking to keep them productive; a few pods left to mature, and the plant will think it's done its baby-making work and stop flowering, so a couple of times a week you'll have to squat and pick them — which, if you're a market gardener or have trouble bending, can be hard on the spine. This is one of the many reasons I'm so enamoured with their taller relatives, the climbing beans. Walking along rows and harvesting without the need to kneel is far gentler on my body.

I'm working on positive self-talk, as we're all encouraged to do, consciously making the change from calling myself 'lazy' to more helpful terms like 'efficient' — which is why I'd love to change the name of a favourite climbing bean, 'Lazy Housewife', to something kinder. A German heirloom, Lazy Housewife earns her name for her generous bounty from one sowing, and from the fact that her tender, green pods are stringless, meaning they can go straight from vine to pot, saving the labour of cutting the ends from the beans and easing the strings from their sides for more pleasant eating. If left to mature, the pods are filled with perfect white beans that are just the thing in braises or white bean purées. If sowing a seed that offers so much can be called anything, it's certainly not lazy. Miraculous, efficient and just as magical as Jack's fairytale beans.

Another useful trait in climbing beans is colour. 'Purple King' beans are, as their name suggests, purple, and 'Climbing Butter Bean' a beautiful gentle yellow. When you're scouring your verdant, leafy row, a pop of colour makes it far easier to spot the bunch of beans you're after among the lush foliage. They are both tender, flavoursome varieties, and the Purple King is a delight to cook while children watch, as the beans magically turn from dark purple to bright green the instant they hit hot water.

Flat-podded Roman or 'Romano' beans are excellent cooked in olive oil, scented with garlic and herbs, and braised in some liquid — crushed tomatoes, salted water or stock — for a gentle half-hour on the stove with an occasional stir, or covered in a slow oven if you've other things to attend to. Cooked for longer than we're used to, the beans become yielding to the tooth, and flavours are absorbed right to the middle of the pods. If you do use the oven, you can top them with herby, garlicky, olive-oily breadcrumbs for a crisp and crunchy contrast to the tender beans.

Runner beans are divisive at our family dinner table, where likes and aversions are discussed with great fervour. Their slightly rough exterior bothers people with delicate tongues, and if they're left on the plant too long, the need to string them can seem arduous. But I think they're the most flavoursome of beans at every stage in their growth — as tiny snap beans, left to become a little bigger to be braised like the Roman beans above, or, at full maturity as the most magical-looking of all dried beans with their wondrous black and purple speckled skins. After soaking overnight, then simmering for an hour or so with bay leaves and garlic cloves, they're perfect in a vegetable soup.

The diversity of the bean world is half the fun. We owe much of our garden's leguminous range to local plant breeder and collector Bob Reid, who has travelled the world collecting useful and delicious varieties, then trialled them at the Cressy Research Station here in northern Lutruwita (Tasmania), before making them available to farmers and home gardeners. From his bean collection we've grown the high-yielding 'Estonian Black', which we use as dried beans, and the peculiar 'Pea Bean', which produces tiny pea-like pods that are delicious young, then ripens copious amounts of half-white, half-burgundy dried beans. My favourite snap bean is a bush variety, 'Deuil Fin Precoce', a slender green bean with the prettiest purple stripes and a fine flavour. Found closer to home is 'Lohrey's Natural Salt', a Tasmanian heirloom climber from the north-west coast that is said to need no seasoning, but a little salt is always welcome — and its tan seeds, marked with peculiar black curves, are hypnotic to behold.

Jack knew what he was
about, trading the cow
for those beans.

Broad beans

VICIA FABA

I'm sitting at my desk with a tray taking up the space where my broad bean reference books should be, because beauty is an equally important form of information.

One of a gardener's great pleasures is pushing your hands wrist-deep into a bucket of seeds and lifting them out, letting seeds trickle between your fingers. The smooth coolness of the seeds on your skin, the whisper of the trickling seeds falling back into the bucket, the visual grace of the fall as each seed finds its place nestled among the others, and the sense of promise — one handful of seeds able to feed entire families in perpetuity — is heart-filling. If they're seeds you've grown, saved and even bred yourself, the satisfaction and awe are multiplied.

The tray that clutters my desk is filled with a rainbow of seeds. Large cream-coloured seeds sit beside smaller tan, green, black, scarlet and lilac ones, and as I run my fingers through them I know each one. The plump cream ones are descended from a packet of Egyptian broad beans and will most likely form short plants and flat pods with three large, loosely packed seeds. They bring to mind an image of Pat Nourse, my writing mentor, atop a camel eating Egyptian *ful medames*, a staple Egyptian stew made with dried broad beans that he described eating during a trip to Egypt.

'Scarlet Cambridge' is a dense, red-seeded variety, the first red one I'd ever seen. It was sold to me by my seedsman friend Sam Bayley, who keeps it as part of his vast collection of edible and ornamental seeds. When harvested in a basket with other varieties, it helps entice children to help with the task of podding: the novelty of not knowing what colour bean is hidden inside the pod you're about to shell is almost as good as the allure of a Kinder Surprise egg — a joyful motivation!

'Crimson-Flowered' broad beans actually carry bright pink blooms (rather than the 'crimson' of their name) and form densely packed pods of plump, bright green beans that keep their vivid colour when dried, making for the sweetest, greenest falafel. These make me think of my friend Lindy Campbell, another collector of edible plants, who declares this one the most delicious of the broad beans.

I found a chocolate-flowered form on The Diggers Club website, and my chef friend Vince Trim from Mona loved using the gothic, almost-black flowers as a garnish when he prepared a dish of all-black foods for a colour-themed feast that was served on a giant glockenspiel. These thoughts of friends bring layers of meaning to my work, and their faces and kindnesses run through my mind as the seeds pour through my hands.

For about a decade I've been growing every broad bean cultivar I can find in the same plot, pulling out any plants that succumb to wind, aphids or rust, and any that don't produce full pods, to make for stronger genetics in the seeds saved. Over time, we've noticed crosses occurring. The plants now produce a rainbow of edible flowers — from the more usual white with a black throat, to a spectrum of pinks, pale greys and rich browns, and occasionally pure white. The seeds have become just as diverse. We began with parent varieties having only red, green, white or tan seeds, and now we open pods to find shades of pink and lilac, and even some that dry to black.

Running my hands through those seeds also keeps shared meals in mind.

Broad beans are always on our Christmas menu, and podding them with my friend Katie while we sip champagne and watch people open presents is a ritual I look forward to. When I was a child, my mother and I were the only ones in our family who relished the wholesome, almost metallic taste of over-ripe beans — well cooked, never double-podded and served with lots of butter and salt — in an exclusive broad-bean-lovers' club of two. When I met my husband Matt, and his father's partner Katie joined our family, I was delighted to find she could also join our bean-lovers' society, even outdoing me and Mum in gleefully eating the large raw beans straight from their pods.

I've made tiny but delicious ferments loosely based on the spicy Chinese bean paste doubanjiang, which makes for excellent, fast mapo tofu dinners, because our friend, fermentation guru Adam James, let us taste his version. Inspired by another dear chef friend, Jess Muir, we gather immature broad bean pods, cook them for a few minutes in salted water until tender, blend them with salt to taste, pass the mixture through a sieve to remove any fibrous strings, then add a little butter and pepper and enjoy the sweetest, greenest purée.

We love broad beans at all stages of maturity. We spoil ourselves with very young ones podded when they're impractically tiny, and serve them with equally diminutive peas for little bursts of vegetable sweetness in our mouths. Medium-sized ones are a daily vegetable simply podded, boiled and seasoned. When they're old and starchy they make a magnificent dip, puréed and flavoured with garlic, lemon, maybe some tahini, and possibly some cumin; it makes you feel strong and healthy while you're eating it. Felafel made with mature, fresh broad beans are a perfect summer dish — a slippery, delicious treat, quite different to those made with dried pulses. The tops of the plants are an excellent salad green and are brilliant cooked as you would spinach. Plucking the tops from your young plants also promotes stout, bushy growth, an excellent advantage for windy gardens.

So, that tray of seeds holds more than the promise of a good crop to come. As I enjoy the silken fall of the seeds through my hands, there are friends, family meals and feelings of perfect satiety there with me.

And it's lucky we have plenty of seeds, and a garden in which to grow them. We once had the entire staff from the (now sadly closed) Nipaluna (Hobart) restaurant Garagistes come for dinner. Hungry chefs, front-of-house staff and kitchen hands came to cook a joint of pork and raid our garden to complete the meal.

While the fire worked its magic on the pork, we all wandered the garden, cutting lettuce, picking onions, pulling radishes and tasting herbs and flowers with the restaurant crew. It was peak broad bean season, so we gathered a basket full. Chef Luke Burgess (who is also responsible for the glorious photos in this book) showed us how to grill the beans whole in their pods until they began to yield and soften. He had a big bucket of something he called 'Texas Barbecue Sauce' with a basting brush in it, and as we pulled the beans from the fire he anointed them with the spicy, smoky, sweet sauce.

The pork, and the onions grilled underneath it, bathing in its juices, were excellent. Sweet spring radishes disappeared into mouths with no preparation beyond a squirt from the hose. But the broad bean rows rustled all evening as chefs and our guests kept returning to the plot, refilling the bean basket for grilling, brushing the pods with sauce as they left the coals, then gnawing on them — eating the tender ones whole, and sucking the beans from the older ones, edamame style.

I sow broad bean seeds in our cool-temperate garden between March and late September, skipping June and July when the cold soil means slugs or rot can get to the seeds before they grow. It's important to space plants about 15 cm (6 inches) apart, as planting too densely can encourage rust and other diseases. If you plant a patch every month or so within this period, you'll have a continuous harvest, rather than a glut. Staggered sowings also free you to cut waning plants, clear the garden bed and plant some leafy greens to take advantage of that wonderful broad-bean-driven soil fertility, safe in the knowledge that another harvest is on the way.

Grilled broad beans with BBQ sauce

Make the barbecue sauce, light a fire, set up your grill, gather your broad beans and find lots of napkins.

I haven't managed to steal Luke's barbecue sauce recipe yet, but I love the food-recombining alchemy of raiding the pantry for condiments, simply to amalgamate them into yet another condiment.

Start by making the sauce. Toast the ancho chilli in a small dry pan over medium heat on both sides until fragrant. Pop it in a heatproof bowl and pour in just enough boiling water to cover. Leave to soak for 30 minutes, then drain, reserving the soaking water. Purée the chilli with a dash of the soaking water and set aside.

Warm the oil in a saucepan. Brown the onion for 5–7 minutes over medium heat, then add the garlic. When the garlic has softened, add the mustard powder, paprika, salt and a good grind of black pepper. Cook for a minute or two more, then stir in the remaining ingredients, except the reserved chilli water.

Simmer for 30 minutes, stirring now and then, until glossy and thick — an hour would be better, if you have the time. A slow, steady cook gives everything time to settle in together. If the sauce is getting too thick, add the ancho water a little at a time. For a smooth sauce, use a stick blender, or push it through a sieve and return to the boil. Set aside for serving.

Makes about 180 ml (6 fl oz) sauce

a basket of broad beans

oil, for drizzling

BARBECUE SAUCE

1 dried ancho chilli

1 tablespoon oil

1 small onion, finely diced

5 garlic cloves, crushed

1 teaspoon yellow mustard powder

1 teaspoon sweet paprika

2 teaspoons salt

200 ml (7 fl oz) tomato sauce (home-made is always best)

¼ cup (60 ml) apple cider vinegar

2 tablespoons molasses

1 teaspoon worcestershire sauce

To store it for a longer time, pour the hot sauce into hot, sterilised jars and seal. Leave to cool and stash in the fridge, where it will keep for a month or more.

When your fire has burned down to coals, and you're ready to grill your broad beans, place the whole pods in a big bowl, and drizzle over enough oil to lightly coat them. Toss them about until there's a good coating on each pod, then sprinkle with salt and toss again.

Working in batches, if needed, lay them on a warm to hot barbecue grill (or chargrill pan or frying pan) and watch as they turn from bright green to khaki, then flip them. (A fish-grilling basket can be handy for this if you're cooking for a crowd.) A minute or two more and they're done.

Brush the pods with a little of the sauce and serve, preferably under a warm spring sky with excellent companions.

Peas

PISUM SATIVUM

Peas are the first food I remember stealing from the garden. I'd listen to my mum and stepdad debating whether to pick them young and tender — Mum — or let them get fat and get more value from the plot — my stepdad. For me, such deliberations were null and void. If I was in the garden pegging out washing, roller-skating around the clothesline or mucking about with my sisters, I was eating the peas. I did enjoy the little ones, their tiny beads of sweetness akin to candy, but I also loved the way the older ones fitted so snugly in their pods, becoming square-sided to nestle together — so they, too, were scoffed. Not wanting to leave evidence or waste a morsel, my sisters and I learned to eat the pods, peeling away their inner membrane by folding along their edges and slowly easing the papery, inedible part from the sweet, succulent flesh. Luckily for my parents, I'd not yet learned that the new shoots, buds and flowers of pea plants are just as delicious as the peas themselves.

Peas are the first food I remember stealing from the garden.

Now, if I'm ever overwhelmed by a pea harvest — which is a very rare occurrence as we tend to eat or sell them as quickly as they grow — I allow plants to mostly dry off in the plot, then gather the crisp pods, dry the peas completely, and store them in jars in the pantry, ready for growing pea sprouts, or making mushy peas or pea and ham soup.

We grow 'Yakumo Giant' snow peas as much for their glorious, tasty purple flowers as their long, crisp pods. Sugar snap peas are perhaps the most efficient of all peas, being edible in their entirety — thick, succulent pods with flavoursome peas inside. When I see sugar snaps at the greengrocer's they never seem to have full pods, which is a shame. If you let them mature a little, the extra depth of flavour and the satisfying density of the peas inside is well worth the extra effort of stringing the slightly more mature pods as you pluck off their tops.

As with beans, peas also give you a choice between the short, concentrated burst of productivity from bush varieties, or the longer season offered by the climbers. I always grow climbing 'Telephone' podding peas because of their lovely flavour, big pods, disease resistance and long productive season, but my favourite shelling peas are the tiny, sweet pods I steal early from my plantings of the bush variety, 'Kelvedon Wonder'.

Peas can be sown into cool soils, the plants bulking up and beginning to flower when the danger of frost, which may damage flowers, is passing. After you've had your fill of raw peas eaten from hand in the garden, and bowls of barely cooked ones with butter and mint with your dinner, you absolutely should fill your freezer with them. It may not look as romantic as a pantry filled with jars of home-made preserves, but my stash of tiny peas — blanched for just moments in boiling water, before being drained and chilled in ice water, then thoroughly drained again before freezing — is tightly guarded for when I want to add their sweet bursts of flavour to a risotto or potato salad, or serve them as part of a classic meat and three veg.

Shelling peas is an enjoyable chore. I love the satisfying 'pop' you get from a full pea pod when you apply your thumb just-so to the outward curve on its tail end, and the way you can run your thumb down the seam to open it before running it in the opposite direction, making the peas fall into your bowl. But, if I have a kilo or two to work through, I love a companion. The best chats are had when your hands are busy and your minds are free. Moments shared that way are worth growing peas for alone, even if your deep chats are punctuated, inevitably, by somebody shouting, 'I've pead on the floor!'

Fabaceae

Peas
& carrots

In the months before you begin this dish, while you wait for the peas to grow, visit second-hand shops, or your nanna's china cabinet, and find yourself a tureen or vegetable dish with a lid — the prettier the better.

Harvest your peas as close to mealtime as possible. Sugars in many vegetables begin to convert to starches quickly after picking, so keep the time from plot or market to pan as short as possible.

Have your butter by the stove, and a colander sitting in your chosen serving dish in the sink.

Shell your peas.

Wash your carrots, trim their tops and drop them into a saucepan of boiling, salted water. Depending on their size and tenderness, give them a few minutes while you shred your mint. Drop the shelled peas in and put the lid on so your water comes back to the boil quickly. If your peas are tiny, drain them the second they come to the boil; if they're older, give them a minute to turn a deeper shade of green.

Drain them into your colander, so that your vegetable tureen fills with the hot water.

Tip your drained peas and carrots back into the saucepan. Add the butter and mint, season with salt and a grind of black pepper and swirl as the butter melts.

Pour the water out of your now beautifully warmed vegetable tureen. Pour in your buttery baby vegetables and pop the lid on.

Carry your tureen to the table and lift the lid, to release a waft of fragrant steam and delight your guests.

butter

peas — the youngest, sweetest ones you can find

carrots — the youngest, sweetest ones available

a few tiny new shoots of mint

Other things in pods

The legume family offers much more than seeds, greens and pods to be eaten as vegetables and pulses. Often our winter meals are given some refreshing crunch using sprouts, and the Fabaceae clan affords many contenders. Simply wash your clean, viable pea, alfalfa, fenugreek or other sprouting seeds well, then soak them overnight, drain them thoroughly, and put them in a jar with a cloth fixed around its neck (or use a fancy sprouting contraption if you have one), and leave it somewhere out of intense light. Rinse and drain thoroughly every day, removing your cloth covering and flushing out seed husks as they're dislodged. I like to eat lentil and mung bean sprouts young, while they're still short and crisp, but I tip my peas onto trays lined with damp paper towel and let them get a little leafy and develop their pea taste.

We sow **fenugreek** plants in late spring and they look a lot like clover, just a little more upright. As well as a bounty of greens, and nitrogen for the soil, they offer a wonderful gardener's treat inside their scimitar-shaped seed pods — sweet, unripe fenugreek seeds, like tiny peas, that have just a hint of the curry flavour of their ripe form. Dried fenugreek seeds are a wonderful caramelly spice, with a slight bitterness that dissipates a little upon toasting — that same toasting making them a little easier to grind before adding to spice mixes for curries. The greens are delicious — grassy, bittersweet and slightly curry-flavoured. Known as 'methi' in Indian and other cuisines, they're used as a cooked vegetable, salad green or herb.

Lentils are a plant I've not yet grown — but with local producers such as The Grain Family growing the sweetest green lentils, we don't need to. Their Latin name, *Lens culinaris*, is perfectly apt, for lentils do look just like little lenses, and we love their culinary gifts.

Legumes offer sweetness too, none more so than the roots of the **liquorice** plant, *Glycyrrhiza glabra*. Those long, ropey roots take around three years to grow to a useful thickness — and then, when the leafy plant becomes dormant in the winter, takes the patient wielding of a shovel to harvest, following the roots as they wend through the soil. I find dried liquorice root a bit overpowering, can't abide liquorice tea, and wish our local apothecary didn't use it to mask the bitterness in their tinctures — but balanced with molasses and whatever else is in the liquorice bullets and spelt liquorice at our wholefoods store, it becomes delicious.

In lean summers the tips of **vetch**, *Vicia sativa*, find their way to restaurants in Nipaluna (Hobart), as we take advantage of their enterprising nature. They sow themselves where we'd rather they didn't, but also provide us with pretty garnishes when other plants wane from the stress of summer. Their pods are triggered to open in warm weather, and I've spun around on many occasions to see who was throwing things at me, only to find a vetch winding its way up a nearby plant spitting out its seeds.

Braised lamb with lentils

One of the privileges of working at home is being able to put dinner on at lunch time. Around one in the afternoon I soak some of those green lentils from northern Lutruwita (Tasmania) in a bowl of water, put the oven on and prepare lamb to braise. I season a lamb neck with plenty of salt and pepper, brown it in a cast-iron casserole dish, tuck some onions, carrot, celery and garlic around it, top the pan up with an inch of water — or wine if I have it — and leave it in a slow oven to gently braise.

I'll come in for a cup of tea around four, baste the lamb with its juices, top up the liquid so the base of the dish doesn't burn, and put the lid back on.

Around five I'll drain the lentils, gently boil them for about 15 minutes and drain them a little. I'll carefully tilt the lamb dish and skim out as much of the lamb fat as I can, saving that for baked potatoes another day. Then I'll shake the lentils around the lamb, checking there's still liquid in the dish, put the lid back on and return it to the oven while I prepare some vegetables.

By the time I've trimmed, steamed and buttered some broccoli, dinner will be done and my family will arrive in the kitchen, lured by the smell.

Peanuts are on the list of plants I'd love to grow, if only to taste them fresh and watch the ingenious way they thrust their pods underground to ripen, safe from predation in nature, but still vulnerable to hungry gardeners with garden forks. I've managed to germinate them, but gone no further.

One legume that *is* within my reach, as I know it's being farmed in Lutruwita already, is the humble **chickpea** — another ingredient that has happy memories for me. Years ago, I did a horticulture class, where we learned the foibles of cultivating the botanical marvels of Lutruwita. When the course finished, our class formed a walking group that dwindled week by week until there were just four of us left. The bond created by a shared love of this place and its flora was only deepened by our shared love of cooking and eating together, and a regular ingredient of choice just happened to be chickpeas — and so our merry band of biophiliacs became known to our families as the Chick Peas.

So perhaps this summer, as a tribute to those special women, I'll sow some chickpea seeds and watch them grow, then cook up a feast for my beloved Chick Peas.

Lamiaceae

MINT FAMILY

Peppermint humbugs, roast lamb with rosemary, lavender picked from a neighbour's garden and sniffed on the walk to school, twiggy oregano stuffing in a shop-bought roast chicken. Many strong memories from my youth are bound up within this vast plant family, so rich in gifts. I'm sure my children will have their own ties, too, and I wonder which ones will fix most firmly in their minds. The lemon balm and peppermint by the back door, or the lemon verbena we hang in bunches to dry — all three finding their way into our teapots? Perhaps the pineapple sage they suck nectar from, or the oregano that self-seeded under our tree ferns, to season their cooking only a stride or two from the kitchen door?

Lamiaceae members may have magnificent large flowers evolved to feed hummingbirds, or dainty ones that invite the tiniest of insects. Scents and flavours range from the deeply savoury to the minty and brightly sweet, and harvests span whole plants, from their aromatic foliage and edible flowers to mucilaginous seeds, crisp swollen galls and edible underground rhizomes.

This family is relatively easy to identify. Plants have squarish stems, with leaves arranged in pairs or whorls at intervals along them, and the wonderfully diverse flowers are bilaterally symmetrical, most with flattish, rounded lower lips that invite insects to land, and curved upper lobes that push pollen down upon the heads of visiting nectar-eaters.

Oregano
& marjoram

ORIGANUM VULGARE, ORIGANUM
SYRIACUM, ORIGANUM MAJORANA

Once on television I saw Yotam Ottolenghi crouching on a Mediterranean coastal headland amid wind-shorn shrubs, and I felt a strange twinge of recognition. The coastal shrubbery around him was made up of rosemary and Syrian oregano, *Origanum syriacum,* a plant I'd grown and fallen in love with the previous summer. It tastes like oregano with the harshness taken away — a full, complex flavour that I use in my cooking with a kind of elation brought on by its perfection.

I may never have the chance to meet this plant in its Mediterranean home, but now, when I come across it in my garden, a little corner of my mind travels to that windswept headland and the adaptations the plant developed over its life there: the grey fuzz on the foliage, perfect for reflecting the harsh rays of the sun away from the leaves, and for trapping tiny water droplets from the moist ocean breezes. I wonder at the culinary traditions that have made use of this plant, unchanged from its wild state, over millennia as food and medicine.

Origanum species are perennial flowering shrubs that thrive in well-drained, sunny gardens. Some will self-seed with abandon, others respond well to being split with a sharp spade, making it easy to share plants with friends. But despite their similar appearances, and shared horticultural needs, they offer a diversity of flavours and culinary uses.

Greek oregano, *Origanum vulgare* subsp. *hirtum,* is the one most used in my kitchen. It grows quickly and responds well to regular, brutal haircuts — best performed when the plant has formed tight little buds, but is yet to open its white flowers. I cut the flowering stems down to ground level, which not only helps plants adapted to dry, airy environments resist disease in our cool, damp location by enhancing airflow and letting light in, but also provides bountiful bunches to hang in the kitchen and crumble into every savoury dish that sits on my stove.

I wonder at the culinary traditions that have made use of this plant, unchanged from its wild state, over millennia.

Common oregano (how I'd love to change all the 'commons' — common sage, common chives — to 'classic' instead), *Origanum vulgare*, is one you may have pulled out of your garden as a weed, and it is rather tenacious, even growing with abandon where the wallabies graze and all else is demolished. Lacking the concentration of volatile oils its hairy, smaller-leaved Greek cousin has, it can be used generously — it is wonderful stripped from its stems and stirred through tomato sauces right at the end of cooking, or scattered atop pizzas hot from the oven so that its heady scent melds with the pizza's steam for a magnificent sensory overload as you bite into it.

I've barely touched the oregano genus here, with its dozens of culinary and ornamental forms, but I can't leave you without talking about the delightful marjoram, *Origanum majorana* — the wraith of the so-called 'hard herbs'. For a perennial, it has a fleeting lifespan, often prematurely ended in spells of wet or chilly weather. It has the camphor-headiness of other oreganos, but is sweeter, milder and sublime, with its soft, velvety foliage and tiny pink or white flowers. If I want a savoury herb to infuse a fresh cheese, a shortbread or mild fruit with, I'll reach for marjoram. You can dry it, but you'll lose something of the soft magic the fresh, downy leaves offer. Whenever you find it in your hands, I suggest holding a sprig between your palms, crushing it gently, then popping your nose into your cupped hands and inhaling for a moment. Forget about everything else and soak up this gentle treasure.

Rosemary

SALVIA ROSMARINUS

Rosemary is the queen of resilience. A landscaper in the 1980s planted a roundabout near my childhood home with a delightful prostrate form. I've circumnavigated that roundabout thousands of times and very much doubt the plants have ever been watered, tasted a lick of fertiliser or felt the slice of pruners, and yet they thrive. I've snuck onto the roundabout late in the evening, when the threat of being run over is reduced, and stolen a few branches — and the scent is magnificent. Left to fend for themselves, their soil biome uninterrupted since the upheaval of roadworks that formed the mound upon which they live, these plants have likely developed relationships with all of the organisms they share their hummock with, exchanging the products of their photosynthesis with the fungi and bacteria that make nutrients from the sparse soil available to them. This, combined with bright sunshine, a clean sea breeze to blow away all the motoring fug, and the slow, contained growth of plants not pumped along with extra water and fertilisers, leads to a complex, strong scent you won't find in delicate, well-tended garden plants — although I wouldn't eat it from that particular spot until we're all driving electric cars.

An even more resilient rosemary grows in the semi-arid landscape of Boolcoomatta — a Bush Heritage Australia property in South Australia, on traditional Adnyamathanha and Wiljakali land, that dear friends of ours from Lutruwita (Tasmania) managed for two years. They exchanged the comforts of rural suburbia — with a school ten minutes away, friends a short walk to visit and a capital city only twenty minutes from their door — for a place where school was delivered via radio, the nearest groceries were an hour and a half away at Broken Hill, and the neighbours not much closer. And a cool Tasmanian

Rosemary is the queue of resilience.

mountainside, with a gentle cool-temperate climate, for an inland arid environment where long periods of dry are punctuated by extreme rain events, and soaring summer daytime temperatures are followed by frosty winter nights.

The tragic absence of the land's traditional owners, almost two centuries of sheep farming and mining by colonists, and the introduction of feral goats and pigs have all left their mark, which my friends were trying to repair; a consequence of that work was a freezer full of wild pig and goat.

When we visited I was in heaven — with a generously proportioned kitchen, friends who had been cooking for each other week upon week, and what felt like all the time in the world to show my love for them through the medium of food.

Karen had a tiny kitchen garden, sturdily fenced and covered in shade cloth, where she grew little plants of parsley and rocket — just enough to add a freshness to meals cooked largely from a larder and a deep freeze.

The main garden of the homestead is still laid out as it would have been by the colonist station owners, and I wonder if the rosemary was planted not only for its resilience, but for its sympathy with the lamb that was the station's mainstay. Alongside the thriving, beautifully trimmed rosemary was a lovely hedge of Old Man Saltbush, *Atriplex nummularia*, and some lush clumps of the local native lemongrass, *Cymbopogon ambiguus*. I think there may have even been some roses clinging to life.

Left alone all day in the cool house with a haunch of goat and that formal garden with its fragrant mix of plants, I turned on a slow oven, ventured out with basket and garden shears and put together a feast.

Lamiaceae

Slow-cooked goat with rosemary & saltbush

Season the goat with salt and pepper. Put a flameproof roasting vessel on the stove to heat. Pour in some olive oil and brown the meat all over. Set aside and allow to cool a bit while you prepare the herbs.

Finely chop the pale, tender root ends of the lemongrass, reserving the grassy tops, and place in a mortar with a teaspoon or two of salt and a generous amount of pepper. Add a few tablespoons of stripped rosemary leaves, and a few peeled garlic cloves. Pound with a pestle until the garlic is flattened and the herbs nicely bruised. Add about ¼ cup (60 ml) olive oil, swirling with your pestle until you have a bright green slurry. Enjoy the scent! The bruising and liberation of volatile oils by stone-on-stone grinding is an invitation to pop your nose close and spend some time with your herbs, and you'll appreciate them all the more once they've worked their magic in the finished dish.

Cut incisions into the thickest part of the meat and rub your herby slurry all over it, working some deep into the cuts. (My joint of meat was a leg, from a slim desert goat, which is harder to cook to a nice tenderness than a shoulder. If I had my chance again, I'd dig through the farmhouse freezer for a fatty bit of feral pork and cut some lardons to also poke into the incisions on the goat leg, to keep the meat juicy.)

One haunch of goat. You may find a pampered animal from a lush farm, only a year old with a nice amount of fat, or a desert goat with barely a lick of fat, and muscles that have worked hard for years, developing flavour and a texture that responds well to slow, gentle cooking, and turns to inedible leather and sinew if hurried. A leg of mutton or two-tooth will be wonderful here too.

A big handful of native lemongrass. You can substitute any lemony herb here, but choose something like lemon thyme or verbena that gives a little herbaceous warmth along with the sweetness.

Have some butcher's twine ready. Wash the saltbush branches and bend them to soften any rigid ones, to make wrapping the leg easier. Place them on some baking paper, along with the reserved lemongrass tops. Lay the anointed haunch on top and roll it up in the branches, wrapping tightly with the paper and securing with the twine.

Put the leg back into the roasting vessel, then into a 150°C (300°F) oven for the day — maybe 6–8 hours. (I've since made this dish with goat from our friends Kate and Iain from Leap Farm. Their young goat is tender enough that it needs only an hour or two to cook. You'll need to chat with your butcher or farmer and choose the timing best suited to your particular beast and the life it led.)

An hour before dinner, peel some potatoes and turn the oven up to 200°C (400°F). Pop your potatoes in a baking tray with a little dripping and warm in the oven for a few minutes to melt the dripping. Take it out again, roll the spuds so they're nicely coated in fat, sprinkle with salt and roast for 30 minutes.

In a perfect world, all ovens would be the same, and all bunches of saltbush identically steamed at this point — but in this perfectly imperfect one we're taking the lid and paper from the goat and hoping for a soggy mass of saltbush, well steamed but intact. You could perhaps drizzle a little more olive oil over the leaves to aid crispiness, or cross your fingers and pop the unwrapped leafy meat back into the hot oven, jiggling those potatoes while the door is open... and in 20 minutes, while you prepare some buttery chard, peas or beans, or a crunchy green salad, everything should be done.

If the oven gods are on your side, the top layer of saltbush leaves should be crisp and delicious. If the top layer is overdone, discard it and hope for better in the next layer down. Your meat will still be tender and wonderful, and if you have the right kind of guests, they'll be digging the branches from under the goat leg and gnawing the tender, meat-soaked leaves from their stems.

A bunch of rosemary, enough to yield a few tablespoons of stripped leaves, and a few branches kept whole.

Garlic, salt, pepper, olive oil.

A hefty bunch of saltbush. I used this to wrap the goat, to keep in the moisture it needed to cook without becoming stringy and inedible, while imparting its beautiful salty vegetable flavour, and soaking up the cooking juices to become delicious in its own right. If you don't have saltbush, just wrap your seasoned joint in baking paper and cook it in a flameproof roasting vessel with a lid.

Lamiaceae

Sage

SALVIA OFFICINALIS

In our humid mountain garden, sage doesn't thrive. Rather, it hangs tenaciously to life, preferring north-facing gardens with well-drained soils. Occasionally, when the weather behaves like the warm days of the Mediterranean, I'm sure I see my sage relax, unfurling and tilting its leafy faces to soak up the sun.

A silvery-leaved, woody perennial herb with glorious sprays of bright purple flowers, common sage is worth growing for its beauty alone. There are even cultivars with purple, variegated or large silver leaves that are just as likely to find a place in an ornamental garden as an edible one. Common sage can be easily propagated from seed, but specific forms must be grown from cuttings to maintain their unique foliage or growth habits. I find the purple-leaved form a little hardier in my cool garden, and less often in need of pruning than the common variety — and it's just as lovely in the kitchen.

Sage's antibacterial properties have long been used to heal mouth wounds and clean teeth, although your modern, conventional dentist may disapprove. And if by chance you happen to be near a sage bush in the garden and see your lover approaching, you could do worse than rubbing a sage leaf over your teeth and gums to set the scene for a heady, aromatic kiss.

To me sage has a 'round' flavour. Gentle, savoury, soothing and mouth-filling, with a tiny volatile tickle for the sinuses. One of my books says it tastes of sausages, which can probably be attributed to sausages being seasoned with sage — a chicken and egg conundrum — and yet it's true. Most of my books tell me sage should be used sparingly. Perhaps I'm missing some taste buds, or maybe I'm mistakenly conflating gentleness with weakness, but I think sage is simultaneously strong and gentle, the very best way for a companion to be.

I use sage in our rissoles, braised beans, herbal teas and stuffings, and its purple flowers add a mild, honeyed sage flavour to herb cheeses and dips. Most of all I love to pair sage leaves with the savoury decadence of brown butter to make a sauce for gnocchi — or to spoon over the fried livers of roosters on rooster cull day, as a reward for a difficult task done well.

Every year — sometimes in a coop as part of our chicken breeding plan, but more often on nests in hidden the garden by cheeky hens — clutches of tiny chickens emerge from under their mother's warm breasts. Our mother hens are resilient and raise their chicks to adulthood, unscathed by hawks, crows and visiting toddlers, but, inevitably, half of those cute fluff balls will grow into crowing, brawling, beautiful roosters.

Anyone who has raised chickens knows there is an optimal ratio of roosters to hens. Too many roosters and the hens will be harassed, the feathers trodden from their backs, and they'll understandably stop laying. And the roosters fight. My favourite rooster, and most gracious flock monarch, Cockle Shell, was violently dethroned by an upstart araucana rooster because I neglected to cull in time. Excess roosters are also a growing problem here in Lutruwita (Tasmania). People enjoy hatching chicks, but don't have the stomach for dispatch when the crowing of the male birds annoys their neighbours, so the poor roosters get dumped along bushy highway verges and left to scavenge, before starving to death, succumbing to predation or being run over by cars.

Far better to learn to recognise the gender of your young birds early, gird your loins, sharpen your tools and fill the freezer.

I like to cull our roosters in early autumn when the weather is cool and the meat won't spoil, as I'm a very inefficient plucker. And I do weep every time. I think this is a good thing, to feel empathy for your food and be as efficient and humane as you can, and not waste a morsel of meat — although I admit I'm yet to eat the feet, beyond dropping them in a stockpot.

We light a fire, put a large pot of water on to boil, and have at the ready a supply of clean cold water, plenty of buckets and bowls, and a hole in the compost heap for the feathers and other bits that can't be eaten. Matt does the killing and I go to work, often sharing the labour with a friend in exchange for some meat for their kitchen. We scald the birds in the pot of hot water to loosen their feathers, then dunk them in cold water to cool before plucking and eviscerating, taking care not to rupture the bitter gallbladders or otherwise damage the pluckers' treat — the livers and hearts. I like to halve the livers, trim a little of the sinew away, then give them and the hearts a little rinse and a firm squeeze in a wad of paper towel so they're dry and won't spit when you cook them. We put them aside in the fridge while we wash, butcher and pack the carcasses — by which time the fire has died to coals, and we've scrubbed most of the scent of butchery from our hands, changed out of our feathery shirts and opened some cider.

Culling roosters has become an important ritual for me. There can be no eggs without hatching chickens, and half will always be male. Sadness, reverence, labour, squeamishness and plenty are a spectrum of feelings rarely felt all at once in modern life, and I feel all the richer for tasting the bitter alongside the sweet. Perhaps that is the wisdom, the sagacity of sage.

Lamiaceae

Fire-cooked sagey
rooster livers & hearts

I warm a pan, with a few tablespoons of salted butter in it, on the coals. As it begins to foam I throw in a few sage leaves — maybe three or four for each liver — shaking the pan to make sure each leaf is sitting in its share of butter and not scorching. Watch the heat; the leaves should take only a minute or two to become crisp. Then I lift them out onto a warm plate beside the fire with some of the melted butter, leaving a generous slick in the pan, which I return to the coals to get hot again.

The livers and hearts take the same amount of time to cook, so I put them in the hot pan together, seasoning with salt and plenty of pepper, and making sure there's plenty of room. If they're crowded and start to stew, all is lost. We're after crisp, salty edges and creamy middles, so any grey, boiling action in a cool or crowded pan means you'll have to make them into pâté for tomorrow, rather than crisp, salty treats today.

After a minute or two, turn them over and add a little more seasoning. Once the pan is good and hot and they're sizzling nicely, you add a tiny dash of brandy or wine, shaking the pan to loosen all the tasty bits from the bottom.

When the brandy has evaporated, pop the reserved sage butter back in, squeeze some lemon over and spoon the buttery mess over slabs of sourdough you've toasted in the coals.

Mint

MENTHA SPP.

We always had a patch of mint in our garden, a variety I came to know as 'common' mint. You know how I feel about that particular word, so from here I'll refer to it as classic mint instead.

If sensibly grown within a boundary — say a garden bounded by paths, or in a generously sized container — this plant will form a thicket from stout, unkillable runners that you can divide and share with your neighbours. Its broad, dimpled, slightly hairy, lime-green leaves are mildly minty — fresh, herbaceous and bright, without the sinus-clearing coolness associated with its cousin peppermint. This gentle flavour allows you to use classic mint generously, in a mint sauce, as a green in tabouleh and rather nicely in summer drinks.

While common/classic mint is delicious and versatile, it's just the tip of a very refreshing iceberg. Over time, gardeners and cooks have moved mints from continent to continent, and plants that had not previously met were given the opportunity to cross-pollinate, creating myriad species, subspecies and cultivars, each with its own unique culinary and horticultural gifts.

Corsican mint, *Mentha requienii*, is diminutive and, to my mind, carries the most perfect mint scent — sweet, sappily herbaceous and full of the cleanest menthol aroma. It is a tiny ground-hugging plant, lacking the tall stems of its cousins, so you must dig and painstakingly wash runners to use it, or take to your plant with tiny scissors, sweeping the trimmings into your palm. It is said to be the 'menthe' in crème de menthe, and if you wish to heal the wounds gained by stealing sips of lurid, toothpastey liqueur from your parents' drinks cabinet, you could try steeping some Corsican mint leaves in vodka for a month or two, then straining and sweetening with a little sugar syrup for a truer taste of the herb.

The variety of foliage among mint cultivars, and their ability to fill spaces in the garden, make many worth growing for their visual virtues alone. The gold edges and spicy scent of variegated ginger mint, *Mentha × gentilis* 'Variegata', which requires a lot of imagination to find the 'ginger' in, are a delight. The downy, white-edged leaves of variegated pineapple mint, *Mentha suaveolens*, grow with even more vigour and are mild and lovely as a salad mint. Raripila mint, *Mentha × smithiana*, has gorgeous reddish foliage and a fruity scent, making it perfect in fruit salads and cocktails.

River mint, *Mentha aquatica*, occurs naturally around Australia. Here in Lutruwita it is used in a wonderful mint choc-chip ice cream by Kitana Mansell, who runs Palawa Kipli, a Tasmanian Aboriginal Centre culinary enterprise.

Peppermint, chocolate and Moroccan mints are my favourites for teas. I grow them in containers near the back door where German chamomile, fennel and lemon balm self-seed wildly, giving me access to a herbal tea blend to suit any whim — plastic-free and fresh as a daisy.

Lamiaceae

If you think you don't like peppermint tea, I'm not surprised. As with many foods, the commodification of herbs means some very ancient and well-travelled minty dust is put into tea bags, ruining the image of this delightful brew. Pick some mint fresh, give it a wash and steep it in hot water. Add a little honey to taste if you must; a wee sprig of thyme or rosemary can add a bit of savoury depth, if that's what you need. Then, if you still can't stand the tea, maybe a tot of rum with your mint will help.

Mojito

I make my backyard version of a mojito by picking about 10 mint leaves. Almost any mint will do — ginger mint, pineapple mint, lime mint, classic mint and Moroccan mint all sit happily with lime, rum and soda. I think peppermint is too bossy and chocolate mint too sweet, but please do experiment, it's half the fun.

Save the prettiest mint leaf for a garnish. Drop the rest in a sturdy glass with a few teaspoons of rapadura sugar. Use the end of a wooden spoon to muddle or crush the sugar into the mint until the leaves are nicely bruised. (Often I take this step too far and we end up with a pretty green-flecked drink, and not-so-pretty green-flecked teeth — but that matters not among friends.)

Add a measure of rum and a tablespoon or so of lime juice, then muddle some more to dissolve the sugar. Put plenty of ice in the glass, top with chilled soda water and garnish with a lime wedge and the pretty mint leaf you reserved.

This mojito is equally delicious without rum, and if you worry about green-flecked teeth, by all means strain your cocktail and protect those pearly whites.

Mints thrive in cool, well-composted gardens or pots, in morning sun or dappled shade. Some, like river mint, *Mentha aquatica*, are happy growing in ponds. All are quite invasive and persistent, so must be planted where you can control them, or else give them free range.

My mints are bounded by lawn, and any escapee runners delight the nose of the person mowing. I grow a curly spearmint under a shrubby feijoa and lemon verbena garden, where its delicate white and mauve flowers poke up here and there, pleasing the eye and the bees.

Many mints will die back for the winter in most gardens, and all benefit from regular, brutal haircuts to maintain production of the tender, aromatic shoots we most want in our kitchen.

When I prune, I hang bunches of the mints I like for tea under the eaves to dry in the shade for winter teas. The less tea-suitable varieties we use in our chickens' nests, along with prunings of other aromatic herbs, to deter mites and fleas and, I hope, to give the chickens olfactory pleasure.

Thyme

THYMUS SPP.

'You've got too much thyme on your hands.' At every market stall at least one passer-by will utter this joke, or one of its many permutations, as they look at our collection of thymes. And these heckles — which are largely, but not solely perpetrated by dads — aren't too far off the mark.

Spanish, lemon, orange, parsley, woolly, caraway, pizza, creeping, golden, silver posy and common thyme are but a few of our thyme varieties — and their names, in the main, point to their scents and uses. I grow them all together in a long raised bed where they form a mosaic of textures, forms and colours, tangling in a fragrant riot crawling with bees who, no matter how hurriedly I'm pruning or harvesting, never sting me. Perhaps it is the peace we feel surrounded by such beauty that prevents any interspecies animosity.

Spanish thyme, *Thymus mastichina*, is a magnificent thing. Robust in both flavour and growing habit, it boasts massed, tiny white flowers in late spring and early summer, tolerates dry, poor soils, responds gallantly to brutal harvesting, and tastes wonderful. Resinous, thymey and strong, it is the perfect herb to use in a marinade for barbecued meat or vegetables, where more delicate seasonings would be lost.

Lemon thyme, *Thymus × citriodorus*, is equally beautiful and strong, withstanding sun, snow, frost and gale and still glowing with vigour. Its gentle, sweet, lemon aroma and flavour makes for perfect teas, sweetly scents creams, custards and cocktails, and adds another layer of lemon flavour when used with lemons to season fish or poultry. It comes in upright or prostrate forms, and in gold and silver variegated ones. A herb for the ornamental garden indeed, in pots or in the ground.

Caraway thyme evokes a feast I'm yet to prepare. Its Latin name, *Thymus herba-barona*, is said to come from its use in seasoning a 'baron' of beef — a whole sirloin — before it is roasted. I can't help but think of stone walls, candle-lit tapestries, some poor basting boy sitting by the fire anointing and turning the joint as it grilled over coals, and the feast that followed. This thyme grows as a tangled ground cover, forming roots merrily as it goes, and opening tiny, deep-pink flowers through the warm months. It is faintly caraway-scented and very delicious.

If you were to gnaw on a stem of lemon thyme, rosemary or sage, you'd not be all that impressed, but add that same herb to a neutral recipe, and the raw, bitter or resinous notes that seem overwhelming in the fresh plant find context. Simple, tart, milky labneh, and warm, comforting soda bread are both like blank canvases — marrying well with many savoury herbs and allowing the flavours of the plants to shine. An excellent way to get to know the subtleties of any new herbs that cross your path.

In my kitchen common thyme, *Thymus vulgaris*, is as indispensable as salt, pepper, garlic or olive oil. I can't turn on a stockpot, prepare a batch of meatballs or make a casserole without a little bunch of this strong, savoury thyme. I do find its combination of twigginess and tiny leaves makes for tedious preparation, so I'll either throw sprigs in whole and let my dear family spit them out (entirely acceptable!), or, for more refined preparations, hold each sprig at the tip, just below the tender part where it wants to snap, and strip the leaves towards the main stem, before nipping the tender tips off between thumb and forefinger.

I always harvest extra so that I can leave the excess out to dry, at which point the tiny leaves are more easily rubbed from the stems straight into a dish, or into a jar for cooking with later.

Common thyme plants are densely leaved, low-growing, silvery shrubs with exquisite clouds of tiny pink flowers through late spring and early summer. They thrive in sunny, well-drained gardens and are very hardy, but can be short-lived. You can extend their lifespan by regular hard pruning, cutting back to where you can see young new growth, but not into older woody stems, as you'll lose the whole plant that way. If you're lucky, they will naturalise and self-seed through your garden, and you'll have plants here and there ready for harvest, and those masses of pink flowers to entice the bees.

Lamiaceae

In my kitchen, thyme
is as indispensable as
salt, pepper, garlic
or olive oil.

Thyme labneh with herby soda bread

Left-over labneh is excellent on sandwiches, dolloped on braised greens or dropped into spicy lentil soup. It will keep for a week in the fridge, in a sealed container with a little oil on top.

Thyme labneh: Set a sieve lined with muslin (cheesecloth) over a bowl. Mix together all the labneh ingredients, spoon into the sieve and twist the muslin tightly over the top. Place a saucer that sits inside the sieve on top, then weigh the saucer down with a heavy jar or tin of food. Leave in the fridge for up to 48 hours — the longer you leave it, the thicker and more sour your labneh will be. Remember to reserve the whey that accumulates at the bottom of the bowl for your soda bread, opposite.

Serves 4 for a hearty lunch, with extra labneh for later

THYME LABNEH

2 cups (450 g) good-quality plain unsweetened yoghurt

1 tablespoon picked thyme leaves of your choice, bruised

20 g (¾ oz) pecorino, finely grated

1 teaspoon lemon juice

1 teaspoon sea salt

freshly ground black pepper, to taste

Soda bread: Preheat your oven to 220°C (425°F) and line a baking tray with baking paper.

Pour the whey that drained from your labneh into a 1 cup (250 ml) measure and fill to the brim with buttermilk. Set aside.

In a bowl, whisk together the flours, bicarbonate of soda and salt, making sure the bicarb of soda is well distributed. (I also add a bit of black pepper.) Rub the butter into the flour.

Add the whey and thyme and combine gently. Soda bread behaves like scones and needs to be mixed as little as possible, so I use a butter knife to mix roughly, then turn the dough out onto a floured bench and knead ever so slightly before pulling it together into a ball.

Pop the dough on the baking tray, shape gently into a loaf about 5 cm (2 inches) thick, and score a deep cross into the top to allow the bread to rise.

Bake for 15 minutes, then turn the oven down to 200°C (400°F) and bake for another 15 minutes. When it's cooked, the bottom of the loaf will sound hollow when tapped.

Serve warm, slathered with butter and labneh.

SODA BREAD

labneh whey (from making your labneh, opposite)

buttermilk (or milk soured with a squeeze of lemon juice)

170 g (6 oz) plain (all purpose) flour, plus extra for dusting

155 g (5½ oz) wholegrain spelt flour

1 teaspoon bicarbonate of soda (baking soda)

1 teaspoon sea salt

20 g (¾ oz) butter, at room temperature

1 tablespoon picked thyme leaves

Lamiaceae

Basil

OCIMUM BASILICUM

Some long for truffles, foie gras and caviar, but give me a bunch of the first basil of summer and I'm awestruck. Basil has the headiest of scents, even more precious because of its short season in the cool hills of Lutruwita (Tasmania) where we garden. Just touching the plants to release their fragrance is a heart-filling pleasure.

I grow a tiny Greek variety that grows in little domes; its strongly flavoured leaves are perfect to scatter over a tomato and burrata toast. I adore the classic, smooth-leaved Genovese basil for its good sense: so long as you regularly pinch out any stems that look as though they may flower, it just keeps going, producing steadily over the season, and has the fine, classic basil flavour that I spend winters looking forward to. And a giant Italian variety, 'Mammoth', produces flavourful leaves that you can use to make mountains of pesto — the way to my daughters' hearts.

Thai basil is an equally anticipated treat. Salads with an array of herbs as the stars are a summer staple here. A few strands of rice noodles, a handful of bean sprouts, and fistfuls of coriander, mint, laksa leaf, dill and Thai basil — dressed with lime, fish sauce and chilli — can be stuffed into rice paper wraps, find their way into a larb with roasted rice and minced meat from one of our roosters, or into a bowl with hot stock ladled over just before eating.

Persian or Iranian basil is a flavoursome halfway point between Italian and Thai basils. Savoury with a hint of anise and maybe a little cinnamon, it has unique purple-tinted leaves and pink flowers. It becomes a stunning condiment when the picked leaves are layered on a plate with shaved salad onions, and freshly barbecued meats are left to rest on top, as the warmth of the meat frees their beautiful aroma and flavour.

Basil is a fussy customer, though. It likes to be warm, but not sun-scalded, and reasonably well watered — but damp environments encourage fungal diseases. I have most success growing it among the peppers in my greenhouse, where our plants receive diffused light and constant warmth, and where we irrigate only with drippers that distribute the water directly onto the soil, keeping the leaves of our crops dry.

It's also happy planted among the tomatoes outdoors, where the tomatoes shade the basil, and the basil is said to deter pests from the tomatoes. But please don't rush it. In our cooler climate, many gardeners plant basil babies too early in spring, only to watch them wither and rot as the soil is still too cool.

For such a heavenly bounty, I am ready and willing to cater to its every whim.

Basil pesto
with hazelnuts

Roast the hazelnuts in a dry pan over medium heat, shaking frequently, until toasty-fragrant. Tip them into a folded tea towel and wrap them to cool. Rub the tea towel firmly with the hazelnuts inside, and most of the brown skins should come off; there's no need to be too fussy.

Crush the garlic clove in a large mortar. Add the hazelnuts and crush again, leaving a little texture. Tear the basil and pound a little at a time, adding more as the volume decreases. Stir in the lemon zest and juice, olive oil and pecorino.

A bowl of pasta topped with this and my children are happy. I love it on sourdough, as a dip with cheesy crackers, or dolloped on top of cracked-open soft-boiled eggs. It will keep with a film of oil on top, in a sealed jar, for a week in the fridge.

50 g (⅓ cup)
raw hazelnuts

1 garlic clove, peeled

2 bunches, or 2 packed
cups, of fresh basil

grated zest of 1 lemon

1 tablespoon lemon juice

150 ml (5½ fl oz) olive oil

20 g (¾ oz) pecorino,
finely grated

Lamiaceae

Lemon verbena

ALOYSIA CITRODORA

It is hard to believe that the plant with the most sophisticated scent in the garden keeps the hours of a rambunctious teenager. Every spring I wait for my lemon verbena plants to awaken, sometimes scratching at the wood to see if they're green and sappy under their bark so I know they're still alive... and they are, they're just being tardy. By mid-December they usually grace us with their presence. And what a presence it is — the most perfectly balanced lemon scent that begs you to brush your hands over it, crush a leaf and rub it into the tender skin under your chin as perfume, or pop the kettle on and brew a magical tea.

Native to South America, and adopted by gardeners all over the world, lemon verbena grows as a tall, woody shrub or small tree. I like it best pruned into a bushy shrub by regular, brutal harvesting; if left alone it can become twiggy and sparse, and you'd miss the delight of its leaves and massed sprays of tiny white flowers. It loves full sun, and isn't too fussy about soil, but every plant will thank you for compost, mulch and regular deep watering.

In mid-summer, when the chickens are laying with aplomb, the verbena is flourishing and long days make me want to lounge in the garden with friends, I love to make chiffon cakes. Nothing is so simple and so grand at the same time. Eggs, sugar, oil, flour and your flavouring of choice, nothing to it. A bit of practice and precision, I'll admit, and having a chiffon cake tin makes it easier, but it's worth any effort to eat a cloud — and a cloud flavoured with verbena is a wondrous thing.

There's no rush, though. Like all teenagers, lemon verbena stays up as late as it sleeps in. Well into May in our cool-temperate garden I gather bunches of this glorious herb to hang in my kitchen, then pack its dry leaves into a jar near the kettle so that I can brew a pot of sunshine on even the drabbest of days.

It begs you to brush
your hands over it, crush
a leaf and rub it into the
tender skin under your
chin as perfume.

Lamiaceae

Lemon verbena chiffon cake

A cake is a wonderful place for herbs. A few rose geranium leaves to scent a pistachio cake, some thyme to add a serious note to a carrot cake, or mint leaves blitzed into the base of a mint slice can lift a simple treat to something celestial.

I've chosen a labour-intensive chiffon cake here because I love the impossible, almost industrial, fineness of its crumb, but lemon verbena, lemon balm or lemon thyme can be combined with citrus juice in the same way and used to flavour a basic butter sponge or syrup cake, or you can sift good-quality dried herbs into the flour when preparing your batter. Why should we always reach for vanilla when so many other delights lurk in our gardens?

The most important thing when making a chiffon cake is the tin. You need to hang your cake upside down as it cools, and chiffon cake pans are designed to let you easily extract your cake from the ungreased pan once cooled. If you grease or line your tin, then hang your cooling cake upside down it, you'll be courting disaster — and will probably find your cake fallen on the bench. I only started making chiffon cakes after finding a pan at an op shop, and I'd urge you to trawl the second-hand options before buying new.

I use a 25 cm (10 inch) tin for this recipe, and it has some spare headspace when I pour the cake batter in, so if yours is a few centimetres smaller it should be fine.

Serves 10

400 g (14 oz) lemons, approximately, to yield 190 ml (6½ fl oz) juice

1 loosely packed cup (25 g) of lemon verbena leaves (I use lemon balm in winter, when the verbena sleeps)

250 g (9 oz) plain (all-purpose) flour

3 teaspoons baking powder

pinch of salt

280 g (10 oz) caster (superfine) sugar

150 g (5½ oz) egg yolks (7 eggs from my hens; please weigh your egg yolks to be sure)

100 ml (3½ fl oz) grapeseed oil

300 g (10½ oz) egg whites (9 eggs from my hens; please weigh your egg whites to be sure)

½ teaspoon cream of tartar

Like all teenagers, lemon verbena stays up as late as it sleeps in.

Ensure your cake mixer, bowls and whisks are completely free of any trace of grease. Yesterday's slap-dash dishwashing is today's sponge cake failure — any stray fat will keep your egg whites from reaching their lofty potential.

Preheat your oven to 170°C (325°F) and make sure you have a rack in the middle, with enough room above it for the tall chiffon tin. Many times I've had my cake ready to bake, only to have to stop and rearrange the oven shelves, losing precious oven heat.

To get the maximum flavour from the verbena, reserve the zest from one of the lemons, then peel the rest of the lemons, taking time to remove as much white pith as possible. Put the reserved zest and all the peeled lemons through a juicer with the lemon verbena leaves, or blitz them in a smoothie maker and wring the pulp through some muslin (cheesecloth) to extract the juice. If you don't have these gadgets, you can juice your lemons the usual way and pound your verbena and lemon zest in a mortar before adding them to the lemon juice, letting it sit for 10 minutes, then straining it, pressing to get as much green essence from the verbena as possible. Whichever method you use, you'll need 190 ml (6½ fl oz) verbena-scented lemon juice for the batter.

In a bowl, whisk together the flour, baking powder and salt.

Tip 250 g (9 oz) of the sugar into a large bowl. Add your lemon juice, egg yolks and oil and whisk together.

Using a stand mixer fitted with the whisk attachment, beat the egg whites with the cream of tartar on medium–high speed until opaque and stiff. With the mixer still going, add the remaining 30 g (1 oz) of sugar a teaspoon at a time, allowing a few seconds between each addition. You should have a glossy, pliable cloud.

Working quickly so your egg whites don't begin to set in the mixer, sift the flour mixture over the egg yolk mixture and whisk together. Add a few big tablespoons of the egg whites to the mixture and fold it through with a whisk. This is an excellent way to loosen the floury batter to receive the airy egg whites without stealing any of their loftiness. But don't be afraid — whipped egg whites, stabilised with cream of tartar and sugar, are fairly resilient. I'd prefer to fold thoroughly, blending any stubborn whites, than be too gentle and have an uneven cake.

Pour the mixture into your chiffon pan, ignoring the corner of your mind that wants to grease the tin first, and gently smooth the top.

Bake for about 50 minutes, until lightly golden, keeping an eye on your cake; it is done when a skewer inserted in the middle comes out clean.

Now for the heart-in-mouth moment. Sit a sturdy glass bottle on a clean baking tray. Remove your cake from the oven and up-end your cake, putting the mouth of the tube in the centre of the pan over the neck of the bottle. I'm yet to have a collapse, but the clean tray underneath gives me peace of mind that if my cake does fall from the tin, it will still be edible, if rather dishevelled.

I like to serve the cake plain, but sometimes a glaze of warmed lemon juice with enough icing (confectioners') sugar to make a runny paste can be pretty, while adorning it with lots of golden spring flowers and candied lemon zest makes for a grand party cake.

Other fragrant
& textural delights

I was once a plant snob. The only plants I would cultivate were those that grew in my neighbourhood pre-colonisation (to the best of my knowledge), and food plants that could never invade the natural environment. This led me into an unreasonable war with the **lemon balm**, *Melissa officinalis*, that grew unbidden in my garden. Cracks in paths and gaps in the foundations of my house harboured little woody seedlings that were impossible to pull. I hoed, I dug and I gave up. I suspect the universe was telling me something. Lemon balm is a herb said to induce joy and I'd met it with hate. But once I called a truce I saw its beauty. It grew happily under tree ferns and was easily pruned back if it got too leggy. The tiny white flowers cheered the bees, and when I finally thought to put it on our chef's order form, it found its way into drinks, cakes, cocktails and fish dishes all over Nipaluna (Hobart). Now I step to that crack in my garden path most evenings, pluck a sprig and brew a pretty, pale green cup of calming, heart-gladdening tea before bed.

Above the lemon balm arch the branches of **pineapple sage**, *Salvia elegans*, a plant perfectly framed by my kitchen window. It astounds me that it is happy in cool-temperate gardens, sometimes becoming bothersome with its vigorous rhizomes colonising nearby beds, given that its original home is the Sierra Madre del Sur mountain range in Mexico and Guatemala, where it grows in clearings around pine forests at an elevation of around 2000 metres (6500 feet). I love it for its pineapple-scented leaves, which I use sparingly in tea blends — it's almost too sweet, but I find the creatures who consume its nectar most appealing. The plant outside my kitchen window makes washing up a delight, although it does take a little longer when I'm distracted by a parade of honeyeaters — eastern spinebills, crescent and new holland honeyeaters — taking turns to feed on the spikes of red flowers. The other nectar-eaters are children. We planted pineapple sage in the courtyard at my children's primary school, and before long students had perfected the art of plucking flower tubes and lining them up between their fingers to suck the nectar of half a dozen flowers at once. Children are ingenious in their pursuit of sweetness.

The aromatic gifts of this family are so vast I could write reams. Winter, lemon and summer savory are all generous, hardy plants. **Winter savory**, *Satureja montana*, is a small perennial shrub with masses of mauve-white flowers beloved by bees, and a strong thyme/rosemary flavour. Its cousin **summer savory**, *Satureja hortensis*, is a summer annual, sown in spring and killed by the first autumn frosts. Its young tender leaves before flowering are delicious, having all of the heady flavour of thyme, rosemary and their ilk, without the bitter resinousness that makes you stay your hand when using them. It's known as 'bean herb' in parts of Europe for its affinity with beans; I love it with tomatoes, or bruised with oil and garlic as a dressing for soft milky cheeses. The plant I grow as **lemon savory** I suspect might be misnamed, a hazard all plant collectors face. Nevertheless, it's a heady-scented, easily grown, good-looking plant that I adore in both garden and kitchen, and its name suits it perfectly, as it has the sweetness of all lemony herbs, with gentle, savoury, thyme undertones making it an excellent culinary herb. I love to use it or lemon thyme to simulate the packaged lemon pepper I remember from childhood camping trips. Combine some lemony leaves, plenty of salt and fresh black pepper, and you have a perfect seasoning for potatoes, poultry or fish.

Shiso, *Perilla frutescens*, is a summer annual with finicky needs. It will only germinate from fresh seed, and only if that seed has been chilled. If you buy shiso seeds, keep them in the fridge and sow in early spring. I like to sow them in seed trays outdoors where it will get cold, which will aid germination, but under a little cover so hard frosts won't kill emerging plants. Once it's established it loves to self-seed, popping up at will every spring, and you'll wonder why it caused so much trouble in the first place.

There are many forms of shiso, with just as many uses. When I preserved my first ume plums to make umeboshi, my friend Pauline gave me a bunch of red shiso to use in the pickle. After salting the ume plums for a week to draw out their juice, forming a brine that covers the fruit, you rub red shiso leaves with salt and wring out the juice. You then add the bruised, squeezed shiso leaves to the plum brine and leave for another two weeks, before draining and sun-drying the plums and the shiso. I like the pickled plums, but I love the shiso. A wonderful Japanese cook introduced us to the flavour when she served dried pickled red shiso leaves as a seasoning for rice, where their tangy perfume stood out.

A broad-leafed green shiso, sometimes called sesame leaf, has a savoury, minty flavour. In Korea, its palm-sized leaves are wrapped around mouthfuls of rice, barbecued meat and seasonings. There are also pretty forms with ruffled green leaves that are used as herbs in miso and sushi, and battered and fried for tempura.

The mint family is about more than just flavour and aroma.

Many plants in the mint family — basils, perillas and salvias — have a coating on their seeds that absorbs water and swells to form a jelly, a brilliant adaptation to protect and hold moisture around germinating seeds, and one put to use in many culinary traditions where the seeds are soaked to produce drinks and puddings that can look and feel like frog's eggs. Chia seeds are the one I find most often in my fridge, prepared by my girls into little puddings made with coconut milk and dotted with blueberries.

The chia plant, *Salvia hispanica*, grows happily as a warm-season annual, and boasts large, downy, lime-green leaves and pretty sky-blue flowers. Its ripe seeds remain stubbornly lodged in the spent flowers, though, so without some mechanised threshing to extract them, I don't think I'll ever grow and clean enough for our own puddings. As my daughters still haven't won me over to the joys of chia pudding, I'm happy to just enjoy the flowers for now.

There's a plant growing under my crab apple tree that looks, and behaves, just like mint, with clumps of pale green, downy leaves on squarish stems that arise from underground runners. Crush a leaf of **Chinese artichoke**, or **crosne**, *Stachys affinis*, and you'll find no aroma — but, come late autumn, the stems and leaves die back, storing the energy they've gathered over summer in swollen white underground rhizomes that look like little white caterpillars. It is a labour of love to harvest them. You'll find me kneeling in the mud, scratching through soil, seeking the inch-long, knobbly white crosnes (confusingly pronounced 'crones'). I clean them just before they're to be used, as their pearly white skins are easily damaged and will oxidise quickly, losing their beauty.

Their crisp texture reminds me of water chestnuts, and their flavour is mild, slightly nutty and slightly sweet. I use them in stir-fries for their water-chestnut crunch. They are lovely raw as a crudité, and are also wonderful pickled, remaining crisp and beautifully carrying whatever flavours you pickle them with. But best of all is the French way — braised in lots of butter until they begin to look a little translucent, then finished with a little salt and finely chopped chervil, dill or parsley.

Rosaceae

ROSE FAMILY

At the corners of my nursery benches, seeds fall from potted plants. It's shady and cool there, and constantly being watered — the perfect place for slow-to-germinate cool-climate babies to grow. The most common plant I find there, possibly because I pull out the pesky ones quickly lest they seed, is the alpine strawberry, *Fragaria vesca* (also known as *fraises des bois*), and they are a delightful distraction.

Preparing for markets is both arduous and tedious. Harvesting, washing, weighing, then packing produce. Gathering, tidying and labelling plants and restocking seeds and preserves, then hefting our entire inventory into the van — knowing we'll unload and reload it at market, and then unload when we're home again.

I find myself looking for little rewards — finish labelling this tray of plants, or picking that row of kale, and you can have a treat. There is no sweeter or more conveniently placed treat than the fruit from these diminutive alpine strawberry plants right at my feet. Tiny clumps only 20 cm (8 inches) tall that produce fruit the size of your fingernail, with all the scent and flavour of a larger fruit concentrated into their tiny size.

It's hard to see the family similarities as I reach down to pick a short-lived, herbaceous strawberry or reach up to the woody boughs of an apple tree that can grow to a great age. Apples and roses, strawberries and pears, quinces and bramble berries, loquats and cherries are all so different — but look into their flowers and you may catch a glimpse of what ties these cousins together. Radially symmetrical flowers with loose, fluttery petals, often five of them, and most often white or pink in the fruiting species. A long treatise tells me a distinguishing feature, such as a little stipule at the base of the leaf, is characteristic of the rose family, except when it's not. It seems to be a family where exceptions to rules apply, so we'll just trust the taxonomists and enjoy the feast.

What is summer without the kiss of a peach, the succulence of a strawberry or the fragrant tang of a raspberry? How do we make winter lunchboxes fresh and bright without apples and pears?

Quinces

CYDONIA OBLONGA

In summer and autumn in my childhood home, we'd often take our washing to the laundry only to find the laundry basket sitting on the washing machine, filled with fruit. The laundry was cool, easily accessed from the kitchen, and laundry baskets are strong, well ventilated and easy to carry — perfect for lugging and storing bulky produce. Jam or jelly would have to be made, or fruit stoned, stewed and frozen, before you could get to the machine.

A row of gnarled quince trees grew on the roadside on the way to a quiet beach where Mum would take us for after-school swims, and in autumn when the ripe fruit began to fall, Mum would grab the ever-present laundry basket from the boot and we'd fill it with golden, perfumed quinces.

The quince is a 'difficult' fruit that grows on an easy tree. Once established, quince trees will survive drought, frost, rain and snow, and give you majestic spring blossoms — large for a fruit tree, pink-veined white blooms that look like pinwheels when closed, and when unfurled make the tree look as though it's covered in pale pink fairy wings.

Once the petals fall, and the gorgeous carpet they formed on the ground has turned back to earth, there's still a long wait. All summer you'll watch the fuzzy fruit slowly enlarge, stubbornly staying green until autumn when, all at once — and usually when you have a busy weekend — they begin to drop from the tree. But they're patient fruit and will wait on the kitchen table, perfuming your house until you find a spare afternoon to begin the alchemic work of transforming their hard, yellow, astringent sourness into wondrous rubies.

An Iranian man once told me he relished raw quince as a child, which makes me want to taste quinces that have ripened in longer, hotter summers than mine, and meet the different cultivars that grow there and learn how they are enjoyed. But while I wait for that improbable adventure, my back garden fruit offers myriad uses.

Often forgotten is the quince's affinity for savoury dishes. A Moroccan cookbook and a tagine cooking pot found their way into my kitchen twenty years ago, and every autumn I'll add a peeled, cored and quartered quince or two to my tagine, along with a braising cut of lamb — neck if I'm in eating-with-fingers company, shanks if it's a cutlery-only group — and some chopped onion, garlic, a pinch of saffron threads soaked in warm water, some ras el hanout, salt and sometimes a handful of cooked chickpeas, or sometimes tomatoes to thicken the sauce. After a few hours in a slow oven, the fragrant steam when I lift the lid from the tagine summons family from the furthest corners of the house for dinner.

Poached & roasted quince

The simplest way to cook quince is to peel, core and gently poach it in a saucepan on the stove with a little water and plenty of sugar. It only takes half an hour to become a pale shade of peach, yielding and delicious and ready to use in cakes and crumbles.

If you have more time, simply scrub off the fuzz, trim away the calyx at the base of the fruit, place them whole in a baking dish — there's no need to peel and core. Immerse the fruit in a simple sugar syrup, perhaps with a few cinnamon quills and crushed cardamom pods, then roast them in a slow oven for a few hours and they'll become those rubies I promised you — rich, jelly-sticky, sweet and wonderfully fragrant. Then, when they're soft, simply slice out the seed cavity and the fibres that lead to the stem. If you like, you can slip the skin off, too, but it's fine to leave it on and eat it. I love the slow-cooked fruit in tarts, folded through spiced gingerbread loaves or eaten warm with custard.

Slow roasting is also a shortcut to a quince paste. Weigh your quinces whole and raw, then weigh out a little less than an equal amount of sugar (to allow for the weight lost from your quinces when you trim them). Halve and roast them in a covered casserole dish with a portion of your sugar, and enough water to cover, in a 140°C (275°F) oven for a few hours — 1 hour will do; 6 hours, if you keep the liquid topped up, is even better.

Pass the roasted quinces and their syrup (minus any aromatics) through a food mill into a heavy-based saucepan. Add the remaining sugar (to equal the weight of the puréed fruit), plus the juice of ½ large lemon for each kilo (2¼ lb) of fruit. Stir and let it sit a while for the sugar to begin dissolving.

Cook, over medium–low heat, stirring often, so the heat doesn't build up and cause dangerous eruptions of molten quince paste — a story that is written on my kitchen ceiling. Put a few saucers in your fridge to chill for testing the set of your paste later. After an hour or so, depending on how much moisture is in your roast quince purée, the colour should have darkened and the bubbles become thick and viscous. Drop a blob of paste onto a chilled saucer, allow it to cool, and if the surface wrinkles when pushed, you're done. Pour into sterilised jars and seal.

Your roasted quince paste will keep in the pantry for a few years, ready for lazy cheese-plate dinners, adding to casseroles for some rich, aromatic sweetness or, if you get a good, firm set, rolling in icing (confectioners') sugar and eating as a sweet.

Plums

PRUNUS SPP.

Every February, when our kids return to school after the summer holidays, Matt and I exhale.

It is wonderful having the kids around, but there's a tension any parent working at home will understand. You're sort of there for your children, but you're also at work. I'm grateful to be with them, but I feel guilt at the thought of my kids never having a proper summer holiday, or I stress over leaving seedlings unplanted if I spend time with our girls. Balancing the two priorities, joy and responsibility, is fun but exhausting, and on the day the girls return to school Matt and I race through our morning chores, quickly feeding the chickens, walking the dog, watering the seedlings, before packing the car with our foraging kit — gardening gloves, old doona covers, produce crates, a flask of coffee, lots of drinking water, our snake-bite bandage and plenty of Band-aids. We always need the Band-aids.

It's marked in the calendar as Damson Day — and we look forward to and dread it in equal measure.

Plums are the hardiest of fruit trees, and are happy to sprout and grow wherever a bird drops a seed. The wild plum foraging season in Lutruwita (Tasmania) begins with the early cherry plums just before Christmas. I always keep a clean sheet and a vegetable crate in the car, and when I spy a tree laden with fruit I spread my sheet underneath and give the tree a good shake. Any ripe fruit will fall willingly, but so will any fruit pecked by birds, and any spiders and crawling things living in the tree. I squat and scour through my windfall, picking out blemished fruit and creatures I've knocked from the tree, take the fruit home, then hose it off in the perforated plastic crates, before washing it in several changes of water. Submerging sound fruit is a wonderful way to clean it. Leaves and insects float and can be skimmed off, grit and other things sink, and after a few soaks and a final rinse the fruit is pristine. Early cherry plums often have a loose, bright red skin and sour, deep-yellow flesh, and are excellent for making sweet chilli-style sauces, or very sour, very delicious fruit leathers and cordials.

But later in the season, when Matt and I head off on our Damson Day, it's a very different story. The later plums tend to be dense, sometimes mealy, often sour — and in the case of sloes, very astringent.

In late February, wild damson plums are the prize.

My job is to be the spotter. We have a route stored in our maps app, and every time I spy a new tree we taste the fruit, measure the harvest and make new notes on our map. In late February, wild damson plums are the prize. They look very similar to sloe plums, and I'm sure there are intermediate species, but I can bear to hold a bite of damson flesh in my mouth, whereas a bite of sloe will dry your mouth intolerably, its tannins causing your slippery saliva to precipitate into clumps and make your mouth feel awful. The sloes are sometimes not ready on our February jaunt, and we mark new finds on our map to visit after a frost or two. Sadly, with the rise of big distilleries here, we often find sloe trees brutally harvested by people removing whole limbs, often before the fruit is ripe, leaving nothing for other foragers or the subsequent year's harvests. It is a pity. Wild sloes and damsons seem to stick to hedgerows and roadsides, not invading natural areas, and are a beautiful community resource that needs caring for.

On our foraging days we also look out for elderberries, blackberries, feral apples, hawthorn, fennel seed heads and rose hips, which we combine with the damsons to make hedgerow jams and jellies. Scrambling through hedgerows always draws blood, as almost every plant carries thorns or plays host to vicious brambles — and although we arrive home dirty, wounded and tired, our boot-full of bounty is worth every discomfort.

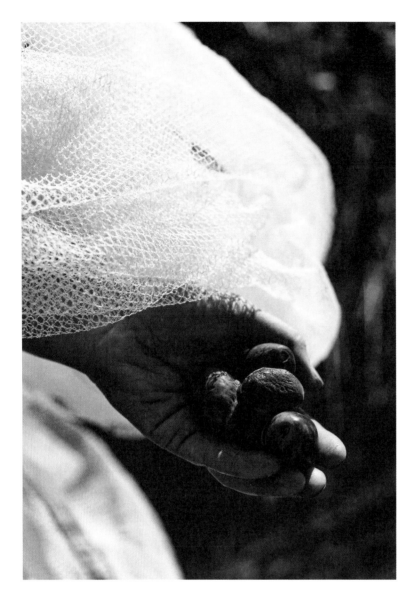

Hedgerow jelly

Hedgerow jelly is one of those wonderful all-purpose condiments that is equally at home on scones with cream, or used to glaze a roasting duck or enrich a savoury sauce.

We thoroughly wash plenty of feral plums, sloes, damsons and not-quite-ripe roadside apples (they have plentiful pectin which helps jellies set) with hawthorn berries, de-stemmed elderberries (all parts of the elder but the berries and flowers are toxic) rose hips and little handfuls of wild fennel seeds. We'll put them all in a jam pan with just enough water to cover them, then simmer until everything is well broken down, squishing them a little with a wooden spoon as all the fruit cooks. Then I'll rinse, wring and scald a few clean old cotton pillowcases, which we keep just for straining jellies, with boiling water, then pour the cooked fruit and all the juices into them and tie them closed. I put sturdy hooks on a clothes airer and hook the pillowcases carefully so they're suspended over a jam pan and leave them overnight to drain. I do love a jewel-like jelly, and my chickens love to peck up the pulp, so I don't bother to squeeze the pillowcases the next morning — but if you want to maximise the yield, you can wring the contents into a separate pot and make an extra batch of cloudier jelly that will be excellent in cooking.

Add one part sugar for each part strained juice, and a little lemon juice to activate the pectin. Return to the stove and warm gently, stirring to dissolve the sugar thoroughly, ensuring there are no sugar crystals stuck to the sides of your pan, before bringing to a rapid boil, skimming off the foam. Turn the heat down a little and continue to boil, staying close to the stove as untended jellies can boil over. Cook until you notice the bubbles thicken, and a few drops spooned onto a cold saucer set into a jelly.

Quickly bottle into warm sterilised jars and seal while hot. The sealed jars will keep in the pantry for a year or two. Once opened, keep refrigerated and use within a few weeks.

Rosaceae

Peaches & nectarines

PRUNUS PERSICA

'Is this a peach or a nectarine?'

A great tragedy of the modern age has befallen stone fruit. More often than not, when you buy a peach or nectarine, the cashier won't be able to tell the difference without asking you — or worse, scanning the tiny barcoded sticker on the cheek of your peach.

I wish everyone could taste the fruit of my childhood, or from my backyard today. There's no way they could forget the distinguishing feature of the peach: the fuzz that can annoy your top lip as you eat, making the most sensuous peach-eaters take the time to nibble the skin off before biting into the unencumbered flesh for the purest hit of sweet, fragrant juiciness. I wish they could know the joy of searching through a bowl of peaches or nectarines for the softest fruit — following a hierarchy of needs perfectly attuned to the glutton. If you don't devour a peach or nectarine the second you cradle it in your palm and feel the slightest give as you apply gentle pressure, then you may miss the moment and find only a browning lump when you next pass the fruit bowl. And if the peach next to it, and the one neighbouring that, is in the same exquisite state of ripeness, then you absolutely must eat them as well.

I remember climbing my grandfather's nectarine tree. The fruit were small, and had a wonderful bitter note to them. The flesh was soft, with a kind of dryness that is difficult to describe — not the floury hideousness of late-season industrial fruit, but a firmness that held that wonderful flesh and allowed my teeth to follow every last fibre along each tiny crevice in the stone, extracting it down to the last morsel.

I found a tree just like it growing on a main road in Nipaluna (Hobart), dropping its fruit down a high wall and onto the footpath. My mum drove into the car park behind the commercial building that hosted the tree and we gathered the fallen fruit, anticipating the ecstasy to come, but some hidden motion detector summoned the building's owner from his Saturday paper and he asked us to leave. Every summer I see the squashed fruit on that path and bemoan the squandering of that bounty. The paradox is that the tree in this city car park, with no water or mulch, no pruning or sprays, and open to possums and vandals, produces so many nectarines. My coddled nectarine tree gives me just a handful of fruit each year that the rosellas eat before it ripens — and leaf curl, the bane of the peach and nectarine lover, bests me every season.

There is a peach tree in our garden that was here when we arrived two decades ago, jammed between two sheds, making it difficult to tend and awkward to harvest. But one of those sheds is made of brick, and faces north, meaning the branches near the sun-warmed wall ripen earlier than those tucked in the shade of the adjacent tin shed. This accidental extended harvest is a boon for our house, giving us sweet, fragrant peaches for a few weeks. I'm not sure of the variety; it ripens in late February and its beauty is dependent on the season. In cool years, the longed-for first bite is disappointing. Cold weather does something terrible to the flesh, making what should be juicy and succulent, dry and floury. But never fear, nothing goes to waste on my watch.

Poached summer peaches

Use a small sharp knife to score a cross in the pointy end of your lovely ripe peaches. Gently drop them into a saucepan of simmering water and give them about 30 seconds to loosen their skins. Lift them out using a slotted spoon, and drop them into a bowl of iced water until they're cool enough to handle.

I am an excellent time waster, but I can't bear the idea of even a whiff of that peach essence going down the sink, so I turn the poaching liquid into a light syrup, dissolving 1 tablespoon sugar to 1 cup (250 ml) water. I pour half the syrup into a bowl and leave the rest in the saucepan.

Peel the peaches and slice in half, placing them in the bowl of syrup to stop them browning. Drop the skins and stones into the pan of syrup and simmer for a minute, then allow to cool before straining it over the peaches. (Sometimes I'll add a sprig of lemon verbena to the cooling syrup, sometimes vanilla, or a few raspberries for a pretty blush.)

Chill the peach halves and enjoy with cool or warm custard, depending on the weather, or freeze and purée them for a lazy person's sorbet — or, most fun of all, blitz them, invite some friends over and mix the pulp with an ice-cold sparkling wine for delicious bellinis.

Rosaceae

Apples

MALUS DOMESTICA

Apples are the most ubiquitous and versatile fruits. What other fruit can be harvested, spend months in cold storage, a day being tortured in a school lunchbox and still be salvaged by thrifty parents to finally find its use in a crumble for dessert?

Storage technology, transport and the sheer diversity of varieties mean we can eat them year-round, but often appearance and crunch are prioritised over flavour. Our friends Coreen Ung and Matthew Tack run an organic apple orchard and have selected their cultivars, prioritising flavour. When it's time for harvest they constantly test fruit, looking for the perfect development of sugars, making for apples that not only store well, but have flavour and aroma when it's time to eat them.

In our home garden we've planted a variety called 'Vista Bella', which is the first to ripen in January; that first, crisp bite after months of cool-stored fruit is bliss. If you choose varieties carefully, and ward off possums and rosellas, you can pick fresh apples until June or July — 'Democrat' being one of the last. The thick, red skin that keeps the apple safe over long months on the tree takes a little work from the jaw to get through, but if the fruit is fully ripened, the sweet, crunchy flesh inside is magnificent.

I could go on about apples — the aromatic delights of 'Cox's Orange Pippin', stealing curls of green skin as Mum peeled 'Granny Smiths' for winter puddings, the mysterious old apple tree in our garden that tastes of strawberries and has red skin that stains the white flesh as you bite into it. Apples are so common, so everyday, that much of their delight has been lost through the commodification that favours storage, uniformity and appearance over flavour. It is well worth finding an apple farmer who will share their favourites with you, fully ripe, fully delicious.

I live a shambolic life, running from chore to chore, using our home for family life, seed-saving, storing produce and running our farm, and the worst possible thing you can do to me is arrive early for morning tea.

I will not have the dishes done, I will probably be wearing my worst track pants, and I certainly won't have picked flowers or swept the doorstep to welcome you. I will have baked, as that is always my priority, but the food will probably still be in the oven and I'll be flustered.

So you can imagine how I felt when my culinary hero Kylie Kwong came to visit and arrived early. Thankfully I wasn't in my track pants, and somebody had done the dishes, but the crab apple tarte tatin I'd baked for her was still in the oven.

Silently panicking, fan-girling inside and unsure whether my tart was cooked, I turned off the oven so I could whisk Kylie away from my unswept stoop and into the garden, where we wandered, tasting dozens of different plants, sharing knowledge and stories, before returning to the kitchen.

If you've ever made a tarte tatin or upside-down cake, you'll know the particular flavour of anxiety that swells in your chest when, after running a butter knife as best you can around the edge of your pie dish to loosen your tart, you pop a plate on top and flip the whole thing upside down, wondering, will there be enough sticky, buttery caramel? Will my carefully arranged apple halves stick to the dish? And did my pastry come out crisp?

Imagine that anxiety — and then imagine you're turning out your tart in front of a culinary goddess.

I placed the plate on top and simultaneously upended the two, one hand precariously holding the warm pie dish, the other the only plate that was big enough to catch any escaping caramelly juices, and felt the gratifying slap as the tart slipped from its dish onto the plate.

It was perfect. I sighed with abject relief and made a pot of tea with herbs we'd gathered in the garden. We opened a bottle of cream and enjoyed the perfect thing that an apple tarte tatin is — crisp and yielding, savoury and sour, burnt-sugar-bitter and caramel sweet.

Little tarts for single serves are delightful, and large ones are grand, although a little more nerve-racking. If you can't find crab apples, use a tart, firm cooking apple.

I am an op-shop Pyrex dish addict, and love using a clear pie dish, so I can see the state of the caramel as it cooks, and also watch for any stuck apples when I turn the finished tart out. And I'm quite sure ghosts of the capable hands of cooks past guide my cooking every time I reach for my vintage dishes.

Crab apple tarte tatin

The following puff pastry recipe comes from one of my grandmother's brittle, yellowing books and is one of our family staples. Once you get the knack, it is quick to make, and if you nail it you'll have a beautiful buttery lamination. We use it for sausage rolls and all manner of pies, tarts and cheese straws. You can easily double the batch, as it freezes beautifully, rolled and ready to use.

Rough puff pastry: Sift the flour, cream of tartar and salt into a bowl.

Slice the butter into 1 cm (½ inch) slabs, lay them on top of the flour and use a butter knife to 'chop' the butter through the flour, aiming for pieces roughly the size of the tip of your little finger.

Pour the water all over the top; don't dump it in the centre. Using the butter knife, stir thoroughly, lifting the dry and wet bits from the bottom of the bowl until most of the flour is clinging to the butter pieces. If you have a large amount of dry flour in the bottom of your bowl, add a splash more iced water, but be sparing. Gather into a rough ball and turn out onto a floured bench.

Use a loose sort of knead to barely work the dough together, then form it into a rectangle. Keep a pastry scraper and extra flour to hand, as the butter will cling to the bench in the early stages.

Dust the top with flour and roll into a long rectangle 1–2 cm (½–¾ inch) thick; your butter chunks will spread out and look like leopard print.

Makes a 25 cm (10 inch) pie

ROUGH PUFF PASTRY

250 g (9 oz) plain (all-purpose) flour, plus extra for dusting

¼ teaspoon cream of tartar

pinch of salt

250 g (9 oz) butter

¼ cup (60 ml) iced water, plus a little extra

APPLE LAYER

20 g (¾ oz) very soft butter

2 tablespoons rapadura or brown sugar, plus an extra tablespoon if your apples are particularly tart

crab apples, halved and cored — enough to line the bottom of your pie dish

Fold the top edge to two-thirds of the way down the sheet and pull the bottom edge up to overlap it. Keeping the dough cool as you work is vital, or your butter will melt into the flour and you won't achieve flaky, buttery layers. If your kitchen is warm, cover and chill the dough after each roll.

Turn the pastry 45 degrees. Lightly dust the bench and the top of the pastry with flour. Repeat the rolling and folding, turn it again and repeat once more. By now you should have a nice, cohesive lump of dough. Flatten it a little, wrap in a beeswax wrap and chill for 1 hour.

Apple layer: Use your fingers to thickly smear all the butter on the bottom of your pie dish. (It may sound odd to do this, but if you don't use all the butter the dish won't work.) Sprinkle evenly with the sugar. Lay out your apples in the dish, cut side down, as tightly as possible. (If I have little red apples, I'll sometimes play with patterns, leaving some skin side down to make a star shape.)

Roll your pastry about 7 mm (¼ inch) thick. Lay it over the pie dish and trim to fit, leaving a generous overhang, as the pastry will shrink, and bubbling caramel will climb up its sides. Cut a few little slashes in the top to allow steam to escape.

Bake for about 40 minutes, until the pastry is golden, cooked through and puffed.

Allow to cool a little; I find the tart turns out best while it's still a little warm. Run a butter knife around the inner edge of the dish, place your serving plate on top and flip quickly and briskly.

Best served in the garden with a new friend, proper china, silver forks, cream and a pot of tea.

Rosaceae

Medlars

MESPILUS GERMANICA

I think we all have a little corner, in some ancient part deep in our brains, where we hold flickering gems of knowledge, so that when encounters occur with precious but rarely seen things, a tiny strobe of recognition flashes, telling us the sound, colour, scent or shape we've sensed is of worth.

I'll often see a plant in my wanderings, in a garden, in a book or a seed catalogue, and those mind sparks will fly, sending me to a corner of the bookcase or to the ear of a friend. It may take moments or weeks, but like the fragment of a song echoing in your mind then becoming whole as soon as you turn your thoughts elsewhere, I'll realise as I brush my teeth that the hedge I saw in the playground yesterday is used as a herb in South Africa, or the vaguely familiar seaweed cast at my feet was the very same wakame that I sprinkle on my avocado toast most mornings.

Many years ago, before I was a mother, when I spent my days cutting hair, and my weekends driving a giant yellow Kingswood station wagon all over the countryside on adventures, I worked at a salon in Nipaluna's (Hobart's) Salamanca Place and would wander up Kelly Street (does that give you the fragment of a song?) into the suburb of Battery Point, where I parked my ridiculous car. This part of Nipaluna has many colonial houses with old European gardens, and it is a delight to wander smelling roses, or enjoying the entire spectrum of pink when magnolias burst into flower. One evening I was walking back to my car, slightly out of breath from ascending the steep Kelly's Steps, and most likely singing that Frente! song under my huffing breath, when a plant overhanging a fence made those strobes in my brain sparkle. I snapped off a small branch so that I could think on it. A tree a little taller than me, covered in glorious russet and gold autumn foliage, with leaves the length of my palm and as wide as two fingers, but it was the fruit that got me — about the size and shape of a stepped-on ping pong ball, and a simultaneously luminous and downy brown, with tiny textured dots on its surface. One end of the fruit was attached to the stem, and on the other was a divot with five flattened faces descending into a dot in the centre, flanked by long, flamboyant calyxes — the leafy structures you see behind the petals of a rose.

I walked to my car contemplating the branch in my hand. The fruit was hard and unpromising, so why had it piqued my interest? I unlocked the door, put the fruit on the bench seat next to me and drove home, my thoughts turning to dinner, and forgot all about it.

Young hairdressers aren't paid that well, and that scary place down the back of the car seat can yield quantities of coin that make sticking your hand into the creepy gap seem worth the risk. A few days after picking that mysterious fruit, I found myself seeking meter money and my fingers found

yielding flesh. I parted the vinyl and there were those fruit — still wearing their outrageous calyxes and still brown, but the russet had eased to a soft, deep tan colour, and when I tugged on a calyx it peeled the tissue-thin skin away from creamy-looking flesh.

Of course I tasted it.

First a tentative flick of the tongue, followed by a front-toothed nibble, then I peeled away as much skin as I could, leaving the now-fragile stem end in my hand and the divot end attached to what turned out to be a central column of hard stones surrounded by sweet, yielding, caramel-coloured flesh. And the knowledge that lurked in that back corner of my mind flooded down synapses and I remembered. It was a medlar (or *cul de chien*, as the French lewdly call it), an old-fashioned, cool-climate fruit. And another example of our tendency to favour larger, sweeter, simpler foods, with the planting of medlars now restricted to curious food growers and ornamental gardeners who enjoy its beautiful spring display of creamy flowers and the russets of autumn. In my hours of reading I must have seen a medlar and read about 'bletting', tucking that knowledge away until the spark of that first taste drew it out.

We pick our medlars in autumn, when the rosellas take their first bites — always an accurate measure of ripeness — or await frost and falling fruit. We lay them in trays of straw, which ensures airflow to prevent the fruit mouldering, and cushions them as they begin softening through the curious process of bletting.

An unripe medlar is hard, astringent and inedible, but lay it on straw, or lose it down the back of a car seat, and wait until it yields to the touch. Bletting is a process similar to ripening, but far more dramatic. Most ripening fruit will travel a familiar path from being firm and tart, to a little softer, a little sweeter, then ending in full ripeness. A bletting medlar will transform from being hard, pale-fleshed, sour and inedibly astringent, to having sweet, fragrant flesh, so soft you can scoop it with a spoon, with no in-between stage. A corner of the fruit will look as though it's bruised, and, within a day or two, the transformation will be complete.

You have several options for your soft, ripe, darkened fruit. You can, as I did on my first bletted medlar encounter, peel back the skin and inelegantly slurp the tender, tangy, aromatic flesh away from the stones. I think, if you truly want to know a new food, you should always try it unadorned — and a medlar sampled like this tastes gentle, like something you would feed a baby, a blend of soft, cooked apple, raisins and a hint of baking spices. I also love to peel them, force the pulp through a sieve, add a dash of lemon juice and a generous amount of icing (confectioners') sugar, then fold it through slightly sweetened mascarpone and whipped cream to make a fool. I serve it with speculaas or brown-sugar shortbread and it's magical.

Medlars also make a wonderful paste to serve with cheese. I prepare medlars as I do the quinces on page 219, although bletted medlars will need less than an hour in the oven before you can sieve out their seeds and proceed with your paste.

Medlar 'cheese'

Roast your bletted (straw-ripened) medlars in a covered baking dish until they become very soft. Force the pulp through a food mill, into a saucepan, leaving the skin and seeds behind. Add a generous lug of lemon juice and one cup of sugar for each cup of fruit pulp, mixing to allow the sugar to dissolve a little. Cook over a low heat, stirring constantly, lest heat builds up, and dangerous hot spurts of medlar lava burn your arms. After a while you'll notice the pulp becomes almost glassy, and when you test it on a saucer, cold from the freezer, the skin on top of a drop of cooled paste should wrinkle when you push it. At that point remove your pan from the heat, then scoop the paste into warm, sterilised jars, where it will keep for a year sealed. Use opened jars within a few weeks and store them in the fridge. Or, if you've made the paste very thick, you can pour it into pretty moulds or slabs and cut off pieces as needed.

Medlar brandy

While I was a hairdresser hunting for change in car seats, my partner Matt was working as a chef in an old Hobart restaurant whose matriarch, Jill Mure, had put up jars of medlar brandy that sat, unloved, in the restaurant larder for years. After a clean-out, Matt brought home a couple of those jars and we upended one over a sieve. The flavour was the closest thing you'll find to drinking Christmas cake.

Using a large pin, prick the skin of your medlars. Pack them loosely in large, clean jars and add brown sugar to taste; I usually use a couple of tablespoons in a 1 litre (35 fl oz) jar. Don't add too many medlars — the ratio of alcohol to fruit must be high or your fruit may begin to ferment.

Fill the jars to the top with brandy and screw the lids on. (Here I come into conflict with some of my booze-loving friends. I feel that if you have a well-grown, beautiful fruit that will age in your pantry for a year or five, you should stretch to a decent bottle of liquor — isn't it a crime to insult good food with cheap brandy? They argue the inverse: what criminal taints a good spirit with sugar and fruit? I'll leave it to you to decide. In a year's time you probably would have forgotten the few extra dollars you spent, and you probably wouldn't taste the difference either!)

Leave the jars in a cool dark spot for at least 6 months to infuse the brandy.

You can press the fruit drained from the brandy through a sieve or food mill and fold it through sweet whipped cream and mascarpone for a tipsy fool, or make the paste on page 237.

a large pin

large clean jars with well-fitting lids

bletted (straw-ripened) medlars

brown sugar

brandy

plenty of patience

Rosaceae

239

Brambles

RUBUS SPP.

In the days before public liability there was a berry farm at Kaoota, just south of Nipaluna (Hobart), on a slope fit for goats, boasting the steepest, longest slippery dip you've ever seen. We'd drive there with jam pans and ice cream buckets, be vaguely pointed towards the best fruit, then left to our own devices in what I remember as heaven.

Here were row upon row of raspberries, probably from a dozen heritage varieties that I was too young to notice — except for golden raspberries growing at the bottom of the farm, whose unique perfume I fell in love with. It had the gentle parts of the raspberry flavour without the zing the red ones give.

The farm stayed open for a few years after my daughters were born, and I loved watching them gather fruit before risking life and limb on the slide. The farmer took up full-time fly fishing and the farm is now a paddock. I often wonder if there are remnants of the plants there, if I might one day visit with a garden fork and salvage a little of that childhood flavour.

Matt's mum Kelsey is a precise jam maker who has raspberry jam down to a fine art. We sell her wares at the markets and they have a cult following.

Nanna's raspberry jam

Having a wide-mouthed jam pan, working in small batches, and selecting ripe (but not over-ripe) raspberries are all vital for success.

Raspberry jam that takes too long to reach setting point will be drab in appearance and flavour. A wide-mouthed jam pan makes for fast evaporation and a shorter cooking time, and the extra pectin in just-ripe fruit means it will reach setting point sooner.

Kelsey heats the fruit in the jam pan until boiling, adds an equal weight of sugar to fruit, and stirs until the sugar has dissolved.

She heats the jam again quickly; she says it should bubble like Vesuvius! She adds the juice of 2 lemons to each 3 kg (6¾ lb) batch of fruit, and throws the lemon halves in the pot to add their tartness and perhaps a little pectin to aid the set.

After 15 minutes of rapid boiling, your jam should be done. You can check the 'set' on a chilled saucer; let a few drops cool and look for wrinkling skin when you push the drops. Bottle quickly into sterilised jars and seal while hot.

It's best to make small batches every month or two. Jam stored for too long loses its vibrancy, whereas jam made fresh, even from frozen fruit, will be sweet, tart and vibrant red.

In the opposite direction to the Kaoota berry farm, north of Hobart at Sorell, there was a pick-your-own bramble berry farm with labelled rows of tayberries, marionberries, silvanberries and boysenberries, all plump in varying shades of maroon, waiting to be tasted and compared — sour and refreshing, rich and winey, aromatic and sweet. We'd fill buckets for Mum to freeze for winter puddings, and sometimes we'd lash out and buy her a little bottle of the silvanberry liqueur the farm made.

Now I scavenge berries from our patch at home — a caged area that the marauding blackbirds I'm trying to keep out find perfect for nesting and raising babies in. Silvanberries and tayberries are the two we have at the moment. I love the silvanberries for their strong, punchy flavour and generous production; their slightly meeker cousin, the tayberry, is less productive, but has a complex, sweet, aromatic tartness that I'll stand in the garden savouring when I should be doing other summer tasks. With our garden devoted to annual vegetables, herbs and fruit trees, I'm yet to plant a raspberry patch, but our other brambles are so easy to grow I may never get around to it.

Raspberries grow in clumps and tend to be upright, not much above head height, whereas brambles grow long arching canes that are most easily harvested — and protected from winged thieves — if trained along a trellis or fence.

At the end of each season I cut out any spent canes, those that fruited that year, and allow young canes to grow through, as these are the ones that will fruit the following summer. And fruit they do. On long summer evenings, no matter how weary I am, I find myself drawn to the bramble patch. My friend Stan taught me the excellent trick of melting a couple of long holes near the top of a plastic, rectangular mop bucket and threading an old belt through the holes, to make a picking bucket that is easily washed and allows you to have both hands free for harvest. I strap the bucket around my waist, and if I'm feeling optimistic I'll take a colander as well, and head out, asking if either of my daughters will come and help.

Did you have the Little Golden Book about the hen who asked for help sowing, harvesting, grinding, cooking and eating her wheat, only to have offers of help with the final stage — the eating? That is how my teenagers make me feel about my berries. Heidi, the youngest, will come out and help cut the blackberries that sneak their way into the patch disguised among their less thorny cousins, so that we can gather berries relatively prickle-free, but rarely joins me when I pick. But as soon as the basket of fruit is on the kitchen bench, it's anyone's game apparently — purple fingers and little cups full of stolen fruit stashed under jumpers, as if I don't see them... so I make a point of secretly squirrelling a few away in the freezer for my own purposes.

Rosaceae

A little gin drink

Pour the gin into a small, pretty glass. Add the berries and lime juice, and top with soda water. As the berries melt a little, your drink will turn the prettiest shade of pink, and berry- and gin-scented bubbles will tickle your nose.

a measure of good <u>gin</u>

a handful of <u>frozen berries</u>, such as logan, boysen or silvan

a tiny squeeze of <u>lime</u>

chilled <u>soda water</u>

Stop and smell them...

The rose family is the one that holds the most pleasurable food memories for me. My happiest Christmas sight was always my mother's platter dripping with cherries, peaches, apricots and strawberries, and us being allowed to eat as much as we liked. Alongside the Christmas pudding there'd be a crystal dish of raspberries with just enough icing sugar folded through to make the juices run from the fruit. After lunch my little sister and I would mix the leftover juice with lemonade into a majestic soft drink that left our favourite pub raspberry lemonades for dead.

Now, in the last days of December, I drive to the same family home, my youngest daughter as my wing-person, and we pull over at a clump of neglected **loquat**, *Eriobotrya japonica*, trees on the way, their honeyed flesh and disproportionate stones a delight and effort only the two of us find worthwhile. So we sit, she and I, sticky-fingered, peeling, slurping flesh from stones, and putting the pips aside for sowing later. I am grateful to have my little fruit fiend, like a voice on my shoulder, telling me 'Mum, it's totally okay to drive forty kilometres for Moorpark apricots. And you should definitely spend the grocery money all on cherries — the season is so short.'

There are more complicated pleasures in the rose family. The cyanide-bitter of **almonds**, *Prunus amygdalus*, in marzipan; the easily overdone power of rosewater that my older sister loves in Turkish delight. There is a Lutruwita (Tasmanian) native plant, called **buzzy**, *Acaena novae-zelandiae*, that has fuzzy seed heads that stick to your socks and your dog, but whose tiny growing tips make a wonderful tea. It is an excellent healer of over-grazed, over-mown landscapes, even if inconvenient for humans.

One summer I spent an inordinate amount of time making umeboshi. My **ume** tree, *Prunus mume* 'Bungo', was raided by possums and only managed to produce five fruit, which made the weeks of salting and drying for such a tiny yield seem ridiculous. You'll find this story on page 212 — but the resulting umeboshi was so beautiful it inspired me to make a cage for my little ume tree.

It is impossible to ignore the aesthetic delights of such a family. We are always reminded to stop and smell the roses, but the blossoms of the fruit-bearing rose family members are just as worthy of resting your eyes upon. On the journey to visit a friend I once witnessed the most perfect moment: a black alpaca was grazing under an old, majestic pear tree and its black pelt, and the ground it had yet to graze, were blanketed in masses of fallen white pear blossoms. Then, when I visited my friend again that autumn, the alpacas in that same field were eating pears fallen from that same tree, which a human with an eye to the future had planted probably a hundred years before.

Rosaceae

Sponge topping for any rose family fruit

This is a sturdy, adaptable, midweek pudding that you can put together with whatever fruit you have to hand. In summer a handful of berries, with just enough sugar to make their juice run, will cover the base of the pudding dish; in autumn I'll use poached pears or stewed apples; and in winter I'll open a jar of the apricots I preserved in summer and feel grateful for my larder. If you don't have a garden or a larder full of fruit, a tin of peaches will make for a warming and delicious pudding.

Preheat your oven to 180°C (350°F).

Butter a pie dish and arrange your fruit in it, with a tablespoon or two of their syrup. (If you're using berries, sprinkle them with sugar to taste, or combine them with cooked apples.)

In a bowl, whisk together the flours and baking powder.

In a separate bowl, soften the butter with the back of a wooden spoon, then beat in the sugar. Add the eggs one at a time, beating well. Using your whisk, fold in the milk and the flour mixture.

Pour the batter over the fruit and bake for 25 minutes.

Serve with cream and any leftover syrup.

70 g (2½ oz) butter, softened, plus extra for greasing

enough berries or poached fruit to generously cover the bottom of your pie dish, cut into bite-sized chunks

170 g (6 oz) plain (all-purpose) flour

½ cup (65 g) rye flour

1½ teaspoons baking powder

⅓ cup (75 g) caster (superfine) sugar

2 eggs

¼ cup (60 ml) milk

OPTIONAL EXTRAS

1 teaspoon ground cinnamon

½ teaspoon ground ginger

a little ground nutmeg, cloves and allspice

Solanaceae

Have you ever had the feeling that your heart would burst because you beheld such great beauty that your soul couldn't fit it in? When I look at babies, oceans or wild places, my heart swells to breaking. It's an intense, magical thing that feels disproportionate when I find myself moved by a perfect crate of tomatoes.

In June I make planting lists for the coming spring, stocktaking and testing seeds before ordering any I need. Every year I tell myself that I'll cut back on varieties to make my life simpler, and I never do. There's always something I've not tasted, or a culinary tradition I find fascinating. Tomatoes from the foothills of Vesuvius that are harvested semi-ripe for hanging indoors and ripening over winter, sourced by fellow edible plant obsessive, Gregg Muller, of Useful Seeds in Bendigo? Sign me up! Blue tomatoes, bred by tomato genius Brad Gates of Wild Boar Farms in California? There's no way I'm not trying those.

And then there are our friends and customers, continually testing my resolve to grow fewer varieties.

When my chef and gardener friend Pauline Mak, a person who really knows flavour, told me to grow 'Moldovan Green' tomatoes, I knew I had to — and she was right. They were meaty, savoury and wonderful, the first variety I'd ever tasted that is ripe while green rather than red. And when countless loyal seedling buyers asked for 'Amish Paste' tomatoes for their passata, I couldn't refuse them. When I trawl the catalogues and find new peppers and eggplants that are suited to my climate, or ground cherries promising scents of pineapple, it is impossible to resist.

In August I'm up to my elbows in spreadsheets, germinating seedlings, muddled labels and seed trays that need sterilising, and I almost regret my wanton seed fetish. But the loyalty and curiosity of our equally obsessed seedling customers make me feel I wasn't too rash saving and ordering all of that seed.

Later, when the tomatoes need trellising, the chillies want stakes and the tomatillos still aren't in the ground, we're all exhausted and I feel the burn of regret. But come autumn this stress turns to bliss, because in southern Lutruwita (Tasmania), as my friend Michelle Crawford states, 'tomatoes are an autumn fruit'.

When your exhaustion stems from the sheer volume of the delicious food you've grown, it is an ache you stretch out with joy as you admire the diversity of flavours, colours and shapes you've conjured from tiny brown seeds.

That moment of heart-swelling beauty? It comes as the low autumn sun glows through our kitchen window and makes the tomatoes luminous. One of my daughters will reach for her favourite tomato, a 'Black Cherry', 'Violet Jasper' or 'Pêche Jaune', and I'll see her eyes light up then close in pleasure as the fruit bursts and the flavour fills her mouth.

Tomatoes

LYCOPERSICON ESCULENTUM

Tuesdays were the best days for my little girls. We'd begin with playgroup — a wild horde of children released into the echoing confines of an old country hall to thunder around on bicycles, and decorate paper, their hair, clothes and limbs with potato stamps dipped in lurid paint, make the world's most unhygienic pizzas, or play in the sand pit. After expending all that energy we'd sweep the hall and embark upon our food shop for the week. I hadn't yet fenced the possums out of the garden, so our home-grown resources were limited to the occasional egg from our lazy Silkie hens, and potted herbs on the back deck. But our region is rich in food, and I knew where to find the very best for my little ones.

Our first stop was the greengrocer for bread, milk and a few vegetables; this grocer also happened to stock huge crates of local apples, with a big basket of free ones for the kiddies. Crunching on apples we'd head for the local butcher, who would hand the girls a little red mystery-meat sausage each, which they'd accept with glee, knowing I'd never buy them such processed 'meat'.

Our favourite stop of all was George the vegie man.

George is from Cyprus and had a house on a couple of sunny acres, and he didn't muck about. Every inch of his land was planted out with grapes, plums, the most succulent peaches, and chestnut and olive trees. There were rows upon rows of annual vegetables, too, including sensational silverbeet with the deepest green leaves. Every Tuesday we drove to his stall, which was always brimming with a cornucopia of beautiful produce that was then the mainstay of our diet.

248

The girls, however, were more enamoured with George himself.

He would always ask after them, and upon hearing that they were hale, hearty and happy, he would fill their little hands and pockets with whatever crisp beans, ripe-to-splitting plums or red bursting tomatoes he thought would make their day. The interaction with a man who probably contributed about half the nutrients their bodies had used to grow from birth to kindergarten was so valued by all of us. What better satisfaction than seeing healthy, robust children grow plump and vital on the fruits of your labour?

At the end of the season, George would sell huge trays of tomatoes for a ridiculously small sum. I would buy as many as I could and roast them to make bottles of sauce and passata.

I wish, when George sold his home, that we'd tried to buy it and been able to continue to nurture and share his work. Our mountain neighbourhood was too much in my blood by then and I couldn't think of leaving. But one thing we saved were the seeds from his beautiful field tomatoes.

He did tell me the name of the variety, but with his strong Cypriot accent, and my mushy mum-of-toddlers brain, it is lost in the mists of time. I chose the reddest, most perfect fruit from a few trays, squeezed the seedy pulp from the little segments between the flesh into a jar, before popping the rest of the fruit into the passata pot.

Saving seeds from tomatoes for home use is pretty simple. Commercial seed growers should separate varieties to prevent cross-pollination, but at home uniformity is less vital. A chance cross is rare, and could even lead to a beautiful new variety unique to your garden. Choose the best fruit from the best plants, ideally from a few separate plants of the same variety, to ensure you don't put your future harvests through the genetic bottleneck of a single parent plant. I consider the traits I'm looking for. Do I want tender skin that yields to the tooth, or am I struggling with splitting fruit and want to work towards a sturdier strain? I might select for early fruiting, or for plants that withstand disease and cold and give me an extended harvest well into the waning season. Or I might prefer a practical short, sharp ripening season for bulk fruit to preserve over a few weeks rather than months. George's tomato is just that, a low-growing bush variety that forms masses of fruit under its low branches.

Despite my best efforts to avoid single-use plastics, little yoghurt pots still somehow find their way into my kitchen. With their sturdy plastic, their straight sides that allow seedy tomato pulp to be tipped in and out with ease, and white surfaces that you can inscribe with permanent marker to keep track of varieties, they are perfect for the task of tomato seed-saving. And a note here on memory. Countless times I've thought I'd remember what I'd planted here, what seed is drying in a saucer there, which purple-fleshed tomato is fermenting in that yoghurt tub, and I always forget. So, grab a permanent marker, even take a picture with your phone — if you're growing and saving an heirloom it's well worth remembering its name.

Squeeze the seedy pulp from the cavities inside your tomato fruit into a labelled container and leave it to ferment, stirring occasionally. After a few days the pulp should be fizzing a little and possibly growing a white bloom on its surface, and that's the time to clean it. Leave it too long and your seed may germinate prematurely or rot in the pulp. Do it too soon and you'll lose the advantage that fermentation gives you — clean seed, free of membranes and pulp, that has less likelihood of carrying disease into the next season. I tip the fizzy mixture into a fine sieve, shake and rinse it to remove the bulk of the debris, then tap the seeds from the sieve into a bowl and fill it with water. Any infertile seeds, membrane and flesh should float and be easily poured away. Add more water and repeat until you're left with only heavy viable seeds that settle at the bottom of your bowl. Drain them well in your sieve and tip them onto a labelled piece of paper towel or clean cloth to dry thoroughly, before sealing in a container to store somewhere cool, dry and dark, where your precious seeds will keep for a few seasons.

Unless there is a furry disaster.

A few years after I'd saved that first seed from George's tomatoes, I began a stall at the Nipaluna (Hobart) farmers' market selling our produce and seedlings.

Selling tomato seedlings sometimes makes me feel like a cult leader. Many people here are incredibly obsessed with tomato growing. During planting season in October we have bustling queues of enthusiastic gardeners mobbing our market stall, and it's all hands on deck! Whether our customers are choosing favourite heirlooms from their ancestral homes, racing to produce the earliest ripe fruit, or wanting a rainbow of cherry tomatoes for their children's lunchboxes, if I've neglected to grow their favourite strain and dare to recommend an alternative, they'll soon let us know their displeasure.

One tragic day some mice found their way into my seed fridge (a broken fridge is an excellent insulated place to store seeds). I'd put wire in the vents, and kept the door closed, but the blighters had pulled piles of insulation out from underneath and gnawed their way in. They ate many seeds — but, worst of all, my entire harvest of George's tomato seed, which meant disappointing many of those loyal, obsessive gardeners who kept our young business afloat.

The community saved us, though. A wonderful pair of gardeners visited us at market every week, and when I shared my sorry tale they came to the rescue with two precious, tiny envelopes of seed — one they'd saved from our 'George' seedlings, and the other from a plump, red staking variety their neighbour's Maltese family had brought with them when they emigrated to Australia.

Since that day 'George', the tomato variety, has spread far and wide. Our market gardener friends have also become custodians, sharing seeds from their garden with friends and neighbours. We've sold tens of thousands of seedlings that have surely produced thousands of tons of fruit, since that first tomato was squeezed into a cup fifteen years ago.

Thank you, George.

Tomatoes on toast

When summer is in full flight, it's too hot to cook and you don't really feel like a proper dinner, plump tomatoes and a good sourdough can be all the meal you need.

I slice tomatoes, lay the slices on a plate and season them with sea salt to balance their sweetness, bring out their umami and make their flavour sing. Then I set a table with whatever tomato accompaniments are to hand.

All, or even just one, of these additions make for a satisfying repast: a fresh, milky mozzarella or a hard, salty pecorino; some fragrant summer basil or tiny picked leaves of thyme; a pepper grinder; perhaps some wakame or other mild seaweed flakes for extra umami; and a bottle of good olive oil to tie it all together.

I toast slabs of sturdy sourdough, one with an open crumb that will soak up all of the wonderful juices, and rub them with cut cloves of garlic before drizzling with olive oil or generously slathering them with butter. Then I summon everyone to the table and let them build their own dinner.

Tomatillo

PHYSALIS IXOCARPA

I am, without doubt, a luddite. I'm sure I'm not alone in longing for an end to the instant-gratification era we find ourselves in.

These days, if I'm curious about a seed variety, I can pick up my phone, find a dozen websites listing it and, biosecurity rules allowing, have it delivered within a week. In the slower times of only ten years ago, I would have to wait for mid-June when the seed catalogues would arrive in my mailbox — and that waiting and sense of anticipation was delicious.

Compiled by seed-growers who used their knowledge to write the listings about plants they themselves had sought out, cultivated and cooked, the catalogues were bursting with personality, opinions and experience. The day they arrived I'd sit down with tea and notebooks by the fire and scour them, ordering my favourite tried and true varieties and keeping a keen eye out for any new ones that needed exploring. The most anticipated catalogue of all was the one from Michael Self of Phoenix Seeds in Snug, southern Lutruwita (Tasmania).

Michael's diligence and curiosity were unmatched. Each of his seed packs came with a little typed story about the variety inside, and every seed germinated and grew as described. Most of all, I'm grateful to him for introducing so many new flavours to my kitchen.

He imported seeds from all over the world — cultivars selected for flavour and for suitability to small-scale growing, bred by seeds-people with an interest in organic growing and patent-free plant breeding. Once a variety was in his hands, he worked to select strains that performed best here, weeding out plants that succumbed to pests and diseases, or lacked vigour, or didn't taste wonderful. He sold me seeds of 'Costata Romanesco' zucchini, the first non-spongy, flavourful variety I'd ever tasted. His squash and pumpkin collection gave us everything from sugary single-serve acorn squash to enormous, long-keeping Hubbard squash. Through him I met delicious, easily grown orach, beautiful 'Lazy Housewife' beans and — the best-spent $3.50 of my life — the tomatillo.

That $3.50 bought me a packet of tan-gold seeds about a millimetre across. As instructed on the tiny slip of paper in his envelope, I sowed them in early spring, in a tray of seed-raising mix, and kept them in a cold-frame — an old window sitting on top of a polystyrene box — and they germinated in only a few days. I painstakingly pricked them out, teasing each tiny seedling apart from its neighbours with the aid of a wooden icy pole stick, and tucked them into their own pots with a compost-enriched potting soil. I watered them in with a seaweed solution to help them recover from the disturbance to their roots, then popped them back into the cold frame to continue growing until the soil had warmed and the danger of frost had passed, and they could be safely planted out into the garden.

Tomatillos are ridiculously productive plants, and the fruit is patient.

I've read of a fossilised relative of the tomatillo, *Physalis infinemundi*, 52 million years old, that was found in Argentina. It is fascinating to think upon the ancient lineage of the foods we eat — the environmental factors that shaped them before they were guided by human hands into the foods we enjoy now. This ancient fossil's modern cousin, the tomatillo, was domesticated by the Aztecs in Mexico almost 3000 years ago, and has since become a common crop throughout the Americas for its productivity, flavour and fecundity.

Tomatillos are feisty, unruly plants around a metre (three feet) tall and wide. I strongly suspect they would do really well with staking or caging, but in the hurly-burly of early summer we tend to focus on their prima-donna cousins the tomatoes, catering to their every whim, while the wilder, hardier tomatillos are left to flop around their beds, eventually cracking their own branches under the weight of their fruit as it begins to set in earnest in autumn.

Tomatillos like to tease gardeners. Seedlings grow with great vigour early in the season, reaching full size within a month or so. They open masses of inch-wide yellow flowers with grey centres, which the bees adore. Once the flowers drop a calyx develops, within which you'd expect to find fruit — but the cheeky tomatillo plants are tricking you into performing the lewd-seeming act of reaching under the foliage, gently cupping each swollen calyx and squeezing in hopes of feeling the heft of developing fruit in your palm. After fooling me into this indignity over many seasons, I've come to wonder if tomatillos might be day-length sensitive. Many plants have evolved to develop with the rhythm of the seasons, investing their energy into ripening seeds at a time that will offer them the most chance of success. But if you're growing any plant outside of its natural range, you may find yourself searching for fruit that won't appear until the plant is good and ready.

It seems this tomatillo tardiness is for the best. We live in a bushfire-prone area, and when they finally deign to ripen, the weather has cooled and it's safe enough to light a fire outside, which is the very best way to cook them.

They are ridiculously productive plants, and the fruit is patient. Tomatillos harvested with no splits or slug nibbles will store in their papery calyces at cool room temperature for months, allowing you ample time to prepare traditional tomatillo dishes — salsas, birrias or moles. But I think they're most delicious when freshly picked and still slightly under-ripe, before their pulp becomes fluffy and seedy, and they're at their firm, tangy peak. My mind always goes straight to recipes from the culinary traditions a plant belongs to, but my dear friend Cassie once served me a salad with ingredients chosen only by what tempted her in the garden, with no such preconceptions or constraints. She piled sliced tomatillos with chrysanthemum greens, coriander, spicy wild rocket, calendula petals and a rainbow of tiny lettuce leaves that self-seed in her garden. Cassie's larder is full of home-made vinegars, and her elderberry vinaigrette brought all of these seemingly disparate ingredients together to make a sparklingly refreshing, vibrant salad.

True to my habits though, when I harvest tomatillos I'll light an autumnal fire, building it up high so that by the time I've husked and washed my tomatillos, it will have died down into perfect cooking coals, ready to prepare salsa.

Braised lamb shoulder wraps with grilled tomatillo salsa

Preheat your oven to 180°C (350°F).

Marinade: Toast the cumin and coriander seeds, pepper and dried chillies in a dry frying pan until fragrant, then grind using a mortar and pestle or spice blender. Add the ancho chillies and their soaking water, along with the remaining marinade ingredients, and pound or whiz until smooth.

Score the outer fat on the lamb shoulder and rub with olive oil and the salt. Heat a lidded, flameproof cast-iron casserole on the stove and brown the lamb, turning it to caramelise every surface.

Pour the marinade over the meat, add an inch of water to the dish, put the lid on, and place in the oven.

Turn the oven down to 160°C (315°F) and roast for 4 hours, checking now and then that there is still liquid in the bottom of the dish, so the delicious sauce doesn't catch and burn.

Remove from the oven and skim off the fat, reserving it for roasting potatoes another day. I like to tease the meat from the bones and fold it through the sticky pan at the table.

While the lamb is in the oven, light a little fire under a grill in the garden if it's safe to do so. You can also use a cast-iron grill pan on the stove, although you won't get the same deliciously smoky result.

Serves about 6

1 whole lamb shoulder

olive oil, for rubbing

2 teaspoons sea salt

wraps, to serve

MARINADE

2 teaspoons cumin seeds

2 teaspoons coriander seeds

1 teaspoon black pepper

dried chillies, to taste

2 dried ancho chillies, soaked in warm water for about 20 minutes

1 bunch of coriander (cilantro), roots and stems washed and chopped (reserve the leaves for the salsa and filling your wraps)

1 brown onion, diced

1 garlic bulb, peeled and crushed

juice and zest of 2 limes

3 bay leaves

2 teaspoons sea salt

Tomatillo salsa: While you wait for your fire to settle, toast the cumin and coriander seeds and pepper in a dry frying pan until fragrant, then grind using a mortar and pestle or spice blender. Add them to a large heatproof bowl with the chopped coriander and lime juice.

Put the tomatillos, onion halves, garlic cloves and jalapeños in another bowl, drizzle with the olive oil and add the salt.

When you have a lovely bed of glowing coals, put your vegetables on the grill, turning often, and adding them to the bowl with the spicy lime juice mixture as they seem done — the tomatillos will soften and turn an unappealing shade of khaki, and some juice will hiss from any wounds you've made in their sides.

You can, if you like, use a blender to make a quick salsa, but I like to get messy and make a salsa with some heft to it. Roughly chop the onion, jalapeños and garlic, put them in a bowl with the tomatillos, then crush them with the back of a wooden spoon to maintain their succulent texture.

Build up your fire a little more so you can sit by it and make wraps with your lamb and salsa — with perhaps some avocado, a little sour cream, lime wedges, coriander and a lick of hot sauce, trying not to let all the fragrant, spicy juices run down your arms as you blink the smoke from your eyes, but find yourself too caught up in the pleasure of eating to move to the lee side of the fire.

TOMATILLO SALSA

1 teaspoon cumin seeds

1 teaspoon coriander seeds

black pepper, to taste

a handful of chopped coriander (cilantro) leaves

juice of 1 large lime

500 g (1 lb 2 oz) tomatillos, husked and washed

1 red onion, peeled, with the root end left intact, halved lengthways

5 garlic cloves, peeled

chopped fresh jalapeño chillies, to taste

1 tablespoon olive oil

salt, to taste

Eggplants

SOLANUM MELONGENA

A bird deposited a seed in my greenhouse. Not an unusual occurrence, but this seed grew, and grew. A more disciplined, ruthless gardener would have hoiked it out, but not I.

It was a Lutruwita (Tasmanian) native kangaroo apple, *Solanum laciniatum* — a culturally significant Palawa food plant — which has fruit that is toxic while green, and is only edible when fully ripe, reddish orange and soft. The plant is also an excellent healer of disturbed land, growing quickly, holding soil together and re-establishing life after fire, landslip or flood.

This hardiness, vigour and the plant's perennial habit enticed me to begin an opportunistic grafting experiment, using the volunteer kangaroo apple seedling as a rootstock. Grafting is an excellent way to marry the traits of one plant with those of another. A rootstock may either enhance the productivity of its scion (the plant that you graft onto the rootstock), curtail its growth, or allow it to thrive under challenging conditions. The robust, perennial kangaroo apple had many desirable traits that I thought it could bestow upon an eggplant scion — a plant with fruit I love to eat, but one that struggles in our short summers. The two plants are closely related, so hoping there would be no issues with compatibility, I went to work.

When the chance kangaroo apple seedling was a metre and a half tall, I cut back every branch into semi-hard wood — a stage of growth where branches have matured enough to bend, rather than break with a sappy snap, and have not yet hardened enough to make a woody bark and to break with hard splinters. I then rubbed off all the buds along each branch, cruelly erasing as much of the kangaroo apple's ability to grow its own leaves as I could.

Then I turned my attention to the closing season's eggplants. Selecting from the healthiest plants, I cut them, choosing the same semi-hard wood, lopping off the sappy tops and woody bottoms until I had a collection of branches with three or four buds on each. Using a sharp grafting knife, I cut a downwards slit into the top of a kangaroo apple branch, then cut wedge-shaped ends onto the base of an eggplant branch, leaving one edge thicker, with a millimetre or so of bark still on it. I pushed the wedge into the slit I'd made in the kangaroo apple, making sure that the bark of the two branches aligned perfectly. When you want a grafted scion (my eggplant) to marry with a root stock (the kangaroo apple), it is vital that the sappy layer just under the bark lines up. This cambium layer under the bark contains undifferentiated cells which, if your graft is happy, will quickly form a kind of callus that allows the scion to receive water and nutrients from the rootstock, and eventually heals — giving your plant a new head.

I bound the wounds with grafting tape and left the plant for a couple of weeks to rest. Semi-hardwood cuttings heal quickly, and after a few weeks

Soft, downy eggplant leaves were followed by the beautiful lilac discs of their flowers.

I took the grafting tape off. It was late autumn by then, so I visited the plant often, rubbing off unwanted buds that tried to sprout from the rootstock, and cutting off any grafted branches that had failed.

The following spring, I watched with joy as the buds on my scions began to sprout. Soft, downy eggplant leaves were followed by the beautiful lilac discs of their flowers. As the season progressed, those flowers were visited by bees, and it seemed every one of those visits was fruitful. The grafted branches were so thick with fruit that they needed support, so we strung baling twine supports from the roof of the greenhouse to stop them breaking, and began to harvest.

I'd grafted three different varieties of eggplant onto my kangaroo apple rootstock: the slender, tender-skinned Greek heirloom 'Tsakoniki', with its white and lavender stripes; the classic plump 'Black Beauty', a century-old cultivar from the United States; and 'Snowy', a white, silken-fleshed beauty that produces well in cool seasons, but whose origins I don't know.

I've been growing eggplants for years. They are slow growing in our cool garden, and it can be very difficult to germinate and grow plants big enough to get in the ground in time for late spring. It's one plant I'd suggest less keen gardeners buy ready to plant, to give themselves a head start.

If it's a mild spring, and my plants are ready, I plant them in our greenhouse in November. In warm gardens you can certainly plant them outside, but they need constant warm temperatures to grow and produce well. Make sure your ground is prepared with a nice layer of compost; I like to add a little extra compost, seaweed meal and a pinch of potash to the soil I backfill around the seedlings. They need plenty of air and light, and benefit from staking to support the heavy fruit, so give each plant a good 50 cm square in which to grow. Resist the temptation to let the fruit grow big. Over-ripe eggplant is seedy, pithy and has tough skin, and takes me back to the days when we were told to salt eggplants to remove their bitterness. Fresh, well-grown eggplants aren't bitter, and it would be a tragedy to salt, wash and wring all of their special creaminess away.

Growing them the usual way, we'd been getting a fruit or two from each plant on my weekly harvest, but upon lifting a branch of this grafted behemoth, the splendid sight of laden branches greeted my eye.

For the first time I could play around with different ways to prepare them. Of course I made baba ganoush, then took advantage of the eggplant's ability to soak up flavours by marinating it in herbs and chilli before grilling it on the barbecue, and used slabs of the plump Black Beauty to make an almost too rich moussaka. But the best on ground was an eggplant pickle. Sour, hot, sweet and well spiced, it was devoured far too quickly.

Solanaceae

Eggplant pickle

Dice the eggplant into 1.5 cm (⅝ inch) chunks. Halve and slice the green chillies, removing the seeds and membranes if you prefer a milder pickle.

In a dry frying pan, toast the cumin seeds, dried chillies and fenugreek seeds until fragrant. Grind to a powder and stir in the turmeric.

Heat the oil in a large saucepan over medium heat and add the curry leaves and mustard seeds. They will jump and pop delightfully. When the curry leaves are a little translucent, add the ginger, garlic and green chillies. Cook, stirring, for a few minutes. Stir in your ground spices until they're fragrant, then add the eggplant. Cook, still stirring, until the eggplant fries just a little. Stir in the sugar, salt and vinegar.

Turn the heat down and simmer gently, stirring occasionally, for up to an hour, until the eggplant is tender and the oil begins to separate and sit on top, being sure not to cook too long and lose the structure of the eggplant pieces. Taste and add a little extra salt or chilli if desired. Stir to mix the oil back through.

While hot, spoon into warm sterilised jars and seal quickly. The pickle should keep in the fridge for a month, and is excellent alongside curries, and wonderful in a cheese sandwich.

Makes about 650 ml (23 fl oz)

500 g (1 lb 2 oz) eggplants (aubergines), picked when young and firm

2 green chillies

2 teaspoons cumin seeds

2 dried chillies; adjust amount or variety to taste

1 teaspoon fenugreek seeds

2 teaspoons ground turmeric

120 ml (4 fl oz) vegetable oil

10 curry leaves

1 tablespoon mustard seeds

40 g (1½ oz) fresh ginger, finely chopped

2 garlic cloves, crushed and chopped

100 g (3½ oz) sugar

1 tablespoon salt

¼ cup (60 ml) apple cider vinegar

It's one plant I'd suggest less
keen gardeners buy ready to
plant, to give themselves a
head start.

Peppers

CAPSICUM SPP.

Chillies, peppers and capsicums can prove challenging for the cool-climate gardener. For years I sowed bird's eye chillies, watched them grow and flower — and only ever picked a handful of fruit. Blocky 'California Wonder' capsicums were the standard seedling variety available in nurseries, and they probably did well in heated greenhouses, but in my unheated mountainside greenhouse they were miserable, shrunken, bitter things.

Gradually becoming wiser, I pored over seed catalogues, choosing varieties that had left their cradles in Central and South America and been taken — most likely by fur traders, foresters and plant collectors — into northern Europe, where local gardeners and cooks selected varieties best able to grow and produce in short, cool summers, and find a place in local cuisines. If a chilli could produce in Hungary, then surely it would feel at home in the foothills of Kunanyi (Mount Wellington)?

Others have been cultivated for millennia in cool and elevated areas from Mexico to southern Chile, and grow and produce perfectly here. Rocoto peppers, *Capsicum pubescens*, are a perennial and can grow into small trees in cool gardens, if protected from frost. Their purple flowers are made of translucent cells and shimmer in the sunlight. Each plant can produce kilograms of golf ball-sized fruit in yellow, brown, red and green, which is where a blessing may become a curse. I've read that a traditional preparation of this chilli is to stuff it with a fresh, white cheese and bake it, but every variety of rocoto I've found is fiery hot. We take advantage of this heat to make all manner of hot sauces — to be consumed in cautious drops, not gallons. Once, when she was only about four years old, my daughter Heidi was helping me sow spring seeds and was scrawling a label for her punnet in charming kindergarten script when she burst into tears. The capsaicin on just a few rocoto seeds had touched her tender child's skin and was enough to turn her face sore, swollen and pink. We soothed the pain with a thick layer of plain yoghurt and a delicious icy pole, but to this day she'll only help in the nursery wearing gloves.

We do have success with Mediterranean peppers, too. Growing Spanish padróns is almost a religion in Hobart. The daring that comes with eating these frying peppers — their savoury moreishness punctuated by a blast of fiery heat that is carried only by one fruit in every dozen — brings out the bravado in the best of us. A few minutes in a hot pan until the skin is blistered all over, a sprinkle of salt, a splash of your best vinegar, and there's nothing nicer to grill outside with friends on a slow summer night, especially when it's seasoned with an extra *frisson* of danger — will this be the bite that bathes my mouth in fire?

Beautiful Basque Espelette peppers fill the niche of paprika in my kitchen. The plants are always productive, the thin-walled peppers easy to dry, and their gentle, rich flavour a welcome addition to any savoury dish. If I want a little more warmth, I'll reach for Aleppo peppers. Both these plants hold the stories of cultures keeping tradition alive in the face of adversity, so I tend and use them with reverence.

'Beaver Dam' is a huge pepper the size of your hand, tapered to a point and ripening to a rich warm red, from a town of that name in Wisconsin, via an emigrant from Hungary. It has heat, but not too much, and I dice them for mirepoix when beginning a meaty braise, grill them to add to summer salads, or ferment them in brine into a glowing red not-too-hot hot sauce that I sprinkle on everything from noodles, to eggs, to cheese sandwiches.

At the end of the season, we pull all of the pepper plants and sow our greenhouse with a green manure crop to feed the soil until next spring. I pick every last pepper, ripe and green, hot and mild. The meatier ones with thick walls — jalapeños, serranos and sweet peppers that won't dry well — get pickled to spice up our winter sandwiches. I poke the stems of the thin-walled varieties — cayenne, Espelette and Aleppo — into the flue of our wood heater to dry the fruits before grinding them into flakes and storing in jars. The heat of my jars of mixed chilli flakes varies each season, so the first meals are seasoned with caution, but magic occurs every year. I find this random cast of peppers more flavoursome than any of my carefully picked single-variety jars. Maybe it's the late season having given these peppers a longer ripening time in which to develop flavour, or just that a choir of peppers has a richer voice than one alone.

Solanaceae

267

Chilli & cheese crackers

Ice-cold work is vital for the crispest crackers. Cube then chill your butter, chill the water you use for mixing, and, if it's a warm day, cool your flour and bowl in the fridge before getting started.

Preheat your oven to 170°C (325°F). Line two baking trays with baking paper and have a cooling rack ready.

Combine the flours and salt in a large bowl and rub in the butter until it looks like coarse breadcrumbs. (Or you can give it a couple of pulses in a food processor.)

Sprinkle the espelette pepper and thyme over, then add the cheeses.

Pour the iced water over and combine with a butter knife. It will look like it won't hold together, but gently knead and the butter will soften just a little and hold the flour. Add a sprinkle more water if needed; flours and humidity all come into play, but you'll get a feel for it once you've made a batch or three. Bring the dough together, turn onto a lightly floured bench and roll out to 5–8 mm (¼–⅓ inch) thick.

I like to be fancy, so I slice the rolled dough into strips about 2.5 cm (1 inch) wide, then slice again on a 45 degree angle to my first cuts to form diamond-shaped biscuits, but any shape you like will work. Arrange on your baking trays, allowing a little room for spreading, then sprinkle with a little extra espelette pepper.

Bake for 20 minutes, or until slightly browned, rotating your trays midway through. Transfer to the cooling rack, and store in an airtight container once completely cooled.

Makes about 70 crackers

150 g (5½ oz) plain (all-purpose) flour

150 g (5½ oz) plain wholegrain spelt flour

generous pinch of salt

180 g (6 oz) cold butter, cut in roughly 1 cm (½ inch) cubes

2 teaspoons ground espelette pepper, plus extra for sprinkling

1 teaspoon picked fresh or dried thyme leaves

1 cup (100 g) grated cheddar

½ cup (50 g) coarsely grated pecorino or parmesan

1 tablespoon iced water, plus extra, as needed

Solanaceae

Potatoes

SOLANUM TUBEROSUM

Potatoes are the stuff of life, and though the work of growing and harvesting is hard, the thrill of unearthing a clump of potatoes never fades. Native to Central and South America, the diversity of species, form and preparation methods for this ancient vegetable is mind-boggling. Round, knobbly, long or tiny tubers in shades of red, black, purple and gold are prepared by freeze-drying in cold high-altitude air, fermented in springs for a year or more, packed in layers of straw, pounded into pancakes, and roasted in wonderful above-ground stone ovens.

A small fraction of that diversity has made its way into countless other culinary traditions. We now take rösti, gnocchi, hot chips and hasselback potatoes (always Hasselhoff potatoes in our house) for granted, and for some the choice in the supermarket boils down to 'washed' or 'unwashed'. But here in Lutruwita (Tasmania) we grow excellent potatoes and revere them, every cook having a favourite variety, and those in the know keeping a keen eye out for the harbinger of the season, the South Arm 'Pink Eye'.

My mother grew up in the home of the Pink Eye, a waxy new potato that aficionados like her know is only authentic if it comes with a fine coating of grey Mutatayna (South Arm) sand and loose skin that slips off in papery layers under the tap. Mutatayna is a hook of land that curls into the mouth of Timtumili Minanya (the River Derwent), and its maritime climate keeps the frosts away, meaning potatoes can grow through the winter and be ready for table in spring. The Pink Eyes that grow there are incomparably buttery, with a fine-textured flesh that is best boiled or steamed until just cooked, then drained, returned to the warm pan and anointed with lots of butter and a little salt, the pan given a firm shake that shatters the skins of the potatoes and allows the butter to soak in.

When the Pink Eyes are done, the potato parade begins.

Fingerlings are my potato salad heroes: 'Pink Fir Apple' that look unnervingly like fingers when I dig them and have firm, sweet, white flesh; waxy 'Banana', with firm, buttery, golden flesh; and 'Kipfler', with a looser texture and more potatoey flavour. The first of these we steal from under the mulch, digging our fingers under still-growing plants, bandicooting out the first sizable tubers we can grasp, being sure to pull soil back over the plants to prevent sun reaching the potatoes left behind. We take them quickly to the kitchen and rinse them before the soil has time to dry and cling to their skins, and drop them into salted water, simmering until just tender. We eat them with butter or olive oil and salt; they need nothing more.

Potatoes are
the stuff of life.

Leftovers are my favourite meal of all. The next day we turn the cooled fingerlings into potato salad. If I'm cooking, I'll dress it with drained yoghurt, chives, lemon zest, parmesan and salt, and serve it with lots of boiled eggs. If it's Matt, he'll cover it in mayonnaise and spike it with plenty of parsley. Potatoes that have been cooked, then cooled, develop prebiotic resistant starch, feeding our gut bacteria and benefiting our gut health, so as well as saving me cooking on hot days, our potato salads are healthy, too.

'Dutch Cream', 'Cranberry Red', 'Tasman' and 'Sapphire' are our mid-season staples, from which we love to make rainbow hot chips, cut with a crinkle-cutter from the tip shop. I've had the crispiest success using dripping rather than oil, a very hot oven and frequent flipping to ensure even, crunchy brown chips, and reducing dinner table arguments over who ate all the brownest ones.

Freshly dug potatoes are best boiled, roasted or used in rösti or scalloped potatoes. Only after a little storage time does the flesh soften, the starches converting to a form that makes a fluffy mash or light gnocchi, rather than giving tight, gluey results. The best mash of all comes in winter when the Kennebecs or other floury types have sat a while in the larder — and, just as I cook extra boiled new potatoes for a salad the next day, I always prepare extra mash for a shepherd's pie, home-made potato gems or Boston bun the following day as well.

When I have the time and inclination, I put whole scrubbed potatoes in a cold pot of water, put the heat on medium and forget about them for up to an hour, only checking now and then that they're not boiling over. When I can insert a knife easily, I drain them and push them through a potato ricer back into the warm cooking pot. I put a small saucepan of milk and butter on the warm hotplate when I drain the potatoes and pour this over the fluffy pile, stirring gently and adding more milk if needed to keep it loose, before checking the salt and adding lots of pepper.

Solanaceae

271

Boston bun

Preheat your oven to 180°C (350°F). Grease a loaf (bar) tin or line with baking paper.

Sift the flour, spices and salt into a large bowl. Rub the butter in.

Put the mashed potato in another bowl. Add some of the milk and stir it through to loosen the potato, then mix in the remaining milk. Stir in the sugar and fruit, then fold in the flour mixture until just combined, taking care not to overwork the dough.

Place the mixture in the loaf tin, smoothing the top, and bake for 1 hour. Allow to cool a few minutes in the tin, before turning out onto a rack to cool.

Pink coconut icing: Sift the icing sugar into a heatproof bowl that sits nicely over a saucepan or bowl and pop the kettle on. Use the back of a tablespoon to spread the butter through the icing sugar. Pour some hot water into your saucepan and sit your bowl on top where the steam will warm it and soften the butter. Add the warm water a little at a time, and a couple of drops of cochineal, and beat until your icing is smooth but not runny.

Spread the icing over the cooled bun and sprinkle with the coconut. Put the kettle back on so you can enjoy a slice of bun with a cup of tea.

The bun is best served with hot mugs of tea on the day it's made. It's also excellent toasted with butter for a few days after baking.

Serves 10

2 cups (290 g) self-raising flour

1 teaspoon ground cinnamon

½ teaspoon ground nutmeg

½ teaspoon ground cloves

pinch of salt

1 tablespoon softened butter

½ cup (115 g) cold mashed potato

1 cup (250 ml) milk

½ cup (110 g) caster (superfine) sugar

¼ cup (40 g) currants

¼ cup (40 g) chopped dried apricots, the mouth-puckeringly tangy kind

PINK COCONUT ICING

1 cup (125 g) icing (confectioners') sugar

2 teaspoons soft butter

2 teaspoons warm water

a few drops of cochineal, or use a dash less water and a few teaspoons of Nanna's raspberry jam (page 240)

1–2 teaspoons desiccated coconut

Nightshades & lampshades

Every autumn when I clean out the 'Cossack Pineapple' patch, I find lacy lanterns, the husks that once surrounded the fruit, eaten by slugs until only the veins remain, sometimes with a few seeds rattling loose inside. I once heard that this was a seed dispersal mechanism — that the lantern-like husks blow away from the parent plant, dropping seeds as they go. Cossack Pineapple is a variety of ground cherry, *Physalis pruinosa*, a fruit largely unknown in the antipodes, but deserving of more attention. Small summer annual plants, sown when you begin your tomatoes and planted out after the last frost, they grow to around 20 cm (8 inches) tall and have the sweetest lemon-yellow flowers with grey dots on each petal. The fruit forms in a green husk that turns gold and papery, and swells as the fruit inside ripens. Mulch your plant with a cushion of hay as the ripe fruit falls; these are easily harvested by just picking up a branch and giving it a gentle shake. If you have children you won't ever see a ripe fruit, as their cuteness and sweetness are irresistible. If you don't have greedy small people you might be able to try drying a few. I like to cut a slice into the base of the fruit to allow moisture to escape and lessen their time in the dehydrator but, if you're somewhere warmer and less humid than here, they dry beautifully in the sun into sweet golden lollies.

A continual struggle is finding the right name to use for a plant. New Zealand is a horticultural powerhouse and has co-opted Chinese gooseberries as kiwi fruit and oca as New Zealand yams. South Africa's Cape of Good Hope has given its name to Cape gooseberries, *Physalis peruviana*, which are actually from Peru and Chile, as their Latin surname suggests. Neither of the gooseberries mentioned here are even true European gooseberries, *Ribes uva-crispa*. And here in Lutruwita (Tasmania), people tried to market Chilean guava (not actually a guava) as Taziberries, but it hasn't seemed to stick. Ideally we'd use names from the cultural groups who are the keepers of the plants, but if I began calling my *Physalis peruviana* seedlings 'topotopo' (from the Quechuan language) or 'uchuva' (from the Aymaran language), my customers would be mystified. On my seed packets or market signs I'll often add the cultural name alongside the more familiar one in the hope of drawing minds to the histories of the wonderful plants we eat.

Cape gooseberries are perennial, and grow into bushy shrubs a metre or two tall. The fruit ripens year-round in our garden and the plant can be a little weedy, but seedlings are easily pulled. If you live in tropical or warm-temperate areas, it can become an environmental weed, outcompeting native species, so I'd avoid planting it there. The plants produce best in the first year or two and are frost-tender, but the bush in my back garden is exposed to frost and barely a leaf is burned. Because of its weedy nature, plants are generally self-sown, and the flavour and quality of fruit varies a lot. There is certainly room for the dedicated connoisseur to sow seeds from the most delicious plants and work on a strain that is tastier than the average. When they're fully ripe I love to serve them with their lampshades peeled back, so they look like badminton shuttles. I've read they make excellent jam, but sparrows steal much of my crop, so only snack quantities find their way to our kitchen.

Tamarillo, *Solanum betaceum*, is the most luxurious of the solanaceous fruits. We halve the red, orange or gold egg-shaped fruit, chop the flesh held inside the thin but firm skin as best we can with a teaspoon, sprinkle in sugar — the quantity varying with the ripeness of the fruit — allow a moment for the sugar to dissolve and the juices to run, then we eat with relish. The firm, bittersweet, yellow flesh melds with the deep winey red of the pulp around the seeds, creating a rich treat. You can scald, skin then poach the fruit in a spiced syrup. We've eaten them with pavlova this way; the strong tang is perfect with the subtler meringue and cream, and any left-over syrup makes for excellent sodas and cocktails. The plant is a small tree with large, velvety leaves, growing to maturity within a year or two, but although they tolerate cold, direct exposure to frost will kill them. The shade of another tree or the radiant heat from a sun-warmed wall is often enough to protect them. I potted an unsold seedling and stuck it in a corner of the greenhouse for 'later' and you can imagine how that went. Untended and unnoticed, its vigorous roots escaped the pot, growing underneath the chilli beds, and that winter a bumper crop of the glorious red fruit formed in an inconvenient spot, but we embraced the chaos and ate with joy.

The nightshade family, with its poisons, belladonna, drugs, tobacco, fruits, vegetables and spices, truly is a cornucopia of wonders.

Other families

In trying to choose a framework to explore the plants I love to grow, spend time with and eat, I decided that botanical families would be a neat way to consider relationships — culinary, geographical and horticultural. But nature isn't neat or simple, and the following plants refused to sit tidily with their kin, so I've put them into this big, happy pot together.

Plants that ask nothing more from you than to be planted, protected from extremes of dry or wet, and offered the occasional feed of mulch and compost in exchange for feeding you, are to be celebrated.

Others make you work harder, asking for rich, well-tended soil, constant moisture and little inputs of worm-wee tea or seaweed solutions as they grow.

Some pop up on their own, year after year, responding to the length of the day or the warmth of the soil.

Rhubarb

RHEUM × HYBRIDUM

There is never nothing to eat.

Remember those hedonistic share house years, with few responsibilities, and even fewer dollars? Living from pay cheque to pay cheque, squandering most of your meagre earnings in the first few days?

Luckily for my sisters and me, Mum taught us how to stock a functional pantry on the cheap, so there was never nothing to eat. Plain flour, self-raising flour, cornflour, oats and breadcrumbs. Caster, brown and icing sugar, golden syrup and honey. Salt, pepper, stock cubes, cumin, paprika, cayenne, bay leaves and oregano. Pasta, rice, butter, oil, tins of condensed milk and tomato. Onions, potatoes, carrots and garlic. Mustard, tomato sauce, Tabasco, soy sauce and Worcestershire sauce.

Add a fruit, a vegetable or protein and we can find you dinner, no stress at all. We can whip up a cake or batch of biscuits… or even a killer rhubarb crumble.

I once visited my sister's share house mid-party, where there was something awful to drink (cheap champagne), cremated sausages on white bread to eat, and an exquisite Staffordshire terrier called Maz to share them with. Squandering summer afternoons, lazing about in backyards with cheap drinks and cute dogs is excellent, but when you've run out of snacks the situation can feel dire. But my sister Belinda and I had it in hand. In the corner of her garden was an excellent perpetual food patch, thriving on nothing more than lawn clippings dumped by tenants over the years, but still pumping out silverbeet — and the target of our afternoon munchies, rhubarb.

My sister and I gathered the rosy-pink stalks, twisting them from the crown of the plant and pulling off the huge, green leaves to discard as our contribution to the future fertility of that otherwise neglected corner of the share house garden, rinsed the stems under the garden tap and took our bounty to the kitchen to transform.

We flicked the oven on to 180°C (350°F), and I washed and chopped the rhubarb, put it in a saucepan on low with a small handful of sugar and enough water to cover the bottom of the pan, stirring now and again as Belinda raided her pantry. We rubbed butter into flour, brown sugar and oats (coconut also often found its way into our family crumbles), sprinkled the lot over our cooked rhubarb, and after 20 minutes in the oven it emerged all crunchy, nutty and sweet on top, sticky and sour underneath — to the gratitude of everyone gathered on the lawn.

Roasted rhubarb

These days I love to roast rhubarb. It concentrates the flavour, and I find it more enjoyable than the 'wet' stewed rhubarb of my childhood. The butter and sugar also ooze together with the rhubarb juices, making for a sticky rhubarb toffee that is the cook's treat, stolen from the edge of the baking tray as soon as it's cool enough not to scald your mouth and fingers. If you have sweet cicely, *Myrrhis odorata*, or culinary angelica, *Angelica archangelica* — not the glossy angelica — in your garden, their stems and leaves (and the roots and unripe seeds of the cicely) are lovely cooked with your rhubarb. They neutralise a little of rhubarb's grabby acid and tannin, and you can get away with a little less sugar.

Preheat your oven to 180°C (350°F). Find a shallow tray that fits your rhubarb and herbs snugly like a brick wall — too much space and the edges will burn, too little and it will stew and you won't get the caramel. Arrange the rhubarb and herbs in the tray.

Dot the honey and butter over the rhubarb, then sprinkle with the sugar.

Bake for 30 minutes. If the rhubarb needs a little more browning to get caramelly, turn the oven up to 220°C (425°F) for another 10 minutes.

Serve with custard, ice cream or yoghurt, and don't neglect to hide in the kitchen when no one is about, Nigella style, and chip all the shards of rhubarb toffee from the corners of the tray.

Serves 8

500 g (1 lb 2 oz) trimmed rhubarb stems, cut into 5 cm (2 inch) lengths

a few stems of sweet cicely or culinary angelica, if you have them

20 g (¾ oz) honey

40 g (1½ oz) butter

40 g (1½ oz) brown or rapadura sugar

Rhubarb is a feisty, hardy plant, thriving, as this one did, on neglect, dying back to its large, tough root stock to sleep through the winter and wake in early spring. In a dry summer, a neglected plant may look feeble, only producing reedy, thin stems, but if you give that struggling plant a deep watering, a few shovelfuls of compost and some mulch to keep its roots cool, it will reward you with plump, tender stems aplenty. Don't fret, either, if your rhubarb has green rather than red stems, as there are rhubarb varieties that span the spectrum from green to pale pink to deep rosy red, and each is delicious in its own way. Nor should you worry if your rhubarb seems to mutate, with a giant flower spike bursting from its heart. I tend to lop these off, thinking it leaves the plant more energy to put into its edible stems, but I have friends who leave them to enjoy the masses of creamy flowers and they always have plenty of rhubarb for crumbles.

Though it can survive neglect, mollycoddled rhubarb is a delight. That extra dash of manure and cool root run can be taken a step further by covering dormant plants with cloches. In the garden of my dreams these are lovely earthenware ones; in my reality, a clean, black rubbish bin works well. The awakening plant will send up its spring stems and, excluded from the light, they'll grow pale pink and extra sweet.

Oca

OXALIS TUBEROSA

A knee-high, clover-like plant grew near our back fence, squashed up with the asparagus near weathered timber palings. A brilliant use of space, the asparagus had its short harvest window in spring, and the clover-like oca, *Oxalis tuberosa*, was harvested in winter and happily grew in the shade of the asparagus fronds. When it was ready for digging, the first knobbly, golden tubers would heave themselves out of the earth, signalling Mum to find a lamb roast and pop the oven on.

Oca is a knobbly, smooth-skinned, firm-fleshed, stem tuber that comes in shades of cream, gold, pink and red. Each tuber can grow up to 8 cm (3¼ inches) long, and 2–3 cm (1 inch) thick. They can contain high levels of oxalic acid, as its Latin genus name alludes to, and once harvested, the tubers are left in the sun for a few days, which greatly reduces the levels of oxalates. In the Andes, their traditional home, they're roasted, added to soups or stews, or dried and ground for use in pancake-like dishes, and even used in sweet conserves similar to marmalade. In Mexico, the larger, red-skinned variety common there is dressed in a salty lime and chilli sauce and eaten raw. I tried this at home with our oca, and it wasn't delicious. The different varieties vary greatly in taste and texture, and I suspect the Mexican cultivar is needed to make this a successful dish.

Its cradle, and the area with the greatest diversity of cultivars, is the high Andes. From there oca made its way to Mexico, and then to the rest of the world. In the 1860s gardeners took it to New Zealand, from whence I suspect it found its way here to Lutruwita (Tasmania). It brought with it the epithet 'New Zealand yam' — which is confusing, as it's neither a yam, nor from New Zealand.

I use the name 'oca' which, from what I understand, is a Spanish corruption of the Quechuan word 'uqa', which in turn is a Latin-alphabet interpretation of the original Quechuan word. I think it is vital to use pre-invasion — in this case, pre-Columbian — words for plants whenever we can find them. Without the cultural groups who continued to grow traditional foods in the face of oppression and dispossession, we wouldn't have them in our kitchens and gardens today, and we wouldn't have the diversity that is a vital tool in our food-security armoury for our changing climate. And I hold hope that recognition can lead to greater impetus to support seed-keepers to maintain crops in their traditional homelands.

I learned to use the name 'oca' in the heady early days of blogs, Facebook and Instagram. Following every person with a vegetable garden, I entered my ideal alternate universe filled with edible plant collectors and breeders. The one who taught me about oca was just a pair of hands (like the

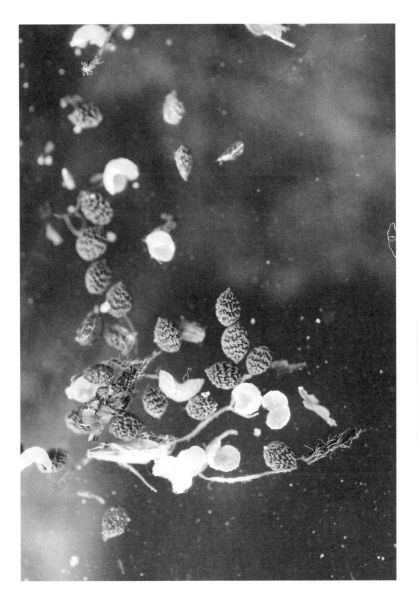

dentist in the toothpaste ad), and a name, Rhizowen (which is not his real one), and he remains mysterious to this day. He posts about the origins of the hundreds of uncommon plants he grows, and botanical and horticultural details such as the length of anthers in oca flowers and how they affect one plant's compatibility with another. Without learning from people like Rhizowen, and his encouragement — asking if my seeds have germinated, or offering the valuable advice that if I pick stems bearing almost-ripe seed and put them in a vase under an upturned bucket, the ripe seed will be trapped when the spring-loaded seed pods release them, rather than me futilely searching for unopened but ripe pods in my garden — my collection and my knowledge of plants would be far smaller.

Our collection of oca was limited to four cultivars. One golden, pink-eyed variety from my childhood garden; a fat yellow one from the Cygnet grocery shop; a productive pink one from a friend's market garden; and a sturdy, high-yielding orange one from the Royal Tasmanian Botanical Gardens in Nipaluna (Hobart). Four varieties seems like enough, right? But whether you're into stamps, cocktail ingredients, cars or tropical fish, you'd know that a sensible amount is never enough. My entire collection was made up of clones from planting one tuber and getting a yield of genetically identical ones at harvest time. But if you sow true seeds, the progeny will have multiple combinations of genes from both parents, giving you an assortment of babies to select from for their desirable traits — better flavour, higher yields, colour or resistance to pests and diseases.

We sow the seeds we're lucky enough to catch in winter, the cold days triggering germination and giving us tiny oca babies to grow on.

The main crop of tubers is planted in spring, often where we've cleared a crop of winter greens. They grow well in any reasonable soil with good drainage and plenty of organic matter. We plant around six tubers for every square metre of garden bed, and they are delightfully decorative all through summer. Clover-like foliage forms mounds on succulent stems to about knee height, and the colour varies depending on variety, from pale green to deep burgundy. The leaves are a lovely lemony garnish, best used sparingly due to the oxalic acid — and if you're lucky, in late summer your plants will carry a haze of pretty yellow flowers above their foliage that open when the sun shines on them.

The trickiest thing about oca is their need for diminishing day length to trigger the plants to form tubers. This means yields are limited closer to the equator where day length changes little, and in cold regions where early hard frosts can kill plants before they've formed a crop. Here at a latitude of 43 degrees south and 300 metres (100 feet) above sea level, we seem to have found the perfect spot. It seems that our late mild frosts help trigger tuber formation, and our day length diminishes enough to give the plants the cues they need.

As I was working with Mum in the potting shed last autumn, we were talking about how she loves her roast oca, and I was telling her how I'd just enjoyed some of the fiddly little ones simmered in a spicy tomato soup, where they became tender in minutes and made the soup feel filling. We looked up from our work and saw a wonderful bird, a green rosella — the largest rosella in the world and endemic to Lutruwita — fly up from the garden clutching a huge oca tuber, which it ate with relish while perched in my apple tree. I walked to the patch and found a dozen rosellas enjoying a picnic in our oca plot.

Oca are also enjoyed by mice, and a few soil-borne pests like weevils and wireworms, so we plant our oca where no root crops have been grown for a few seasons to prevent pest numbers building up — although there's little we can do about the rosellas, besides enjoying their magnificent presence and viewing their feast as a tax from Mother Nature.

Crisp roast oca with labneh

Oca's tangy, neutral flavour and satisfying potato-like heft makes it an excellent vehicle for other flavours. This is a quickly prepared but fancy-looking snack — the scattered herbs and flowers resembling dainty gardens.

Preheat your oven to 200°C (400°F).

Scrub the oca, pat them dry, then cut in half lengthways. Place in a bowl, pour over a generous amount of olive oil and sprinkle with salt. Toss the oca in the oil until they're well covered.

Spread the oca on a baking tray, cut side down, making sure they're well spaced.

Bake for 15 minutes, then take the tray out, flip the oca cut side up and bake for another 5 minutes, or until the outside is crisp. Allow them to cool a little.

Beat the labneh or sour cream with a little salt to loosen it. Dab a little on each oca and serve topped with a scattering of herbs, and those flowers if you have them.

These are best served with a cold glass of white wine in one hand, and the other hand free for oca eating.

Serves 4 as a canapé

500 g (1 lb 2 oz) oca

olive oil, for drizzling

labneh (page 202) or sour cream

soft herbs such as dill, chives, coriander and/or parsley, picked as small, tender leaves

small edible flowers, if you're feeling extra fancy

Corn

One evening I piled up blackberry canes and scrappy bits of timber and lit a small bonfire. We had a freezer full of pork from pigs we'd raised, and hosting outdoor feasts was easy. A spiced shoulder of pork in a slow oven all day, a bucket of ice ready to hold drinks, a pile of robust crockery and hay bales to sit on was all we needed.

I wanted to cook from the garden, and slow-cooked pork, collard greens and grits sounded like a good idea. I'd been talking about collard greens with Nipaluna's (Hobart's) American Creole culinary oracle, Honey Child — aka Toni Burnett Rands — about collards, and she'd told me to cook them long and slow with a ham hock in the pot to make them taste right. This flew in the face of how I'd always cooked greens — usually aiming for a bright, barely cooked brightness — and her teachings have served me well in all manner of cooking.

How I wished we'd talked about grits.

There was, for a long time, a quarantine ban on importing corn seed to Lutruwita (Tasmania) without expensive and onerous biosecurity checks that were out of reach for the small-scale grower. My curiosity was curtailed until the ban lifted and small seed companies suddenly fleshed out their catalogues with wondrous rainbows of corn.

I will always want a sweetcorn patch. Summer isn't summer without buttery, sweet cobs — nibbled typewriter-style by some in my family, or attacked with gluttonous, messy vigour, squirts of juice messing up our faces and butter running down our hands. But open a seed catalogue and see listings for wonders like 'Painted Mountain' corn — a grinding variety developed in Montana in the 1970s by a grower wanting to achieve a diverse, adaptable strain that could tolerate short seasons and dry conditions — and it's impossible to resist. The Montana grower used genetics that have been nurtured for thousands of years in Central America by Native American people. I can only find one vague reference to the people whose seeds were used. This erasure is tragic. Their stories should be woven into this one, their centuries of stewardship acknowledged, and their sovereignty over these seeds upheld.

I grew a patch of it and was astounded. Right from the beginning there was diversity. Plants with green, red and striped leaves, and, as it grew, an equal diversity of corn silk: green, pink, white and gold. Finally, harvest was like Christmas, unwrapping the cobs to reveal kernels of white, burgundy, rust and gold. I mostly use 'Painted Mountain' for grinding and adding to crackers and sweet biscuits for a pleasing gritty crunch, or for slightly thickening a savoury broth for a more filling soup.

Most corn is hungry, in need of well-composted soil with extra nitrogen (composted poultry or stable manure is excellent), regular feeds of compost teas and seaweed solutions as it grows, and consistent watering. They're fast-growing, thirsty plants and will be set back by dry conditions and produce disappointing cobs if you're stingy with them.

Corn is wind pollinated. The male pollen falls onto the corn silk, is trapped by tiny hairs and grows a filament through the silk into the female ovary which, when fertilised, becomes a seed. If your sweetcorn is pollinated by a grinding corn, or a popcorn, it can change the quality of the pollinated cob, making it starchy rather than succulent. Corn needs to planted in blocks rather than rows, to ensure the silks have maximum exposure to the pollen falling from the tassels, but you need to ensure you plant different varieties a good distance apart, or stagger the timing of your plantings, to prevent cross-pollination (and ensure true-to-type seed if you're saving it) and starchy sweetcorn.

We sow ours in plugs of potting soil in October, to plant out when the soil warms in November. Corn planted in cold soil will never thrive, so it's best not to rush. In warmer areas, corn thrives when direct sown, but seeds and young plants are vulnerable to birds and mice.

When I'm working near tall corn plants, I'm always looking over my shoulder. They're large, imposing plants and whisper to one another in the breeze, making me think there's someone behind me. They're also excellent frog habitat. On still days you can see leaves boinging as frogs leap from one plant to its neighbour.

For our ill-fated grits I scoured the internet and found dozens of contradictory methods, so I shut the laptop and winged it. I used 'Black Aztec', a grinding corn with dark grey kernels that are delicious eaten as fresh corn, but chewier in a very good, satisfying way, and can take a little longer in the pot. When I'd harvested it, it was a little unripe for drying, but there was an impending frost and I had to use it or lose it. I husked and ground the grains into a pale blue–grey flour. Being a romantic optimist, I foresaw no problems with cooking my grits on the open fire. I always set up a little range near the bonfire, some bricks supporting old barbecue grills into which I shovel coals from the bonfire as needed. This is a great arrangement for reasonably quick grilling or hands-off cooking, but for grits that needed constant stirring it became a smoky, teary affair, over a pot of what looked like cement.

Luckily my friend Jess Muir, who can make a silk purse from a sow's ear, was there. I was, by that stage, weeping, mostly from the smoke, but partly because I like to serve carbohydrates with my greens and protein. The slightly under-ripe corn lacked the right kind of starch to cook out into something soothing and creamy; it was instead creepily translucent, and had the look of a gluggy sauce that's been thickened with cornflour, which I guess it was. Jess, like a calm spot in a storm, asked me for butter, salt and water, and turned my cement-looking grits into something well-seasoned and palatable. We spooned it onto our plates, topped with shredded pork and dreamy, tender collard greens, and ate together by the fire.

Flowers for feasting

When we first started growing for market, edible flowers, along with foraged foods, headed the culinary zeitgeist. We chose flowers for their flavour, although whimsy occasionally won the day, earning a few subtly flavoured blooms a place in the garden for their beauty alone. The tragedy was, as with all zeitgeists, this one ran its course and a cultural cringe grew. Never was a more beautiful baby thrown out with its bathwater.

I'd adored wandering the garden using my 'rule of thumb' to gather succulent, spicy-sweet heads of black-veined white rocket flowers. I came to know which point of the stem, when grasped between thumb and forefinger, would come away from the plant with no force and a juicy 'snap'. If a stem could be plucked this easily, I knew it would be tender when it found its way onto a plate. We gathered all kinds of brassica flowers this way — fluttery pink radish blooms, lairy gold 'Hon Tsai Tai' choy sum flowers, and big lemon-yellow cabbage blossoms. Brassica stems, when the plants begin to flower, are sappy and full of sugars, but still carry a hint of the flavour of their parent vegetable and the sweetness of nectar from the flowers. A scattering of succulent radish stems and flowers used as a garnish for a beef tartare can bring a little of the quality of horseradish to the dish, and ever so much whimsy. A tumble of sappy cabbage shoots thrown onto a hot barbecue for just a moment is a delicious consolation for the failed cabbage crop that bolted to flower to produce it.

When we have a family build-your-own dinner of nori or rice paper rolls, san choy bau or steamboat, there are always flowers on the platter with the herbs. A few chive or garlic chive flowers scattered on a rice paper roll give all the onion kick you need, and when our Thai basil is done for the season, we'll instead scatter broken-up flower heads of anise hyssop for an anise hit.

When we were working with the Nipaluna (Hobart) restaurant Garagistes, Luke Burgess, the chef, would only use garnishes that added to the dish. Nothing was there for beauty alone, but flavour and visual pleasure often go hand in hand. I remember waiting for my chef–gardener husband Matt to finish work one night as I sat at the bar, with little plates of food made with exquisite care placed in front of me. One plate held slices of potato cooked into delicate crisps, with a smoked eel mousse piped on top, and then a garden of herbs and flowers placed upon it. Salty and crisp, then creamy, smoky and savoury, with a different flavour from each piece of plant coming to the fore as you chewed — the sweetness of anise from lacy white chervil flowers, a little warmth and sweetness from mustard and radish blooms, and a spike of onion from pink society garlic. This memory may be an amalgam of many of the beautiful things that sat before me as a visual feast whenever we went to Garagistes, but to see our garden so fresh and alive and in the perfect context with other ingredients was reassurance that, zeitgeist or not, beauty and flavour will always be relevant.

I can see why the cringe began. Who wants to hoist a huge calendula bloom, sticky with icing, from their cake before they can eat — and where are you supposed to leave it on your plate? And there is no appeal in withered flowers with curling petals languishing in a fading salad or sticking up your nose when you're trying to enjoy a cocktail.

When used with thought, edible flowers have the power to elevate, to add another layer of flavour or story to your food or drink. Imagine that same cocktail made with blackcurrants. The rich, almost medicinal flavour of the fruit is one I relish, while the blackcurrant flowers and foliage carry some of the same chemical compounds as the fruit, but without the sugars, so you experience them differently. If you hang a tiny bundle of blackcurrant flowers on the lip of your glass the scent will enhance the flavour of your drink, but as I love the fruit so much I'm very judicious about stealing those blossoms for the fleeting time they're out.

Onion flowers taste of onions; rosemary flowers of rosemary and nectar. Pea flowers unsurprisingly taste of peas, but dianthus and ladies' smock both carry hints of cloves. If you gather them before the birds and bees visit, the flowers of edible salvias — including common sage, pineapple sage and blackcurrant sage — can be full of nectar. And few will refuse a cheese-stuffed, fried zucchini flower.

We sow a green manure crop every winter that's laden with legumes, including peas and broad beans, that we mow to feed the soil before it produces any vegetables. We gather blossoms from that crop with abandon — a salad of pea flowers is a luxury only gardeners will enjoy, and tastes ethereally of peas. You can only apply dressing moments before eating, and you have to flick it on with the bristles of a pastry brush; if your flowers are drenched with dressing they will quickly shrivel, but a dash of shallot oil, a smidge of salt and a hint of Meyer lemon juice, and you have food of the faeries.

I can't remember where I read of a dinner party begun with a posy of herbs and flowers, tied with a ribbon that was snipped to allow the herbs to fall loose on the plate so guests could dress their whimsical salad and whet their appetite, but once, when I decided to gather friends for a dinner party, that was how I had to start it. I picked heartsease, miner's lettuce, radish, mustard and rocket stems, chervil and sweet cicely flowers — all things that can be eaten without the need for trimming or plucking from stems. I bulked up my salad posies with tiny lettuces, sprigs of sour sheep sorrel and tender baby chives. In the story I'd read, each guest had a pair of silver grape scissors to cut their bouquets from their bindings, but I only had little sewing scissors to hand. Everyone talked as they helped each other snip and dress their salads, waving their forks at each other, identifying and tasting as they went. A perfectly convivial beginning to a dinner party.

And if sweet flowers abound, begging you to pluck them and make desserts, how can you refuse? I make a dessert that tries to take what's good from the addictive Pocky stick, but leaves out the problematic palm oil and plastic packaging. A sweet pastry that's tender enough to bite, but robust enough to withstand being dipped in chocolate and rolled in ground nuts, crunchy pralines, candied peels and sugared flowers. They bring out the child in even the biggest food snob, and make for a pretty addition to a party table.

Candied flowers

Always make sure your flowers are pesticide-free. Flowers that have been shipped for floristry or bought in garden centres may have been treated to satisfy biosecurity requirements and may not be safe to eat. Be absolutely sure of edibility — hemlock and oleander are common plants with pretty but very toxic blooms. Many specialty grocers will have edible flowers for sale or will order them for you, but this always comes with a lot of plastic packaging, so learn to raid your garden or those of friends if you can.

Any edible flower is suitable. Just consider their size and flavour, and whether they're robust enough for crystallising with sugar and coating your chocolate-dipped poky sticks (page 294).

It's often recommended to use powdered egg white here to prevent any risk of salmonella. I use home-laid eggs that I know are clean and fresh.

Put a sheet of baking paper on the tray from a dehydrator if you have one, or on a cake cooling rack. Pour some sugar into a shallow bowl.

Use a small, clean paint brush to apply a fine layer of egg white on both sides of your clean flowers and petals. Sprinkle on the sugar, gently pressing the flower into your sugar bowl and shaking it off to remove the excess before laying it on your baking paper. (Flowers on heads like anise hyssop can be brushed with egg white, working it into the head and doing the same with the sugar. Once dried, snip the tiny florets from the heads with scissors.)

Put the flowers in a very slow oven with the door held ajar, or in a dehydrator on a cool setting. Flowers are delicate and can brown easily if bruised or overheated.

Once the flowers are thoroughly dry, store them in an airtight container in the dark until needed.

1 fresh egg white, thoroughly whisked

caster (superfine) sugar, for coating

SUITABLE FLOWERS

Clove dianthus, *Dianthus plumarius*

Sweet violet, *Viola odorata*

Johnny jump-up or other violas, *Viola* spp.

Anise hyssop, *Agastache foeniculum*

Sweet cicely, *Myrrhis odorata*

Roses (small petals are best), *Rosa* spp.

Scented pelargoniums (rose, peppermint, nutmeg), *Pelargonium* spp.

Gorse, *Ulex europaeus*

Poky sticks

When Matt was working as a chef, every Christmas and birthday brought another fancy restaurant cookbook into our house. Most sit untouched as quite impractical objects of beauty, but the desserts by Katrina Kanetani in the *Pier* book were things I wanted to, and could, make at home. Her version of Pocky sticks have become a festive staple for me. I decorate them with candied herbs and flowers and toasted hazelnuts — a guilt-free version of the over-packaged, palm oil–laden treat we are all secretly in love with.

The recipe has evolved over the years in our kitchen. I've scaled down the volume, but by all means scale it up again. And I couldn't resist throwing in a bit of rye flour grown and milled by our friends The Grain Family, as it makes everything more wholesome and delicious. The unfinished biscuits will wait happily in the biscuit tin for weeks until you need them.

Add the yeast to the warm milk and set aside.

In a large bowl, whisk together the flours, sugar and salt. Sprinkle the mandarin zest on top and make a well in the centre.

When the yeast begins to froth, pour it into the flour and stir, pulling in the flour from the edges. Begin to add the water, then knead in the tahini and butter. Knead for a few minutes on a lightly floured bench, or in a stand mixer with a dough hook, until smooth. It may look as though

Makes about 50

5 g (⅛ oz) dried yeast

¼ cup (60 ml) warm milk

100 g (3½ oz) baker's flour (also called strong flour or bread flour)

75 g (2½ oz) plain (all-purpose) flour

50 g (1¾ oz) plain (all-purpose) rye flour

40 g (1½ oz) rapadura sugar

¼ teaspoon salt

zest of ½ mandarin

25 ml (¾ fl oz) water

20 g (¾ oz) unhulled tahini

40 g (1½ oz) soft butter

Chocolate and garnishes of your choice, to decorate

it won't come together, but keep kneading and the tahini and butter will yield and bind the mix. If you need to, add just a little extra water. Shape the dough into a ball, then cover and chill in the fridge for at least 1 hour.

Preheat your oven to 170°C (325°F). Roll the dough out 5 mm (¼ inch) thick and slice into strips about 7–8 mm (⅝ inch) wide and 15 cm (6 inches) long. Arrange the strips on two baking trays.

Bake for 15 minutes, rotating the trays and keeping an eye on any extra-slender biscuits or those near the edges, and removing them if they look like overcooking.

Leave to cool completely on wire racks, then store in a sealed container until you're ready to dip them.

Other families

The fun part: Select the chocolate of your dreams. White chocolate is ethereal with sugared dianthus and rose petals, perhaps with a few shards of pistachio for its pretty green. Dark chocolate and hazelnut poky sticks are the ones I steal most from my festive stash. And milk chocolate and anise hyssop flowers will make you think of liquorice bullets.

Warm the chocolate in a heatproof bowl set over a saucepan of boiling water. (My ingenious mum used to put jars of chocolate in an electric frying pan full of water set to low. If you're working for a while over a task like this, it does make life easier.) Line baking trays with baking paper, fill plates with your garnishes of choice, invite the children into the kitchen and have fun.

Dip the baked poky sticks in the melted chocolate, using a spoon to ladle it along the biscuit — give the chocolate a moment to cool before rolling it in nuts, sprinkling it with candied angelica pieces or artfully placing sugared flowers along it. The poky sticks look magnificent standing in a cocktail glass on a party table, and also make a beautiful gift as they keep so well.

Further reading

Everything I know I learned from someone else.

My favourite way to spend a rainy afternoon is in learning. I'll often have more than one resource in use at a time. Sometimes the Tasmanian Herbarium's *Census of the Vascular Plants of Tasmania* is on my laptop, a copy of *Weeds of the South-East* and my well-thumbed *Cornucopia II* open beside me. I might find an unfamiliar brassicaceous weed in the census, have a look in *Weeds of the South-East* to see if it looks tasty, flip through my beloved *Cornucopia II* to see if it has a record of being eaten, and how it might be prepared, then scroll through the Plants for a Future database to see if it has a listing for it.

Or, following the same multimedia approach, I might open *Larousse Gastronomique* or Time-Life's *Foods of the World* to find a vegetable and see how it's prepared, before checking its climatic range and suitability for growing in my garden. If I have a plant that is yet to find a context in my kitchen, I'll think hard on what it reminds me of, then find a recipe for a similar herb, fruit or vegetable in a favourite cookbook, and experiment with substitution until I learn what works.

Some books have shifted my perspective, making me kinder (I hope!), more respectful, and grown my sense of what it is to care for land, community and the planet as a whole. Others have taught me how to cook — although I rarely use a recipe as written, my food preparation most often driven by what is in my harvest basket rather than a dish I've been wanting to prepare. The best of these gives me a technique or a feeling that I can use as a jumping-off point.

But that's not an end to it. If you do a web search of a plant's Latin name, along with 'ethnobotany', you may stumble upon a researcher's list of the edible, medicinal and cultural plants of a region you might never be able to visit, but whose plants may well be self-seeding on a footpath near you. Some of these documents can be upsetting, with a colonial, 'discoverer' bent to them, but recently I've found some that are undertaken by researchers in partnership with community Elders, working together to document and preserve traditional knowledge.

To think

Dark Emu: Black Seeds: Agriculture or Accident? Bruce Pascoe

Braiding Sweetgrass Robin Wall Kimmerer

Animal, Vegetable, Miracle Barbara Kingsolver

Living the Good Life Linda Cockburn

The Gastronomical Me M.F.K. Fisher

To meet new plants

Cornucopia II: A Source Book of Edible Plants Stephen Facciola

Lost Crops of the Incas: Little-Known Plants of the Andes with Promise for Worldwide Cultivation Ad Hoc Panel of the Advisory Committee on Technology Innovation

Discovering Fruits & Nuts Susanna Lyle

Vegetables, Herbs & Spices Susanna Lyle

A Taste of the Unexpected Mark Diacono

Instagram and other social media. I follow countless farmers, seed savers, cooks and biodiversity advocates, and learn something new every day.

To garden

My bookcase heaves with gardening books. I'm always learning something new and discarding an old methodology for a new one, but the texts I list below are foundational for me — talking about the soil that supports us, plant varieties and their particular needs, or tools and techniques that make for efficient and flavoursome harvests. If you look locally you'll find garden clubs, crop swap groups, radio talkback shows and nurseries that will offer advice suited to your region and season.

Soil Matthew Evans

The One-Straw Revolution Masanobu Fukuoka

The Complete Book of Fruit Growing in Australia Louis Glowinski

The Lean Farm Guide to Growing Vegetables Ben Hartman

The New Organic Grower Eliot Coleman

The Milkwood Permaculture Living Handbook Kirsten Bradley

Good Life Growing Hannah Moloney

To forage

Eat Weeds Diego Bonetto

The Weed Forager's Handbook: A Guide to Edible and Medicinal Weeds in Australia Adam Grubb & Annie Raser-Rowland

Plants For A Future database pfaf.org

Food Plants International database, Bruce French foodplantsinternational.com

Weeds of the South-East F.J. Richardson, R.G. Richardson & R.C.H. Shepherd

A Census of the Vascular Plants of Tasmania, Including Macquarie Island M.F. de Salas & M.L. Baker, 2023 edition flora.tmag. tas.gov.au/resources/census

To cook

Larousse Gastronomique Prosper Montagné

Italian Food Elizabeth David

Foods of the World Time-Life

The 21st Birthday Cookery Book of the Country Women's Association in Tasmania

The Cook's Companion Stephanie Alexander

Wholefood Baking Jude Blereau

The entire internet. I was inspired to make my skirret pie when I searched Trove, compiled by the Australian National Library, for 'skirret'. A wealth of information is there — horticultural and agricultural advice from old research papers, and a recipe from a 1975 *Australian Women's Weekly* column, 'At Home with Margaret Sydney'. If you've a rainy afternoon to spend, a full teapot, some biscuits to hand and Trove open, a search for a favourite plant is a mind-expanding thing to do.

Any new edible plant that crosses your path will have been cooked, and somebody will have written about their experience. I always search first for people who have cultural ties with the plant I'm learning about; the stories will have richer roots and expand your understanding beyond the basics of cooking time and seasoning.

Acknowledgements

Thank you.

To my mother, who taught me to nurture the ones I love with food, and who is still feeding and caring for me and mine today. You are the world.

To my family, Matt, Elsie and Heidi. Thank you all for your lifelong love and inspiration, and for the time and space you gave me to put this together.

To my darling sisters. Katie who taught her sister — the one who couldn't even get a pen licence — to write. And Belinda who shared her capable hands, cooking with me to test the recipes in these pages.

To my friends. Whether you're near or far, whether I've fed you, or you've fed me. We may have traded seeds, shared ideas or shown each other new perspectives. We may have enjoyed years spending time together, or we may have had only fleeting conversations. Every interaction is a chance for us to enrich each other, and I am happier, wiser and more curious for having known all of you.

To Jane Willson, my wonderful publisher, who sought me out and coaxed me away from my habitual 'I'm too busy' response, winning my heart by eschewing hire cars — hiking four kilometres to meet with me at a country bakery and explore and refine ideas, guiding me through this process. To my editorial manager Justin Wolfers, whose kind, wise and genuine encouragement (including one of the nicest emails I've ever opened) helped me when I was daunted by this task, and my editor Katri Hilden, who patiently corrected, clarified and rearranged my tangled thoughts into a cohesive form.

To Jamie Graham-Blair, a Trawlwoolway and Plangermaireener Pakana, who took the time to read passages that spoke about this precious island of Lutruwita (Tasmania) and its significant cultural plants, as well as some references to plants significant to other First Nations peoples. The firm, kind feedback he gave will be part of my ongoing work into cultural awareness and becoming a better ally. And to Kitana Mansell for talking with me as we stood in the mud harvesting kunzea boughs and giving me a greater understanding of the significance of plants to her and her people. Any mistakes are mine.

To my friend in vegetables, Luke Burgess, who has not only taken the exquisite photographs for these pages, but has always been a companion in my explorations of culinary plants, and helped me refine some of the recipes here. Our relationship has made the photographs for this work feel like a collaboration and an absolute joy.

To the Veggie Growers Group, an excellent assemblage of local market gardeners who supplied me with their magnificent produce for our photographs.

For the care taken by head of creative Megan Pigott, and by designer Klarissa Pfisterer to bring these stories to life, and for the drawings that have captured the spirit of the plants we grow in a few magical strokes. It all fills my heart with gratitude.

To my dear friends Sam and Werner, Natalie, Felix and Esther, Phil and Kelsey, Karen and Al, and Vanessa and Tony, who all lent me their beautiful homes so I could have some time to focus. Thank you for the peace and quiet, the beaches, pooches and jostaberries.

To the brilliant Pat Nourse, who years ago took a chance on a vegetable gardener and taught me how to shape my stories.

Most of all, thank you to the stewards of seeds, culture and country. You are everything.

Index

Index

Published in 2024 by Murdoch Books, an imprint of Allen & Unwin

Murdoch Books Australia
Cammeraygal Country
83 Alexander Street
Crows Nest NSW 2065
Phone: +61 (0)2 8425 0100
murdochbooks.com.au
info@murdochbooks.com.au

For corporate orders and custom publishing, contact our business development team at salesenquiries@murdochbooks.com.au

Publisher: Jane Willson
Editorial manager: Justin Wolfers
Design manager: Megan Pigott
Designer and illustrator: Klarissa Pfisterer
Editor: Katri Hilden
Photographer: Luke Burgess
Production director: Lou Playfair

Murdoch Books UK
Ormond House
26–27 Boswell Street
London WC1N 3JZ
Phone: +44 (0) 20 8785 5995
murdochbooks.co.uk
info@murdochbooks.co.uk

OVEN GUIDE: You may find cooking times vary depending on the oven you are using. For fan-forced ovens, as a general rule, set the oven temperature to 20°C (35°F) lower than indicated in the recipe.

TABLESPOON MEASURES: We have used 20 ml (4 teaspoon) tablespoon measures. If you are using a 15 ml (3 teaspoon) tablespoon add an extra teaspoon of the ingredient for each tablespoon specified.

DISCLAIMER: The information provided within this book is for general inspiration and informational purposes only. While we try to keep the information up-to-date and correct, the author and publisher do not assume and hereby disclaim any liability to any party for any loss, damage, or disruption caused by errors or omissions, whether such errors or omissions result from negligence, accident, or any other cause. Be sure to check with your local council and use common sense when handling any potentially harmful equipment or materials. Individuals using or consuming the plants listed in this book do so entirely at their own risk. Always check a reputable source to ensure that the plants you are using are non-toxic, organic, unsprayed and safe to be consumed. The author and/or publisher cannot be held responsible for any adverse reactions.

ISBN 978 1 92261 687 6

 A catalogue record for this book is available from the National Library of Australia

A catalogue record for this book is available from the British Library

Colour reproduction by Splitting Image Colour Studio Pty Ltd, Wantirna, Victoria
Printed by 1010 Printing International Limited, China

10 9 8 7 6 5 4 3 2 1

MIX
Paper | Supporting responsible forestry
FSC® C016973